DEFENDING RIGHTS

Frank Askin has been in the forefront of legal struggles to expand individual rights for thirty years and has been General Counsel of the American Civil Liberties Union for the past twenty. A Distinguished Professor at Rutgers Law School, in 1970 he founded Rutgers' pioneering Constitutional Litigation Clinic, where he has trained a new generation of public interest lawyers. He has interspersed his activities in the courtroom and classroom with several stints on Capitol Hill as special counsel to congressional committees and has run for Congress twice.

DEFENDING RIGHTS

A LIFE IN LAW AND POLITICS

FRANK ASKIN

GENERAL COUNSEL
ACLU

HUMANITIES PRESS

NEW JERSEY

First published in 1997 by
Humanities Press International, Inc.,
165 First Avenue, Atlantic Highlands, New Jersey 07716.

© 1997 by Frank Askin

Library of Congress Cataloging-in-Publication Data

Askin, Frank, 1932–
   Defending rights : a life in law and politics / Frank Askin.
    p.   cm.
   Includes index.
   ISBN 0–391–04006–5 (pbk.). — ISBN 0–391–04005–7 (cloth)
    1. Askin, Frank, 1932– . 2. Law teachers—United States—
Biography. 3. Civil rights—United States—History. I. Title.
KF373.A83A33 1997
340'.092—dc20   96–8819
                      CIP

Printed in the United States of America

10 9 8 7 6 5 4 3 2 1

To
Steve, Andrea,
Jonny, and Danny

' so you will
always know
what Dad was
doing during
the (Cold) War

Contents

PART III: TALES OF POLITICS

PART IV: REFLECTIONS

Glossary

BURGER COURT. Warren Burger was appointed Chief Justice by President Nixon in 1973, in partial fulfillment of his campaign pledge to undo the work of the "liberal" Warren Court. With the assistance of other Nixon and Reagan appointees, the Burger Court accomplished much of what the political conservatives had promised to do, especially in the area of criminal justice and the restoration of capital punishment. Burger was succeeded by William Rehnquist in 1986. The Rehnquist Court has generally continued in the tradition of the Burger Court.

CLOTURE. A vote to terminate further debate. In the United States Senate, the general rule is that no issue may come to a vote so long as any member wishes to continue debate. This gave rise to the art of the filibuster, used by opponents of proposed legislation to block action and force its removal from the floor. It requires a super-majority vote to invoke cloture and cut off further debate by a time certain. Under present rules, the cloture requirement is 60 per cent.

CONTRA AID. The Sandinista Revolution overthrew the autocratic Somoza regime in Nicaragua in the late 1970s, but the former Somoza supporters (known as "contras") refused to surrender and continued the civil war. The Reagan Administration accused the Sandinista government of being aligned with Fidel Castro and provided support to the contras. Congress voted to cut off contra aid on several occasions in the 1980s, but the Reagan White House continued to provide such aid surreptitiously, leading to the Iran-contra scandal and Congressional hearings.

COURTS OF EQUITY. *SEE* SITTING IN EQUITY.

DENNIS CASE. *United States v. Dennis, et. al.* was the prosecution of Communist Party general secretary Eugene Dennis and the other members of the party's National Committee. The defendants were convicted under the Smith Act of conspiracy to teach and advocate the overthrow of the United States government, and sentenced to jail. Their convictions were upheld by the United States Supreme Court in 1951, with Justices William O. Douglas and Hugo Black dissenting. 341 U.S. 494.

IMPEACH EARL WARREN CAMPAIGN. The Warren Court came under political attack by conservatives as ultra-liberal and "activist," particularly for its decisions protecting the rights of persons accused of crime. Led by the ultra-right wing John Birch Society, a movement sprang up demanding the impeachment of Earl Warren as Chief Justice. Richard Nixon made criticism of the Warren Court a major theme to his 1968 presidential campaign, pledging, if elected, to appoint only "strict constructionists" to the federal bench.

BURT LANCE. Lance, a Georgia attorney, was a chief adviser of President Jimmy Carter and a leader of the Carter White House from his position as director of the Office of Management and Budget.

LYNDON LAROUCHE. A perennial presidential candidate with a cult following. Starting as an off-shoot of the left-wing Students for a Democratic Society (SDS) and for a while involving themselves in Democratic Party politics, the LaRouchites seem to be continually reinventing themselves.

GEORGE MEANY. President of the American Federation of Labor beginning in 1952 and president of the merged AFL-CIO after its merger with the Congress of Industrial Organizations in 1955, Meany was a supporter of a hard-line U.S. anti-Communist foreign policy during the Cold War era and was generally viewed as conservative on matters involving race, abortion, and other social issues.

PANAMA CANAL TREATY. Negotiated by President Carter, the treaty provided for a gradual takeover of the canal by the government of Panama and the withdrawal of U.S. troops to be completed by 1999.

PORT HURON STATEMENT. Students for a Democratic Society, the institutional center of the 1960s' New Left movement, was founded in 1960. In 1962, 59 leaders met in Port Huron, Michigan, to draft a 63-page platform, critiquing the Cold War and the materialistic complacency of postwar American life.

REPUBLICAN-DIXIECRAT FILIBUSTER. The Democratic Party had totally dominated politics in the former Confederate states since the end of the Reconstruction Era following the Civil War. But as the national Democratic Party began to become more responsive to the interests of non-white urban dwellers in the second half of the century, southern Democratic members of Congress (called Dixiecrats) began to form political alliances with conservative Republicans. This alliance of conservative Republicans and Dixiecrats was instrumental in blocking much civil rights and social welfare legislation, especially in the Senate, where a super-majority vote was required to end Republican-Dixiecrat filibusters. Finally, many of the conservative white southern Democrats abandoned the Democratic Party altogether and ran for office as Republicans.

SITTING IN EQUITY. The British legal system was divided into common law and equity. The equity courts were administered by the Chancellor, did not recognize trial by jury, and provided more flexible remedies, such as injunctions. In the Middle Ages, the British Parliament, which viewed the Chancellor as an agent of the crown, enacted legislation forbidding equity courts to assume jurisdiction of matters in which the law courts could provide an adequate remedy. That division was carried over to the American continent, where most states and the federal court system were divided into law and equity branches. Even today, where law and equity have been merged in most American jurisdictions, courts still distinguish between actions at law and actions in equity, and the judge hearing equitable actions is said to be "sitting in equity."

TAFT-HARTLEY ACT. Adopted by Congress over President Truman's veto in 1947 and an issue in the 1948 presidential election, the act amended the National

Labor Relations Act to place restrictions upon trade unions and to make federal labor law more friendly to the interests and desires of the business community.

WALKER AMENDMENT. In the late 1970s and early 1980s, Representative Robert S. Walker, a Republican from Pennsylvania, regularly offered amendments in the House of Representatives to forbid various affirmative action programs designed to provide racial minorities better educational and employment opportunities.

WARREN COURT ERA. Earl Warren the former governor of California and the Republican candidate for vice-president on the Tom Dewey ticket in 1948, was appointed Chief Justice of the United States by President Eisenhower in 1953. He is credited with having orchestrated the unanimous opinion in *Brown v. Board of Education*, holding school segregation unconstitutional, in 1954. With the support of holdover Justices Douglas and Black, William Brennan (appointed by Eisenhower in 1954), Justices Arthur Goldberg (appointed by President Kennedy), and Thurgood Marshall and Abe Fortas (appointed by President Johnson), Chief Justice Warren led a Court majority (through the 1960s) which was firmly committed to the protection of constitutional principles and the reinvigoration of the federal judiciary as the primary enforcer of individual rights.

YATES OPINION. Following the *Dennis* case, regional Communist leaders were prosecuted throughout the country. The *Yates* case involved the prosecution of the party's California leadership. By the time the *Yates* case reached the Supreme Court in 1957, there had been substantial change in the composition of the Supreme Court. In an opinion by Justice John Marshall Harlan, who had been appointed by President Eisenhower, the Court reinterpreted its opinion in the *Dennis* case and reversed the convictions. 354 U.S 298. The new legal standard (requiring advocacy of action and not mere advocacy of ideas) made it practically impossible to obtain further convictions under the Smith Act and resulted in dismissal of the other pending prosecutions.

Preface

Americans almost unanimously celebrate that ours is a government of laws. But consensus quickly breaks down if we try to define just what is meant by that.

Law in our pluralistic society has many sources and takes many forms. Huey Long, Louisiana's celebrated "Kingfish," was not the only bureaucrat who insisted that the law was whatever he said it was. The law clearly *is* what the United States Supreme Court says it is—especially when the focus is federal constitutional law. Congress, however, has the final say on federal statutory law—as long as the president agrees or his opposition is overridden by two-thirds of the votes in both houses. State courts or state legislatures have the last word on the laws of the various states. And the people collectively have ultimate power in our democracy to impose their will on the governing branches, including the power to change federal and state constitutions as well as their elected representatives.

Because there are so many buttons that might be pushed, the process of making, changing, and enforcing law in these United States is complex and often messy. I have been involved in trying to influence the development of public policy—which is, at bottom, the making of law—in one way or another all of my adult life. The effort has often been frustrating, but it is always exhilarating.

I actually began working in a law office at the age of seventeen, but for reasons that will become apparent, I did not enter law school until I was thirty-one. In the interim, I attempted to shape the law by public agitation: gathering petitions to public officials, organizing public meetings and demonstrations, writing and disseminating printed materials, reporting for newspapers and magazines, and running political campaigns. At any given moment, I usually had a pretty good idea of how I wanted to influence public policy, even if my own goals were revised from time to time.

Once I had a law degree in hand, I discovered that my opportunities to influence changes in the law were increased manyfold. I was no longer relegated to urging others to importune some distant power center to do something. My law degree and bar admissions were my passport to the inner sanctum of the law—to courthouses and the judges who presided there, who had the authority and power to actually order new rules for governance.

I admit that not all lawyers look at the practice of law that way. For most of them, law reform is not a major objective. They represent clients who seek not to change the law but to attain some specific relief according to its traditional rules. In contrast, I have always viewed myself as a *public-interest law-yer*, a calling that is unique to the United States, where our constitutional system has made courts of law into potent vehicles for social change. Although my clients had specific personal objectives that I tried to realize for them, to me, their cases represented opportunities to establish or implement legal principles that would have wider social impact: protecting individual privacy against harassment by police officers; establishing principles of racial justice; implementing rights of free speech, especially for grassroots organizations without large advertising budgets; defending political activists against intrusive and threatening government practices, including electronic and physical surveillance; expanding the right to vote; protecting the rights of the poor and the powerless to some minimum level of human essentials.

I also discovered that being a lawyer gave me special entrée to the legislative halls where statutes were debated and enacted. Early in my career, I had taught labor law. This background led to my first official posting on Capitol Hill, where I was thrust into the center of the legislative battle over labor law reform. A decade later, after I had established something of a reputation as a civil liberties lawyer, I was invited back to Washington to serve as special counsel to congressional committees dealing with broad constitutional issues of national security, separation of powers, and official accountability.

Involvement in partisan politics and two failed campaigns for election to the House of Representatives were natural outgrowths of my early brush with the workings of Congress, together with my lifelong commitment to influencing public policy. But through it all, the two most stable aspects of my professional life over the last thirty years have been my training of future lawyers as a member of the faculty of Rutgers Law School in Newark, New Jersey, and my activities on behalf of the American Civil Liberties Union, for which I have served as general counsel for two decades.

This is the story of my life in the law. It is not a story of constant triumph. My side lost as many battles as it won. It is a story of the unending struggles that take place throughout our land in a wide variety of forums in an effort to expand personal freedom and keep government off the backs of the people, which, to my mind, is what our constitutional system is all about.

PART I:

IN THE BEGINNING

1

Red Days

Johnson had Boswell. I had the Federal Bureau of Investigation. When one is trying to reconstruct events that occurred as much as forty-five years ago, it is a great convenience to have contemporaneous reports of trained FBI agents. Not that they are always accurate or at all complete. They tend to be subjective and episodic, but they are still an invaluable source.

An example: On our thirtieth anniversary, my wife decided to take me on a mystery drive. When we passed the sign "Welcome to Harrison, N.Y.," I realized that she was retracing the path of our elopement. However, when we reached our destination, the only thing either of us could remember was that the justice of the peace had been named Venezia. Despite driving around town for about forty-five minutes, we could find no house that looked familiar. The telephone book listed no Venezias, and no one at the police station could remember him. We began to think that maybe he was an imposter and we had never been properly married.

My wife's mistake was not having told me in advance where we were going. If she had, I could have consulted my FBI file, an expurgated copy of which I had obtained under the Freedom of Information Act in the late 1970s. A belated search revealed, as I had suspected, that the FBI knew all about JP Venezia. His name was Charles, and we had been married in his living room at 3 Calvert Street on August 6, 1960.

No, the FBI did not accompany us on our elopement. Agents discovered a report of the event after the fact on the *New York Times* social page, which listed the names of my new in-laws. A telephone call to my mother-in-law by an agent posing as an old friend from Baltimore provided other relevant details for the FBI's insatiable files, including the revelation of a proud mother that her daughter was "attending a graduate school at Columbia University under a scholarship."

The FBI file also comes in handy in various other circumstances, such as when filling out government security forms on which you have to list every address you ever lived at and every job you ever held. For most people my age, that's a real nightmare. I just let my fingers do the walking.

3

The FBI opened its file on me on January 25, 1950, about two weeks after my eighteenth birthday and about six months after I had walked into the Communist Party's Baltimore headquarters and announced that I wished to become a member. The catalyst for my decision was the Maryland legislature's passage of the Ober Act, which outlawed the Communist Party in the state. What else was a red-blooded (no pun intended), patriotic civil libertarian to do? Actually, my act of political bravado was not greeted with enthusiasm by the local Communist chieftain, who told me that I could not become a party member until I was eighteen.

I don't know whether the FBI had the same rule regarding accepting individuals as Communists, but I did not receive any official attention until after my eighteenth birthday. Even then, my status caused something of a bureaucratic nightmare for the Baltimore FBI office. The first item in my file describes an administrative investigation of the agent who was initially assigned to my case. It seems that this anonymous agent (anonymous to me because all such names have been expunged from the documents turned over to me) did absolutely nothing about it until May 12, at which time he informed a superior that he had been tied up with another matter. Even then, nothing happened until September 14, when my case was reassigned to another agent, who finally filed a formal report on my activities on January 29, 1951, more than a year after the original assignment. In the meantime, agent number one was on the carpet for his dereliction. His defense:

> During the period that referenced case was assigned to me, I was engaged in various phases of the [deleted] case, in addition to handling an added number of Loyalty of Government Employee cases with Bureau deadlines, that ordinarily would have been assigned to other agents. The Loyalty case deadlines had to be met and as a result no investigative report was prepared in referenced case prior to its reassignment. I fully appreciate the need for prompt handling of assigned cases and a diligent effort will henceforth be made to correct this condition.

The agent in charge of the Baltimore office demonstrated compassion. He ruled: "I am convinced that the delay in this case was caused by a shortage of personnel, and it is noted that a report has been prepared. No administrative action is recommended." It appears that in mid-1950 the FBI was overwhelmed by the demands on its resources caused by the growing Red menace.

When an agent finally got around to ferreting out my subversive activities, he reported that I had been active in the Baltimore Council for Jobs and Peace, which "was agitating for more adequate unemployment and relief legislation"; was a member of the Young Progressives, identified as an organization that was "used by the Communist Party to further its own aims and purposes"; had written a letter to the editor of the *Baltimore Sun* criticizing a statement by the president of the University of Maryland that he would deny admission to any students who had participated in a New York high school strike; had participated in a picket line in front of the White House in support of a fair employment practices bill; had been seen distributing literature on behalf of the Henry Wallace presidential campaign on a Baltimore street corner; and had collected more than one hundred signatures on petitions to bring the aforementioned Ober bill to a referendum.

*   *   *

Actually, my formal association with the Communist Party was the natural outgrowth of my involvement in the Wallace presidential campaign in 1948, during my senior year in high school. My older brother, Stan, a decorated World War II veteran and the first president of the United States Ranger Battalions Association of World War II, had become something of a world-government pacifist after the war and had come back to Baltimore as an organizer for Wallace. He involved me in the Young Progressives of America (YPA), of which he was the state coordinator. It was my first experience with anything that might be described as civic activity. Prior to that, I had spent my teenage years dribbling, throwing, kicking, or hitting a ball of some sort. In school at Baltimore City College (despite its misleading name, a high school), I spent most of my days in the newspaper office, where I served for two years as sports editor.

Even my first paying job other than delivering newspapers was in professional basketball. In 1944, my uncle Babe, a prominent local sportsman (read gambler), had organized the Baltimore Bullets, and I was paid $2 a game to work the manual scoreboard at the old Baltimore Coliseum. The salary was pretty good, considering that the players were getting only $10 a game. After each basket, I had to change the big wooden numbers. Fortunately, games were relatively low-scoring in those days.

The summer of 1948 opened up new worlds to me. My rooting interest in the Wallace campaign caused me to start thinking about matters other than those discussed on the sports pages. I became caught up with two overriding public issues: the threat of nuclear war and racial segregation. It was the start of the Cold War. As I understood the world, Harry Truman had turned his back on the heroic FDR's foreign policy and was joining with Churchill to turn against our former Soviet ally. As someone who had spent World War II rooting for the Red Army to turn back Hitler's hordes, it was difficult to understand why we were now threatening the already war-devastated Soviet Union with nuclear annihilation. Only Henry Wallace spoke out for a renewal of the wartime alliance engineered by Roosevelt and the prospect of world peace.

Baltimore was a Jim Crow city. In all honesty, I had not thought much about that before. My household, in Stan's absence, was a typical racist environment. I had lived a totally segregated life. The Wallace movement and the Progressive Party grabbed the city by the throat and challenged its smug racial assumptions. Once I was confronted with the issue, the answer was apparent. I enthusiastically enlisted in the movement for racial equality. In the YPA, for the first time in my life I became acquainted with people of color. Some of them became close friends. I discovered that the only place I could socialize with them was in their community. They were not allowed in mine.

Baltimore was rocked in the summer of 1948 by the Druid Hill Park tennis court sit-in. There are probably a number of events that can lay historical claim as the beginning of the civil rights movement, and the tennis court incident was certainly one of them. The public clay tennis courts in Druid Hill Park, several blocks from my house, were a local landmark. I had spent many summer afternoons there as a boy. If someone had asked me why there were never any Negroes at the courts, I probably would have said that if there were Negro tennis players, they weren't interested in playing there. I was unaware that the Baltimore Parks Department had unwritten rules forbidding blacks to use the "white" courts.

The YPA and the NAACP (National Association for the Advancement of Colored People) decided to challenge those unwritten rules. After being denied a permit for an interracial tennis meet, the organizers publicly announced that they would challenge the Parks Department policy by holding the matches anyway on Sunday morning, July 11. When the police appeared on the scene and asked them to leave, the tennis players refused. Most of them sat down on the courts and forced the police to carry them off. According to subsequent reports, an interracial crowd of about three hundred had gathered to watch. The defendants were ultimately convicted of conspiracy to riot. My brother, who had been the primary organizer, received the longest sentence, a two-year suspended term.

*   *   *

By the time the November election was over, I was ready to become an active member of the radical youth movement (in hindsight, "movement" is a vast overstatement), and I soon became the leader of the nascent YPA in Maryland. It didn't take me long to discover that many of the most active and committed "progressives" I had met in the Wallace campaign, those who continued to play leading roles in the peace and racial justice movements after the election, were Communists. For some who had become active in the Progressive Party, that discovery resulted in disillusionment and a recognition that the press' Red-baiting of the Wallace campaign had been well-taken. It led me to an opposite conclusion: Maybe Communists weren't so bad after all.

I had always envisioned a career as a journalist, particularly as a sportswriter, but my recent experiences led me to start thinking about law school. One of the lawyers I had met during the Wallace campaign, Maurice Braverman, lived in my neighborhood. The home of Maurice and his wife, Jeanette, was a social gathering place for the left-wing community in northwest Baltimore.

I talked to Maurice about law school, and he finally offered to hire me as a law clerk/gofer for $10 a week if I would enroll at the University of Baltimore at night. The university had a five-year prelaw/law program that was accredited in the state of Maryland and permitted graduates to take the Maryland bar exam upon completion. I spent the next two years working in Maurice's law office on Gay Street during the day and attending the prelaw program at night. I was free to carry out my YPA activities at the office, in addition to helping Maurice with his own political involvements, most of which centered around the local chapter of an organization called the Civil Rights Congress (CRC), which was appropriately called a "Communist front." I use the term descriptively and not disparagingly. I still believe that the activities it engaged in were of the highest order of patriotism and directed at the defense of fundamental constitutional rights. All the activities I can recall involved either attacks on racial segregation or opposition to the McCarthyism that was sweeping the country and threatening freedom of speech and association in the name of combating the "Communist menace." Of course, the Communist Party and the CRC were largely concerned with trying to protect the party's members and supporters who were being persecuted. All over the country, officers and leaders of the Communist Party had been indicted under the Smith Act for teaching and advocating the overthrow of the government by espousing the principles of Marxism-Leninism.

Whatever you may think of Marxism-Leninism, most of the Communists I knew were peaceable and gentle people, concerned with issues of justice and equality and the possibility of nuclear war. They also believed—quite erroneously, as I later came to realize—that the Soviet Union was truly an egalitarian workers' state. If it engaged in authoritarian and undemocratic practices, it was assumed that they were necessary for self-protection from the threats of Western capitalist imperialism.

My own activities during this period as a leader of the local left-wing youth movement were centered on issues of Negro (the politically correct term at the time) rights and world peace. It was the time of the Stockholm peace appeal, and my colleagues and I spent much of our time on street corners handing out literature in favor of nuclear arms control and gathering signatures on petitions addressed to the United Nations and the U.S. Congress.

Even my basketball playing took on a political tint. A local Progressive Party leader was leading a campaign to get the city to end segregation in its recreation program. He organized an interracial team and attempted to enroll it in the all-white municipal league. He had signed up many of the city's top black scholastic players and needed credible white players. I was not quite up to the competition, but he was desperate for white faces. So for two years I was one of three white players on what was probably the best amateur basketball team in the state.

* * *

My idyll in the Braverman law office was shattered when Maurice was indicted under the Smith Act, along with the leaders of the Maryland Communist Party. By then, the original Smith Act trial of Eugene Dennis and the party's national leadership in New York had been completed, and the government took to prosecuting the so-called second-string party leaders all across the country. As in the other Smith Act trials, the basic evidence consisted of testimony by a parade of FBI plants inside the party about the meaning of the party's Marxist-Leninist doctrines. The basic charge was "conspiracy to teach and advocate," which focused on the nature of the party's ideology.

In all the Smith Act cases that went to trial, the essence of the government's case was that the party believed and instructed its members that a Marxist socialist state would never be achieved peacefully and that armed revolution was therefore inevitable. To my knowledge, none of the many informants called to testify ever claimed that any acts had been undertaken pursuant to such beliefs. Despite the absence of evidence of anything beyond the discussion of abstract doctrine, the U.S. Supreme Court, to its shame, upheld the convictions in the *Dennis* case over the strenuous dissents of the Court's First Amendment stalwarts Hugo Black and William O. Douglas. The high court thereby lent its support to the view that Communists were political pariahs and legitimized the anticommunist hysteria sweeping the country.

It is one of the vagaries of U.S. history that but for the untimely deaths of Justices Harlan Stone, Frank Murphy, and Wiley Rutledge early in the Truman administration, we might have escaped the worst ravages of the McCarthy era. Certainly Murphy and Rutledge (leading New Dealers), and most likely Chief Justice Stone (who had been appointed to the Court by Coolidge but elevated to the chief's spot by FDR), would have agreed with Black and Douglas. Latter-day historians have rescued the reputation of Harry Truman, and many now place him in the pantheon of great presidents, largely for his role in joining with Winston Churchill to create the Western alliance against the Soviet Union after World War II. I remain skeptical about the wisdom of Truman's foreign policy and the necessity of the forty-year Cold War that resulted. What I am absolutely certain of is that his selection of Supreme Court justices earns him failing grades. In place of the brilliant jurists Stone, Murphy, and Rutledge, Truman appointed three political cronies—Chief Justice Fred

Vinson, Tom Clark, and Sherman Minton—who could be described as mediocre only through excessive generosity. Despite Truman's own occasional objections to the McCarthyite hysteria of the times, his Supreme Court selections meekly subscribed to the *Dennis* convictions, with Vinson himself writing that opinion for the Court.

It is one of history's ironies that it took the conservative Dwight Eisenhower to right the constitutional balance on the Court. By the time the second Smith Act case, involving the Communist Party leadership in California, reached the tribunal, Ike had made three appointments—Chief Justice Earl Warren and Associate Justices John Marshall Harlan and William Brennan—all of whom joined in the *Yates* opinion to guarantee that there would be no more prosecutions of Communists under the Smith Act. Without directly overruling the decision in the *Dennis* case, the opinion written by Harlan held that conviction under the Smith Act required proof that the defendants advocated action, not mere belief.

Unfortunately for Maurice Braverman, the federal courts in Baltimore were among the most efficient in the nation. By the time the *Yates* decision was handed down, Maurice had completed most of his three-year sentence. Defendants in the other second-string Smith Act cases were still awaiting either trial or appeal and never went to jail. Maurice had been disbarred, and after his release he spent the next twenty years working as a bookkeeper, mainly for his former legal clients. In the early 1970s, I assisted Maurice in his successful application to be readmitted as a member of the Maryland bar, a process that was complicated by his refusal to express contrition for the political activities and relationships for which he had been convicted.

*   *   *

With the onset of full-blown McCarthyism and the conviction and imminent disbarment of Maurice, my own aspirations to become a lawyer appeared doomed. I was now convinced that the powers that be would never allow me to practice law. So when I completed the prelaw segment of the University of Baltimore's joint program, I decided not to go on to law school. By this time, I had also graduated from the politically amorphous YPA and was helping to organize an incipient Labor Youth League (LYL), a relatively short-lived successor to the Young Communist League of the 1930s and 1940s. Unlike the YPA, the LYL proclaimed its Marxist leanings and its fraternal relations with the Communist Party of the United States. As the local LYL organizer, I settled into the life of a radical youth leader.

One of the left-wing union leaders in town informed me that there was hiring going on at a small metal-cabinet fabricating plant in west Baltimore that was organized by the United Electrical Workers (UE), one of the unions that had been expelled from the CIO for being Communist controlled. Since UE-organized plants were constantly being raided by the CIO's newly created anticommunist International Union of Electrical Workers (IUE), the party was interested in having loyal left-wingers involved in the union to fend off the raiders. Thus began two and a half years of employment at Miller Metal Products, most of it on the final assembly line, where Beautyrest kitchen cabinets were put together and crated for shipment to the homes of the well-heeled.

*   *   *

It must appear to be paranoid delusion when I write that FBI agents would actually trail a twenty-year-old as he went about the city of Baltimore organizing activities on behalf of arms control and racial integration. However, my files are replete with memos from agents describing my travels about town and meetings with various individuals, although the identities of the parties I met with have been excised from the documents turned over to me. Nor did the agents make much of an effort to conceal themselves. It was well known among party activists that the agents drove easily identifiable Fords and that many of their cars had consecutive license plate numbers. The obvious conclusion is that they were as intent on frightening me (and others in their sights) as in determining who I was meeting. In any event, whenever I was going to see someone whose identity I wished to conceal, I used circuitous routes until I was reasonably certain that I had lost my tail. I would always leave myself an extra hour of travel time when I set out for a meeting of a confidential nature. In retrospect, I seem to have been reasonably successful in that endeavor. There are no documents that indicate that the FBI knew of a meeting with a contact whose identity I had made a concerted effort to protect.

There is one report in my files of two FBI agents who attempted to interview me personally. They approached me as I was leaving the house on my way to my car. I knew immediately who they were from their easily recognizable "uniforms" of topcoats and brimmed hats. Their report describes the encounter as follows:

> A fisur [physical surveillance?] was instituted by SAs . . . and . . . on the morning of ll/3/54 in the vicinity of subject's residence, 3505 Woodbrook Ave. At approximately 10:45 a.m., the subject was observed departing from his home and proceeded to his automobile which was parked some distance away. Both agents approached subject just prior to his reaching his automobile.
>
> Upon approaching ASKIN, the agents identified themselves as Special Agents and informed ASKIN that they desired to discuss a serious matter with him. ASKIN was visibly shaken and uncertain as to just what he should

do. . . . ASKIN only commented that he had nothing to say. Agent . . .
persisted in attempting to talk to him and placed his foot in such a manner
that he could not close the door. Agents continued to engage him in conversation hoping that he would give them an opportunity to enter into a
discussion concerning communism.

After approximately five minutes, it became apparent that ASKIN either
from fright or some other reason, had no intention of entering into any
discussion with the agents. He deliberately closed the window and deliberately closed the car door. It was obvious that subject intended breaking off
the interview and was using this means to isolate himself.

In a final evaluation section, the agents reported: "The approach to Askin,
although cordial and polite, completely upset him. He was unable to talk co-
herently and was completely off balance during the original minutes of the
interview." I have no recollection of the interview that would contradict anything in the FBI report. I have no doubt that I was unnerved by two federal
agents accosting me in this accusatory fashion, even though I had long been
aware of their attention to me and my activities and knew that in their eyes I
was some sort of danger to the nation. It seems almost comical that they
could have viewed their assault on me as "cordial and polite."

*   *   *

Meanwhile, back in the shop, I had become the leader of the union. Miller
Metal had about ninety unionized employees who were a small minority of an
amalgamated union local. Our sister shop, which contained about 80 percent
of the local's total membership, supplied all the union's officers. As chief shop
steward, I was Miller's only representative on the union executive board. I
was also the only Communist among the local union leadership, although the
international representative who had arranged my job and ran local UE operations was probably a party member. My fellow union leaders were constantly
embarrassed by the UE's identification as a communist union and flirted with
solicitations from other unions, including the IUE, to change affiliation. One
reason that the UE organizer had wanted me in the local was to provide a
voice against the CIO and AFL raiders. The fact was that the UE had always
provided good, honest leadership and was respected by most of the workers,
who hoped that the allegations of Communist domination were untrue. It was
part of my responsibility to reinforce their loyalties to the UE by denouncing
the IUE and CIO unions as being dominated by corrupt leaders who just
wanted to grab their dues and would sell out their interests to the bosses if
given the opportunity.

As chief shop steward, I was a major thorn in the company's side. I was
always prepared to be an articulate advocate for worker grievances, and I was

a hard bargainer during contract negotiations. My successes at the bargaining table tended to encourage the militancy of the workers. Although we had a good contract and wage structure in comparison to similar plants, the employees continued to be aggressive in their demands, which I generally encouraged. How much of a problem I was to the company became obvious when the president called me in to his office and appealed to me as a fellow Jew to tone down my union militancy. He even had an uncle of mine, with whom he had some sort of business connection, make a similar appeal. Among other things, I was told that I was going to encourage anti-Semitism among the workers if I continued my anticompany rhetoric. There was, unfortunately, a basis for his concerns. As relations between the workers and the company deteriorated, there was a noticeable increase in anti-Jewish feeling among my coworkers. The fact that they knew I was Jewish didn't seem to have much of an ameliorative effect.

As the expiration of the union contract neared, militancy was rampant among the workers. It didn't take much encouragement on my part to put them in a mood to strike. Many of the employees were young men without families or women who were second wage earners. Some even looked forward to the prospect of a strike and several weeks off from work. Meanwhile, company management believed that its wage structure and benefits package were near the top of the industry, and it was not of a mind to negotiate new benefits. When the contract ran out without a new agreement, the workers were ready to walk out.

Based on my own limited experience, I assumed that the strike would be short-lived. It was one of the worst miscalculations of my life. Management had decided that it was time to wage all-out war with the union and attempt to break it once and for all. Maybe it had counted on the divisions within the union. From the beginning, the strike was bitter. By the end of the first week, a truck that had crossed our picket line to deliver supplies was firebombed within fifteen minutes after leaving the plant. I had no doubt that the bomber was one of the young delinquents who worked in the paint shed. Fortunately, the truck driver was not injured.

By the third week of the strike, the company decided to reopen the plant and bring in strikebreakers. Striking workers were invited to return to work and warned that if they refused they would be replaced. This was a rarely used management tactic at that time, but perfectly legal. The nonunion employees, together with a handful of union members, accepted the offer. The striking workers were furious at their former coworkers as police led them through the picket line. An additional forty to fifty scabs were brought in, apparently from out of state. On the second day of renewed operations, massive numbers of workers from other unionized shops joined our picket line in a show of solidarity. Family members also joined in. My son Steve, who years later would become a labor journalist, had his picture in the local newspapers the next day riding in a stroller that carried a sign that read, "You can't break my Daddy's Union." Unfortunately, his first labor prediction turned out to be wrong.

I have always abhorred violence and even attempted to dissuade my young militant unionists from attacking picket-line-crossing truckers. But when the scabs crossed our picket line, I felt that I had to provide some leadership and wade into one of them. The cops grabbed me along with half a dozen other strikers and hauled us off. Strangely enough, considering the scope of my political activism over nearly a decade, it was the only time in my life I was ever held in jail—although my confinement probably lasted less than half an hour. I was convicted of disorderly conduct and fined $10. One of the more interesting consequences of that incident was that it gave the FBI a reason to designate me as a dangerous person. For the next dozen years, the FBI's annual review of my status routinely noted, under the category called "Evidence of Dangerousness," that I had once been arrested and fined for disorderly conduct. It was a major justification for my retention on the FBI's Security Index, which, as I understand it, was the list of individuals to be rounded up and interned in Arizona or New Mexico in the event of a national emergency.

After about five weeks, it was obvious that the strike was beaten. The union finally advised those workers who wanted their old jobs back to apply for them. Many workers did and were rehired. A few other strike leaders and I were obviously not welcome. I certainly had no interest in returning to work in a nonunion atmosphere amid a bunch of strikebreakers, even if the company would have rehired me. In addition, I was mortified by the damage I felt that I had caused to so many people's lives. I wanted to get as far away as possible. It was the end of my active participation as a member of the blue-collar working class.

*   *   *

My days at Miller Metal had been interrupted by a brief stint in the Army. When I received an Army induction notice in the fall of 1952, I consulted my party elders. I was not in school and was ineligible for a student classification. By the time my wife became pregnant with Steven, it was too late to apply for a fatherhood deferment. I was instructed by my Communist gurus to do whatever was required and be a good soldier. Unlike the situation a decade later during Vietnam, there was no antiwar movement within the military. I was strongly admonished that if I was actually sent to fight, I would have no choice but to kill or be killed like any other soldier; North Korean Communist bullets would not distinguish between Communist and non-Communist GIs.

I only vaguely recall it, but my FBI files report that on November 29, 1952, there was a farewell party for me at the Little Folks Theater in Baltimore "occasioned by subject's being inducted into the U.S. Army." The report added that I "was presented with various gifts," although I do not recall what they were. When I showed up for induction, there was no question that the FBI had phoned ahead. As I sat with several dozen other recruits in the reception center at Fort Meade, Maryland, the telephone rang. I heard the officer who picked up the phone repeat, "Askin?" as he looked down his list. He then lowered his voice.

As we went through routine processing during the next few days, among the forms I was given to fill out was a loyalty oath and security questionnaire. I responded with a statement that such inquiries violated my rights under the First and Fifth Amendments of the U.S. Constitution.

Toward the end of May, the sergeant announced one morning at roll call that I was to report to the separation center for discharge processing. My comrades in arms, most of whom were dying to get out, were astounded and wanted to know how I had pulled it off. I told them that I had a relative with political influence.

When on May 23, 1953, I was actually handed my discharge papers and could take off my uniform, I was ecstatic. At the time, I didn't particularly care that my discharge papers read "general discharge under honorable conditions" rather than the usual "honorable discharge." It was several years later when I realized that such a discharge might have negative consequences and that the Army had no business victimizing me because of my political beliefs. After all, I hadn't asked to be inducted, and when I was I had been a perfectly good soldier—better than most. I had done nothing to deserve being stigmatized. If the Army didn't want someone with my political outlook, it should have decided that before drafting me. When I read in the newspapers that a federal court had ruled that the Army could not give a less-than-honorable discharge because of activities that predated military service, I asked a lawyer friend to try to get my discharge upgraded. Shortly thereafter, I received a new "honorable discharge."

*   *   *

It could be said that I found my first professional career in the left-wing youth movement. My efforts at amateur journalism with my various bulletins and newsletters made such an impression on the national leadership of the LYL that I was approached about moving to New York to become editor of the publication *New Challenge*, the communist movement's effort to reach out to mainstream youth. It was one of the early pocket-size magazines (à la *Jet* and *TV Guide*) and hid its political messages among breezy articles about sports and pop culture. The editorship of *New Challenge* was considered one of the four national leadership positions in the LYL.

To say that I was ecstatic over the opportunity would be an understatement. After the debacle at Miller Metal, I earned a living as a door-to-door salesman in the Baltimore suburbs for some of my left-wing friends who had found refuge from the witch-hunters in the home-improvement business, later immortalized in Barry Levinson's film *Tin Men*. (That industry was one of the few major employers that didn't seem to care about the politics of its workers, as long as they could sell aluminum storm windows, awnings, or siding.) The work was lonely and boring, and I had to push myself to get out of the car and start knocking on doors each day. In addition, I was wearying of the day-to-day tasks of trying to build an activist movement in the hinterlands among what later came to be known as the Silent Generation. Doing my political proselytizing in the Big Apple as the editor of a magazine was infinitely more appealing.

My last public splash before packing for New York was an appearance on behalf of the LYL before a House Armed Services subcommittee considering a universal military training bill. Strangely, I was one of the few left-wing activists of the period who was never subpoenaed to testify before a governmental committee investigating communist activities. Although numerous friends and comrades in far less visible positions were routinely pilloried by those witch-hunting committees, I was spared. However, in a sort of perverse counterstrike, I volunteered to testify before a congressional committee in Washington in opposition to the military training bill. The March 2, 1955, edition of the *Baltimore Sun* contained the following news account under the headline "Witness Dodge Brings a Walkout."

> A House Armed Services subcommittee today walked out on a witness who refused to say whether he was a Communist.
> Frank Askin of Baltimore identified himself as Chairman of the Maryland Labor Youth League, and taking the stand, started reading a statement on a proposed new Military Reserve Program. Representative Brooks, Democrat from Louisiana, the subcommittee Chairman, interrupted to say that the Labor Youth League "has been cited by the Attorney General." "Are you a Communist?" Brooks asked Askin. "That question is completely irrelevant," Askin said; he also called it an "invasion of my rights." Askin started reading again and Representative Winstead, Democrat from Mississippi, moved adjournment of the hearing.
> The motion was carried and the four members of the subcommittee who were present started walking out while Askin was on the stand.

It may have been one of the few occasions in congressional history when an entire committee got up and walked out on a witness in the middle of his testimony. (Some years later, when I was serving as a special counsel to the House Government Operations Committee, Chairman John Conyers walked out on a *government* witness who claimed executive privilege in response to the chairman's demand for certain White House documents. No one else in the hearing room realized why I found the incident so amusing.)

* * *

My chroniclers report that my furniture was loaded into a moving van on November 28, 1955, the same day that I filed a change-of-address card at the Baltimore post office listing my forwarding address in Brooklyn. However, the last official political sighting of me in Baltimore was August 6, when, according to a substantially excised report, I was seen leaving my residence in a 1950 green Plymouth with Maryland license plate BJ 98-52, in which I drove to 1801 West Baltimore Street. Unfortunately, the agents "were unable to ascertain the significance of this visit." By December 9, the New York FBI bureau had opened a file on me and had obtained my new telephone number. A detailed New York bureau review of my activities in January revealed, among other things, that I had "participated in the LYL's efforts in New York City to secure food for Southern Negroes."

My year at *New Challenge* was a delight. Although it was a one-man office during the day, the volunteer staff and editorial board, consisting of a talented and fun-loving group of young radicals, often convened in the evenings to discuss plans for articles and forthcoming issues as well as ideas for expanding the magazine's circulation and influence. Foremost among that group was the extraordinarily gifted and charming Lorraine Hansberry, soon to become one of the country's premier playwrights, and her husband, Robert Nemiroff, who became the curator of Lorraine's literary legacy and a theatrical producer in his own right after Lorraine's untimely death in 1965 as a result of a brain tumor. When I took over *New Challenge*, Lorraine was listed as associate editor and Bob as managing editor. Shortly thereafter, Lorraine took a leave of absence from the magazine to devote more time to her writing. To this day, one of my fondest memories is sitting in Lorraine and Bob's fourth-floor apartment on Bleeker Street in Greenwich Village, listening to Lorraine read excerpts from her manuscript of *A Raisin in the Sun*, which was to win international acclaim a few years later.

My tenure as editor in chief saw the publication of only four issues of *New Challenge*. The lead story in the first issue was entitled "Grace and the Prince," a somewhat cynical view of the "fairy-tale marriage" of Grace Kelly and the prince of Monaco. The article admonished our young readers not to be taken in by all the hoopla about the good life of princes and princesses. It criticized the popular media for

> suggesting to too many girls that perhaps marrying for money is the way to get ahead after all. They [the media] are sidetracking too many guys on the

notion that the big thing in a woman is not her love, her good sense, her ability to stand at your side through life—but simply her looks. And that—with money—you can *buy* the girl of your dreams. And love. And happiness.

Our own moral was that real love had to be based on "striving and sharing and experiencing life to the full together." It probably wasn't such a bad idea. The main political story was about Ku Klux Klan terrorism in the South aimed at southern black activists. The centerfold consisted of an open letter to President Eisenhower urging him to provide federal protection for the nascent civil rights movement. A story in honor of St. Patrick's Day highlighted the role of Irish Americans in the building of the U.S. trade union movement. The May 1956 cover featured a picture of Babe Ruth to promote a story on the psychological barriers that baseball players faced in trying to break his record of sixty home runs, entitled "Mind Over Batter." The second lead was about a black Mississippian who had defied the White Citizens Council and insisted on his right to vote.

*   *   *

A short time after I moved to New York, two events occurred on the other side of the world that were to change the course of my life as well as the left-wing movement in the United States. One was the crushing of the Hungarian uprising by Soviet troops, and the other was Nikita Khrushchev's speech to the Soviet Communist Party Congress. In retrospect, it is hard to explain why Khrushchev's revelations about Stalin's terror came as such a shock to reasonably well-educated, politically alert individuals like myself. After all, the same allegations had been made by writers, historians, and political scientists, including a number of former Communists, for many years. But it seems to be a common human failing that once someone commits to a cause or movement—be it a religion, a cult, or some other equally intense affinity group—it becomes nearly impossible to believe negative information about the group, and all attacks are dismissed as the work of enemies with ulterior motives. What else could explain the many irreconcilable tribal rivalries that exist among factions whose adherents are certain about the rightness of their respective causes—Arabs and Jews, Irish Catholics and Protestants, Hindus and Sikhs, Greeks and Turks, Croats and Serbs and Muslims? In each of these conflicts, there are thoughtful people on both sides who are equally certain that God and right are with them.

Once the leader of the Soviet Union confirmed what the enemies of communism had been saying, it was difficult to deny the obvious—unless, of course, Khrushchev was himself a secret capitalist tool, which was a conclusion that some hard-core Communists were quite willing to accept. But those of us who had adopted the communist ideology after World War II, mainly as a result of the U.S. party's domestic agenda, did not have a great investment in the myth of Soviet probity. The possibility that Stalinism was an aberration and that, by discrediting it, the new leadership would be able to transform the Soviet Union into a model state was rebutted by the brutal Soviet response in Hungary. The impact on the communist youth movement was particularly devastating. The LYL was in total disarray. *New Challenge*, whose fiscal status was already a bit shaky, was jettisoned. A national conference was called to discuss the future. I did not hang around to find out the answer.

I was living in Brooklyn with a wife, a child, no job, and a failed ideology.

2
Newspaper Days

Fortunately, I had found a trade. With a year of experience as the editor of *New Challenge*, I decided that I was a journalist. I answered an ad for a job as a reporter for a weekly newspaper on the Jersey side of the George Washington Bridge. I explained that I had been editing a magazine that went bankrupt and invented some experience on weekly newspapers in Baltimore. Fortunately, nobody investigated my résumé or asked to see copies of my magazine.

Like most weekly newspapers, the *Palisadian* was a one-man band. I reported on everything from town council meetings in the four municipalities we covered to the police blotter and local obituaries. I also wrote all the headlines. It was the latter skill that gained me a job fifteen months later on the copy desk of the daily *Bergen Record*. It was a bit embarrassing years later when I found my *Record* job application in my FBI files, it included a largely bogus history as a journalist and a college degree in English from the University of Baltimore.

Meanwhile, two things occurred that would greatly influence my future plans. I had abandoned my Communist connections, and as the influence of McCarthyism receded, it occurred to me that there were no real barriers to my ambition of becoming a lawyer. I started attending City College of New York (CCNY) part-time, hoping to complete enough credits to apply to law school. The second happening was the onset of a union organizing drive by the American Newspaper Guild. The *Record* was a family-owned paper, and its patrician publisher, Donald Borg, expected absolute personal loyalty from his staff, who were expected to work a six-day week with no overtime pay. Longtime employees were generally well treated, but the salaries of the mostly young and transitory reportorial staff were dependent on a semiannual profit-sharing bonus that could be curtailed at the owner's whim in favor of the purchase of a forest to provide newsprint. With my background, it was inevitable that I would become the leader of the union organizing drive. It was also inevitable that the management would discover that I had been moonlighting (actually daylighting) at the *New York Daily Mirror*, an infraction of company policy for which I was summarily fired in the fall of 1960.

19

I challenged my dismissal as an unfair labor practice before the National Labor Relations Board but dropped the case when I was hired as the executive director of the Democratic Party of Bergen County, which was preparing for the 1961 gubernatorial election. I couldn't be the Democrats' chief spokesperson while waging a legal battle against the county's only daily newspaper.

*   *   *

Since going to work for the Bergen Democrats in 1961, I have been involved in Democratic Party politics to one extent or another—usually in a "reform" capacity. In the late 1960s, I was active in New Jersey's New Democratic Coalition; in 1972, I was an unsuccessful candidate for delegate to the National Convention on George McGovern's slate; in 1976, I was the New Jersey treasurer of the short-lived presidential campaign of populist Senator Fred Harris of Oklahoma; in 1980, I was elected as a Kennedy delegate to the National Convention and was an appointed member of the National Democratic Platform Committee; in the early 1980s, I was a leader of the reform Essex County Democratic Coalition; in 1982, I was an unsuccessful candidate for Congress in the Democratic primary in the Eleventh District of New Jersey; in 1986, I was the official Democratic candidate for Congress in the Eleventh District; in 1988, I was a Jesse Jackson delegate to the National Convention. Through much of the 1980s, I was an elected member of my Democratic County Committee.

I generally describe myself as an independent or progressive Democrat. But from 1961 to 1963, I was part of the backbone of the Democratic establishment in New Jersey and Bergen County. If there were party reformers around, I was part of the system they were out to reform.

The Democratic candidate for governor in 1961 was Richard J. Hughes, an obscure superior court judge and former Mercer County Democratic chairman, handpicked by the party bosses to succeed the retiring Robert Meyner. For the next several months, the big political question in New Jersey was "Who's Hughes?" To most people, he was a political nonentity. The Republican candidate was James Mitchell, a prominent member of President Eisenhower's cabinet and the uncle of movie actor Thomas Mitchell. The early odds listed Hughes as a longshot.

Dick Hughes was a politician's politician. He loved politics, and he loved the Democratic Party. He even seemed willing to suffer political scoundrels gladly, as long as they were loyal Democrats. He also loved being a public servant. During the 1961 campaign, we always addressed him as "Judge." He had a marvelous judicial temperament and was adept at bringing warring factions together. Congressman Frank Thompson, who was part of Hughes's Mercer County Democratic organization and whom I came to know some years later, referred to Hughes as "Two Buckets" because, he explained, he was so adept at carrying water on both shoulders.

As executive director of the Democratic Party in Bergen County, a loose federation of seventy municipal party organizations, it was my job to prevent a Republican landslide in the county, where the GOP was used to piling up majorities of up to 150,000 in gubernatorial elections. We figured from the start that if we could keep Mitchell's Bergen majority under 90,000, our candidate would stand a chance statewide. In an effort to establish the candidate as a man who cared about Bergen County and its people, I rashly issued a statement early in the campaign promising that Hughes would visit every one of Bergen's seventy municipalities before the election in November. It took a Herculean effort, but he actually fulfilled the promise, as the local newspapers kept a running tally during the course of the campaign.

It was part of my job to accompany the candidate on these rounds. I also made it my business to provide him with a brief memo that he could peruse while we were on the road with all the pertinent information about the upcoming event, including the names of our hosts, significant local concerns, and information about local political and community leaders who might be in attendance. I would suggest how he might incorporate local references into his regular stump speech. I felt great pride when, midway through the campaign, Hughes addressed the Democratic State Committee and passed out copies of my memos and asked that party leaders elsewhere in the state provide him with similar guides.

I must confess that I am a bit fuzzy as to what the major policy issues of the campaign were. To a large extent, Hughes ran on the coattails of Bob Meyner, who had been a popular governor with a reputation for integrity. I do recall that Hughes spent a great deal of time talking about improving public education in New Jersey. Reviewing our campaign literature, I note that we bragged that the past Democratic administration had kept the state from adopting an income tax, but I find no pledge to oppose such a tax in the future. Indeed, as governor, Hughes was constantly frustrated in his efforts to have the legislature adopt an income tax to provide funds for public education, which at the time was totally reliant on local property taxes. It was not until he became chief justice of the state supreme court following his retirement as governor that he was able to force an income tax on the state by ruling that reliance on property taxes violated the state constitution's requirement of a "thorough and efficient education" for all its children.

Whatever the issues and whatever the reasons, the people of New Jersey had the good sense to choose the wise and steady Hughes over the nationally prominent Mitchell. In Bergen County, the results exceeded our wildest dreams—a mere 39,000-vote margin for the Republican.

In 1968, after completing law school, I was cocounsel in a lawsuit against

Governor Hughes. The American Civil Liberties Union (ACLU) was suing on behalf of a class of black residents of Plainfield whose apartments had been searched by the state police without warrants in the wake of civil disturbances there. I was told by a member of the governor's staff that when he found out that I was representing the plaintiffs in the Plainfield case, he replied in amazement, "Askin is a friend of mine; he won't hurt me." In his final act before leaving office in 1969, Hughes got the legislature to agree to appropriate $40,000 to settle our suit, since he didn't want to leave office with the threat of personal liability hanging over him. It may be a sign of his generous and forgiving nature that when I ran for Congress some years later, he was willing to come and speak for me.

*　　*　　*

Although I considered myself a good and true Democrat, the FBI still had me on its Communist-watch list. It was October 20, 1961, two weeks before the election, when the Newark office reported to Washington that I was employed by the Democrats and working on the Hughes campaign. The memo noted that the information was being provided for headquarters "in view of the fact that public media have indicated that President Kennedy might travel to New Jersey to stump for Hughes in his candidacy for Governor."

The director of the FBI immediately informed the attorney general of the United States of this startling discovery, repeating the information that President Kennedy was planning a trip to the state. Interestingly, a copy was also directed to Deputy Attorney General Byron White, soon to become a justice of the U.S. Supreme Court. There is no indication that anything further was ever done in connection with this information, and I have no reason to believe that the FBI ever disclosed anything about me to officials of the Democratic Party in New Jersey or Bergen County. If so, the Democrats apparently did not consider it significant.

*　　*　　*

People tend to remember traumatic public happenings from personal perspectives. To me, the Cuban Missile Crisis was the event that wrecked my first congressional campaign. I use the term *my campaign* in a professional sense. The campaign director always views the campaign as his or her own, the candidate is sort of an afterthought. Of course, I had a somewhat different perspective when I became the candidate.

In any event, in 1962, I signed on to direct the campaign of Donald Sorkow, a Democrat in the Ninth District of New Jersey. Shortly after the gubernatorial campaign, the Democratic Party found that it could no longer afford a full-time director, so I took a job as managing editor of a chain of weekly tabloid newspapers in Bergen County. But I found running political campaigns more exciting, and when Don offered me the chance, I jumped at it. He was a young lawyer starting a private practice and figured that he couldn't be hurt by the notoriety of a congressional campaign, even though he was challenging a longtime Republican incumbent and had no chance of winning. Especially in those days, when lawyer advertising was absolutely prohibited by ethics rules, running for public office was one of the few ways lawyers could promote themselves and build a reputation. It was pretty much a no-lose situation for the candidate.

Don was young and idealistic, and we were extremely compatible. Our biggest crisis of conscience came when Lou Harris, the professional pollster who had been hired as a consultant, suggested that the only issue we could exploit against the incumbent was federal aid to parochial schools. The district was heavily Catholic, and the incumbent was a Protestant who had opposed such aid in the past. Don was a Jew who had been active in the Anti-Defamation League of B'nai B'rith and was a strong believer in church-state separation. On principle, I also opposed public aid to religious education, but I had never considered it a burning issue. I sympathized somewhat with religious parents who had to pay taxes to support the public school system and then had to pay separately for their children's education. However, on balance, I felt that diverting public funds to private education would guarantee the destruction of the public school system, especially in the inner cities, while private schools for the well-to-do would flourish. I agonized along with Don about what to do. The more we studied the demographics of the district, the more convinced we were. Our only hope of an upset was the shifting of a significant part of the Catholic vote.

Don decided to act on Harris's advice, and I did not try to dissuade him. We started to build a mailing list of district voters who were active in Catholic communal organizations, such as the Knights of Columbus, and prepared material to be sent only to people on that list. Obviously, we couldn't keep the contents of the mailing a secret, and we knew that our opponent would use it to try to discredit Don with other constituencies, especially the Jews. But Don believed that, with his background, he could minimize damage in that quarter.

Then came the Cuban Missile Crisis. For most of the last ten days before the election, U.S. and Soviet warships steamed toward each other in the Atlantic, and the world waited nervously for the nuclear holocaust. People sat anxiously in front of radios and TV sets. No one cared about aid to parochial schools. The only thing we could address in public campaign statements was the missile crisis, and the only thing we could say was that the candidate stood 100 percent behind the president in this time of crisis—which, of course, is exactly what our opponent was saying. There was no longer any difference between them on the issue that was suddenly the only one that mattered. The crisis was defused several days before the election, but between then and the actual voting, people were too busy breathing sighs of relief to have any more interest in petty political squabbles. The district voted pretty much according to historic pattern, and our Republican foe coasted to an easy victory. The good news was that nuclear war had been averted.

An election campaign is a tumultuous ride that ends abruptly and precipitously—especially for losers. But this time, I had new goals in mind. I had completed almost enough credits at CCNY. I signed up to take the Law School Aptitude Test and began filing law school applications. I had hoped to attend evenings, but the only schools in the area that would consider admitting me without a bachelor's degree, Columbia and Rutgers, had no night schools. Undeterred, I promptly accepted when Rutgers offered me admission and a full scholarship. I was ready to embark on my next voyage.

PART II
TALES OF LAW

3

The Portal of the Law

When I enrolled in Rutgers Law School in September 1963, I was suddenly a full-time student for the first time since graduating from high school fifteen years before. Financially, the decision made no sense whatsoever. I was paying alimony and child support, had a second wife with a one-year-old child and another on the way, and had almost no savings. Fortunately, I found a convenient job—working on the copy desk of the *Newark Star-Ledger* from 6 to 11:45 every night.

Toward the end of the first year of law school, I also started working Sunday nights on the *New York Post* copy desk. Since the *Post* was an afternoon paper, the copy desk worked midnight to 7 A.M., after which I would drive straight to Newark to go to school. The pay at the *Post* was much better— $65 a night, compared with $23 at the *Ledger*. Because of something that happened at the end of that first year, the *Post* gig turned out to be a godsend.

One evening, the editor in chief of the *Star-Ledger* called me into his office and told me that the paper was getting rid of its part-time copy editors and I would be let go at the end of the week. The news was astounding. None of the other copy editors had mentioned it, and most of them were part-timers too, working full-time on New York newspapers and moonlighting one or two nights a week at the *Ledger* to pick up extra money. (Some referred to the *Ledger* rim as the "alimony desk.") The following evening, I confronted the editor over this glaring incongruity. After hemming and hawing for a while, he finally asked me if I had ever worked for the *Daily Worker*, the Communist newspaper. I told him no, but explained that I had edited a left-wing youth magazine at one time. He insisted that he had information that I had been employed by the *Worker*. When I pressed him for the source of his information, he claimed that it had been an anonymous telephone call, which made no sense in view of his adamancy in the face of my denials. Despite my pleas, he told me that the only way I could keep my job was to get clearance from the FBI.

It seemed obvious to me that the FBI had spoken to him about me, but he stuck to his story. I thought that I could probably work an additional night at the *Post*, so I was less upset about losing the measly $23 a night the *Ledger* paid me than I was at being fired because of my past political associations. I was especially concerned because I knew that when I went before a bar character committee, I would have to state whether I had ever been fired from a job and, if so, why. I did not want to have to explain this away, but I had no intention of seeking absolution from the FBI.

The next day, I asked for an audience with Dean Willard Heckel and explained everything to him, including my past associations and my concern about having to face a bar committee. The dean was outraged and promised to try to help me. Several days later, he reported to me that he and another faculty member had gone to lunch with the *Star-Ledger* editor and had gotten him to agree to rescind his edict. He had assured the editor of my trustworthiness and castigated him for permitting the FBI to dictate his personnel practices. The agreement was that I could continue to work for the *Ledger* on Saturday nights only, which was fine with me, since I could work at the *Post* on Fridays and Sundays. And since I expected to be part of the Law Review staff the following year, I knew that there was no way I could continue to work six or seven nights a week.

Although I must assume that the FBI made direct contact with the *Star-Ledger* management, there is an FBI memo that at least clouds the issue. A memo from Newark to bureau headquarters dated March 25, 1964, about a month before the incident, states that I would not be personally interviewed by agents because my employment by the *Star-Ledger* "might cause embarrassment to the Bureau." It says nothing about approaching the *Ledger* management without my knowledge, although presumably such a course would threaten the same embarrassment. On the other hand, some years later, when I sued the Newark FBI office on behalf of a client, I obtained through discovery a document describing how the bureau had gotten a member of the Socialist Workers Party fired from a job with another New Jersey newspaper. So it was clearly within FBI operating procedure to pay secret visits to employers—including newspapers—to "expose" those on the FBI's watch list.

* * *

This may come as a shock to many generations of lawyers who suffered through law school, but I loved being a law student, despite my onerous schedule. Maybe it was because I had never really been to college, and this was my first opportunity since high school to be a full-time student. Also, because I was older and had been dealing with legal issues for a number of years as a journalist and a political organizer, the material came fairly easily to me. I found Rutgers Law School to be a compatible place with a marvelous faculty, many of whom were deeply involved in real-world activities.

In my second year as a law student, Arthur Kinoy joined the faculty. Arthur, who was to become my legal guru, was one of the master constitutional litigators in the country. He had been an architect of the legal strategy for the southern civil rights movement and, along with Bill Kunstler and Mort Stavis, was to establish the Center for Constitutional Rights in New York.

Ruth Bader Ginsburg (now Supreme Court Justice Ginsburg) joined the Rutgers family the same day I did—I as a student, she as a professor. She was my civil procedure teacher during my freshman year. We were about the same age, and we traveled the same road for the next decade and a half, until Ruth was appointed to the U.S. Court of Appeals by President Jimmy Carter as he was leaving office in 1980. Ruth and I were faculty colleagues at Rutgers from 1966 to 1972, when she left to join the Columbia Law School faculty; from 1976 until her appointment to the bench, we were two of the four general counsel of the ACLU. Indeed, when my student days were over and I joined the faculty, I also made the course in civil procedure my main teaching venture and regularly looked to Ruth for guidance. Even on her first day as a teacher, Ruth's knowledge of the subject was encyclopedic. She was a workaholic who obviously cherished the subject matter of the federal judicial process, an obvious plus for a future member of the U.S. Supreme Court.

It came as something of a surprise to everyone who knew her when Ruth suddenly emerged in the 1970s as the country's foremost legal advocate of women's rights. She was probably the least ideological member of our faculty. In the late 1960s, the Rutgers faculty was pretty well split along political lines. (Some wryly referred to the two sides as the "Russian" and "Chinese" factions.) But Ruth never took sides. No one ever knew in advance which side Ruth would be on when it came time for faculty votes, although she could usually be relied on to support affirmative action efforts to diversify the law school student body and faculty. She was almost exclusively a scholar, with apparently little interest in "political" issues, either internal or external to the law school. When students attempted to capture Ruth's essence in the annual parodies they put on in those days, they would portray her intensity. The 1970 law school yearbook featured scenes from a show in which a male student stood behind the oblivious Ginsburg impersonator and stripped her down to her underwear as she lectured on an esoteric procedural issue.

Apparently, Ruth started examining the subject of gender discrimination as a scholarly and intellectual endeavor at the prodding of her female students and found herself drawn into the issue on a personal level as a consequence of her own experiences as a woman trying to succeed in what had formerly been a male bastion. In any event, she began to take on cases of sex discrimination for the ACLU and, in 1972, established the ACLU's Women's Rights Project. Over the next few years, she argued most of the gender discrimination cases before the Supreme Court and was responsible for establishing most of the constitutional law in the area.

Ruth Ginsburg was not the only woman who came to Rutgers Law School in the fall of 1963 destined to achieve national prominence. Among the four female classmates of mine in the class of 1966 was Hazel Rollins, who in 1993, was to became President Clinton's secretary of energy under the name of Hazel O'Leary. Hazel, one of three African-American students in my year, had been one of the most popular members in the class—a function of the fact that she was not only smart but also quite stunning looking. I thought Hazel did Rutgers particularly proud when it was reported in July 1993 that her counsel was decisive in convincing President Clinton to continue the moratorium on nuclear testing that had been scheduled to end that summer.

In contrast to the class of 1966, by 1970, the entering classes at Rutgers were almost 50 percent women, thanks in part to the efforts of Ruth Ginsburg.

*   *   *

My years as a law student were marked by the assassination of John F. Kennedy and the explosion of the southern civil rights movement. I found it a bit bizarre when the struggle for black freedom actually became a popular cause in the country. Just a decade before, my comrades and I in Baltimore had been condemned and placed on the FBI's Security Index of dangerous subversives because we advocated such a cause.

The outcasts of the 1950s became public heroes in the 1960s. But to the FBI, I was still suspect. A memo dated March 1964 reported that agents had conducted a physical surveillance of my Leonia residence on March 9, 10, 11, and 13, but that I was not observed. Of course, unless they conducted their surveillance between 12:30 and 7:30 A.M., they were not likely to find me at home.

They interviewed at least one neighbor, who reported that I was a little "weird," an observation that was explained by the fact that I would "on occasion grow a rather long beard and generally gives the impression of being different from the rest of their neighbors." In fact, I had briefly sported a goatee but had shaved it off before starting law school the year before. The FBI could not determine that I belonged to any organizations other than the Leonia Democratic Club but decided to continue my placement on the Security Index, a status that would not end until 1967, after I had graduated from law school.

I confess that all through law school I was obsessed with the possibility that my past Communist associations would be used to deny me admission to the bar. Every bar applicant has to be passed by a character committee, and I was concerned that some conservative lawyers were going to block my admission. The Supreme Court had not yet decided some important cases that would make it impossible for bar committees to reject applicants solely because of past Communist associations.

I had discussed my concerns about the character committee with Assistant Dean Helen Hoffman, the school's placement director and a sensitive and caring human being. She arranged for me to talk with a senior partner in a leading Newark law firm who would be sympathetic. His advice was quite simple: move out of Bergen County. Bar applicants in New Jersey face a character committee from the bar association in the county in which they reside. He said that the only obstacle might be running into some conservative suburban lawyers without any appreciation for civil liberties. He felt certain that if I went before a sophisticated committee from urban Essex County, there would be no problem. I followed his advice. Before my senior year, we sold our house in Leonia and moved to an apartment in Newark. I had no problem with the character and fitness committee, although it did routinely ask the FBI for derogatory information.

*   *   *

Although there was not much political activism among law students in those days, we did organize at least one march down Broad Street, Newark, to the Federal Building to urge the Department of Justice to provide protection for the civil rights workers in the South. Most of our contact with the civil rights movement was derivative, coming through Professor Kinoy's lectures in civil liberties class. Through him, we lived the historic case of *Dombrowski v. Pfister*, which he argued before the U.S. Supreme Court during the first week of the spring 1965 semester and was decided as the semester was about to end in April.

The *Dombrowski* case involved an ingenious attempt by Kinoy to obtain an injunction from a federal court sitting in equity against the criminal prosecution of a group of civil rights workers by the attorney general of Louisiana under a state sedition statute. Kinoy contended that the statute was an abridgment of speech that violated the first Amendment of the U.S. Constitution and that the purpose and effect of the prosecution were to intimidate civil rights activists. The suit ran counter to two well-entrenched legal doctrines: (1) that courts of equity do not enjoin criminal prosecutions, and (2) that a federal court may not interfere with judicial proceedings in a state court. Our civil liberties class was jubilant when the Supreme Court voted five to four, in an opinion authored by Justice William J. Brennan Jr., to uphold the authority of a federal court to protect constitutional rights in such circumstances. The decision was a high-water mark of the Warren Court era, one of its most far-reaching determinations of the special role and duty of our federal courts to protect fundamental constitutional rights from overreaching government agencies, both state and federal.

Although the *Dombrowski* precedent was short-lived and was quickly eroded by a series of decisions handed down by a new Supreme Court majority shortly after Richard Nixon's election as president, for me, it was the beginning of a new faith. Having tired of the street activism of my youth, I began to see that as a lawyer I could continue to be an effective advocate for social change on behalf of causes about which I felt deeply. The lawyer as hired gun, which seemed to be the model for our training, had never appealed to me. I certainly did not visualize myself going off to some high-powered law firm to represent corporate or other private interests. While my classmates were all interviewing with law firms, I expected to remain a journalist. My role model was Anthony Lewis of the *New York Times*, and my aspiration was to become a press correspondent at the Supreme Court. However, the Warren Court, and especially Justice Brennan, had provided me with new inspiration. Suddenly, I could see myself practicing law the way Professor Kinoy and his associates in the civil rights movement did. Maybe I would become a practicing lawyer after all, a public-interest lawyer—or, as Professor Kinoy liked to call it, "a people's lawyer."

* * *

At about the same time that I started to change my career perspective, some members of the faculty began suggesting that, in light of my outstanding academic record, I consider going into teaching. The idea of becoming a law professor was immediately appealing. I figured that it would allow me to make a decent salary while taking on volunteer legal cases, like Professor Kinoy did.

Rutgers had never before hired one of its own graduates for the faculty, let alone one just graduating. Law schools outside the first rank of the Harvards, Yales, and Columbias believed that they had to populate their faculties with graduates of the elite law schools, as most members of the Rutgers faculty were. I put my name in for the annual law schools hiring meeting, referred to as the "meat market." Several schools, notably New Mexico and Indiana, seemed genuinely interested. I felt that in order to avoid future embarrassment, I had an obligation to reveal to them my past political associations. I asked members of the Rutgers faculty—most of whom were aware of my past history and the dean's intercession with the *Star-Ledger*—to make discreet disclosures on my behalf.

For whatever reason, the only firm offer I received was from Rutgers itself. After a divisive fight, the faculty voted to offer me a job as an assistant professor. I happily accepted. Thus, I had a job on the Rutgers Law School faculty even before I had completed my final examinations. I was ready to begin a whole new career in the autumn of 1966.

*   *   *

The highlight of my first semester on the faculty was the dedication of a new law school building, Ackerson Hall, on University Avenue across the street from the main Rutgers campus. We had actually moved into Ackerson, from a former YWCA building on Washington Street, during my senior year, but the official dedication had been put off until the fall of 1966. Among the dedication participants were Chief Justice Earl Warren and Supreme Court Justices William Brennan and Abe Fortas. Since I was the junior member of the faculty, Dean Heckel asked me to pick up Chief Justice Warren at Newark Airport and be his chaperon for the day. I told the dean that I was embarrassed to drive the chief in my beat-up old Buick, but he said that Warren was a very modest man who would not mind at all. In any event, I got one of my students to borrow a relative's Cadillac.

Airport officials gave me permission to drive out on to the tarmac and pick up the chief justice as he stepped off the plane. When we drove away and sirens began to blare around us, I realized that we had a police escort. Warren seemed a bit uncomfortable, and he commented that the first thing he did when he became governor of California was to ban the unnecessary use of sirens by the state police because of his concern over noise pollution.

After the morning session, Justice Brennan joined our little entourage as we drove the several blocks to the Robert Treat Hotel for a luncheon program. On the way, Brennan, a native Newarker whose father had once been police commissioner, commented to the chief that the car trailing us contained plainclothes Newark detectives. Warren, who was being denounced by law-and-order types all over the country because of his Court's many decisions protecting the constitutional rights of criminal defendants, responded, "Who are they afraid of—us or somebody else?" After lunch, Brennan suggested that we walk back to the law school so that he could show Warren the sights of downtown Newark. As we walked through Military Park and Brennan was pointing out buildings where he used to have offices, I spotted walking toward us Joel Jacobson, president of the New Jersey Industrial Union Council and a member of the Rutgers board of governors. As he strolled past, I nonchalantly greeted him. Never in my life have I seen anyone do a double take like Joel did—his head practically spinning on its axis—as he recognized the figures on either side of me. When we arrived back at the law school building, we were greeted by a picket line of jeering marchers carrying "Impeach Earl Warren" signs. "I was wondering where my friends were," Warren commented good-naturedly. "They usually show up wherever I go."

To be honest, I remember nothing about the dedication ceremonies other than my brush with these judicial giants. At the end of the day, I drove Brennan and Warren back to Newark Airport. When the car stopped for a light at

Broad Street and Central Avenue in the middle of downtown Newark, I saw
a guy on the street corner peering into the car and then, in a stage whisper,
asking the motorcycle escort in front of us, "Hey, is that Earl Warren?" When
the cop nodded in the affirmative, the guy cupped his hand over his mouth
and shouted for all of downtown Newark to hear, "Hey Earl, you're a good
man, but a little too far to the Left." To which Brennan commented, "Well,
Chief, you can't please everybody."

* * *

In the late 1960s, Rutgers Law School had a reputation for being politically
divisive. But it is probably true to say that academic politics is to politics as
military music is to music. That is, it is not politics in the ordinary sense that
most people understand it—as in Democrats and Republicans or liberals and
conservatives. The divisions at Rutgers were more along the lines of elitists
versus populists and scholars versus doers and teachers. The self-described
scholars tended to view their jobs as adding to the storehouse of legal knowledge and considered their occasional classroom obligations as unfortunate di-
versions from their main activity. They viewed legal education as an academic
discipline akin to Ph.D. programs and dismissed courses designed to teach
students lawyering skills as "trade school" education. Of course, their coun-
terparts insisted that the scholars' pedagogical predilections merely reflected
their own inadequacies as lawyers. I was soon categorized by the scholars as a
"practitioner" and clearly felt an emotional and intellectual attachment to the
teacher-activists. Dean Heckel was most decidedly part of the latter camp. He
considered teaching a high calling and had little use for the faculty elitists
who considered it beneath them to waste much of their valuable time on mere
students. Dean Heckel also had a great commitment to public service. As a
lay leader of the Presbyterian church and, for several years, its national mod-
erator, he was a force for modernization of church practices, including the
ordination of gay priests. Heckel himself was most certainly homosexual, although it was only at the end of his life, when such things were becoming at
least minimally socially acceptable, that he began to exhibit a more openly
gay lifestyle.

Dean Heckel also felt strongly that the law school had an obligation to be a
servant to the community in which it existed. When the War on Poverty was
launched during the Johnson administration, he became the president of the
Newark Community Corporation, the main arm of the poverty program in
Newark, and made law school resources available to it. He was a strong supporter of the embryonic Legal Services for the Poor program. When black
activists in Newark accused the contractors building the new law school of
discriminating against minority construction workers, Heckel sided with them,

even though it meant a delay in the completion of the building. When Newark, like many other cities, exploded in urban rioting in the summer of 1967, he opened the law school as a headquarters for community forces trying to restore peace to the city and to resolve the many grievances of the urban poor against the city administration and police department.

Heckel and his associate dean and longtime roommate Malcolm Talbott had long been concerned about the scarcity of students of color attending the law school. My graduating class had three out of 150, which was about par for the course. Malcolm, who handled admissions, would give special consideration to nonwhite applicants, but there were not many of them. Willard asked me in the fall of 1967 to chair a special faculty committee to deal with the problem of minority admissions, and we determined that there were only about fifty black lawyers in the entire state of New Jersey, about one-half of 1 percent of the practicing bar. We could not identify more than three lawyers of Puerto Rican background, despite a large Puerto Rican population in the state.

My special committee worked throughout the year to devise a feasible program to increase minority admissions that the faculty would support. In part because of a fairly widespread belief that there were few minority college graduates who were interested in attending law school, our discussions foundered. When the assassination of Martin Luther King Jr. in April 1967 sparked more urban unrest and increased public concern about the grievances of the black population, some of us decided that the time had come to push through a serious program of minority admissions so that we could train substantial numbers of indigenous lawyers to represent the urban community.

Our proposal set a rather ambitious goal of admitting twenty minority students the following year and forty each year thereafter, which would represent about 25 percent of each entering class. Although proponents acknowledged that we might not be able to meet our goals, we included a standard that any applicant who had graduated from an accredited four-year college in the top half of his or her class was presumptively qualified for admission. In other words, all minority applicants who satisfied that standard were entitled to admission until our goal had been fulfilled. Perhaps because some of our colleagues assumed that we would not have enough qualified applicants to achieve our goal, our proposal was overwhelmingly adopted before the end of the 1967–68 academic year for implementation the following September. Thus was born the Rutgers Minority Student Program (MSP), probably the most successful such effort in U.S. legal education. For the next quarter century, it turned out many of the outstanding African American, Caribbean American, and Asian American lawyers now contributing to the legal and political life of our country. Among the members of the first MSP class were at least two future judges, a future executive director of the National Legal Services

Corporation, one of the most prominent trial lawyers in Mississippi, and the executive director of a state civil rights agency, in addition to a number of successful practicing lawyers. I consider my role in the creation and establishment of this program to be one of my most important contributions to the life of our nation.

4
Advocating for Racial Justice

The urban riots in the summer of 1967 also launched my career as a practicing lawyer. Although I had been admitted to the New Jersey bar in late 1966, the only occasion I had had to practice law was representing a neighbor in a small-claims dispute with a laundry that had ruined her dress. But the summer of 1967 brought a huge demand for lawyers who were willing to donate their time to riot-related cases. I undertook the criminal defense of one Newark resident accused of looting and joined a team of civil rights lawyers, including several other members of the law school faculty, planning to bring a class action against the Newark police department for violation of civil rights. After a decade-long absence, I suddenly found myself back as an active participant in the civil rights movement.

My representation of an alleged looter was my introduction to criminal law. It was more educational than a semester in a criminal law class. The main thing I learned was that litigation was mostly about *facts*, not law. My client was a fifty-year-old Newarker with no criminal record. He had gone to the bus stop at the height of the riot to meet his wife when she came home from work. As he waited, a police car pulled up and two cops jumped out, threw him to the ground, and handcuffed him. He was charged with looting. I was convinced that my client was telling the truth and that the arresting officers had picked a random black man off the street.

The only other eyewitness to the events was an unknown juvenile who was already handcuffed in the police car when my client was taken into custody. After a six-week search, I was able to locate a juvenile who had been arrested by the same two cops at about the same time. Without prompting, the kid corroborated what my client had told me about his arrest. I was ecstatic; I felt like Perry Mason. I subpoenaed the juvenile to testify at my client's trial, and he repeated what he had told me. Since the charge was for a misdemeanor, my client did not at that time have a right to jury trial, so the case was heard by a judge. In his ruling, the judge said that he had no reason to disbelieve the testimony of the police officers. I was stunned. Since there had clearly been no opportunity for my client and his witness to fabricate their story, it was obvious that the cops were lying. Even though my client was sentenced to time already served while awaiting bail, I appealed. I called to the attention of the appellate court the findings of numerous federal and state crime commissions that white police officers frequently fabricated criminal charges against black defendants in riot-type situations, and I insisted that a court could not take an inflexible position to favor the testimony of police officers in such cases. The appeals court denied my appeal without opinion.

*   *   *

There was much disagreement over the immediate cause of the Newark "riot." The police and city administration placed the blame on civil rights agitators such as playwright Leroi Jones (later to become Imamu Amiri Baraka) and Tom Hayden. Hayden and some of his comrades from the Students for a Democratic Society (SDS) had set up shop in Newark's central ward under the name of the Newark Community Union Project (NCUP) shortly after the formation of SDS and the issuance of its famous Port Huron statement. There was no doubt that the black population of Newark was seething with grievances against the predominantly Italian city administration. The immediate spark was a demonstration in front of the police station protesting the arrest and beating of a cabdriver named John Smith. When some members of the crowd began throwing bottles and rocks, the police attacked, launching four days of police vengeance against the essentially defenseless black community and resulting in twenty-six deaths. A report commissioned by Governor Hughes and issued the following February called for an investigation of the Newark police department, which it accused of "the use of excessive and unjustified force and other abuses against Negro citizens." It further accused the state troopers assigned to riot duty of engaging in "a pattern of police action for which there is no possible justification."

The post-riot legal response was organized by the young Newark Legal Services, the local arm of the national Legal Services Corporation spawned by Lyndon Johnson's War on Poverty, and by the New Jersey Chapter of the ACLU, then guided by a dynamic young lawyer named Hank di Suvero. It was Hank who recruited me for the legal team, which was attempting to provide representation for the hundreds of people arrested during the disturbances as well as to organize a federal civil rights suit against the police forces for the needless death and destruction unleashed against the black community. That endeavor was also my introduction to Mort Stavis, the dean of New Jersey's civil rights lawyers, who was masterminding the federal litigation. After much brainstorming, we filed a complaint alleging such massive violations of constitutional rights by the Newark police that the only effective remedy would be to place the department in receivership and have the court appoint a master to oversee its operation. Like many such lawsuits, this one did not result in a legal remedy but turned out to be an effective "political" tool in the interests of the client—Newark's black community. It was one of the many public actions that helped mobilize the majority population of Newark to elect the city's first black mayor, Ken Gibson, in 1970.

*   *   *

I confess to having had some misgivings about involving myself with the ACLU. I still harbored some lingering resentment over the organization's failure to aggressively defend the rights of my Communist comrades during the McCarthyite hysteria. As the ACLU itself belatedly acknowledged in the mid-1970s, its attempts to curry favor with J. Edgar Hoover and congressional witch-hunters had caused it to be less than vigilant in defending the First Amendment rights of Communists. I was proud to be a member of the ACLU national board several years later when it did its mea culpas for the McCarthy era and even rescinded its 1940s expulsion of Communist leader Elizabeth Gurley Flynn.

I was impressed by Hank di Suvero's forthright stand and the leadership he displayed in the tumultuous summer of 1967, and I decided to enlist as an ACLU volunteer lawyer. As the legal aftermath of the Newark events proceeded, Hank came to me with another legal project involving nearby Plainfield, where there had been some parallel occurrences. The unique aspect of the Plainfield situation was that in the midst of the civil unrest, there had been a burglary at a gun factory in a nearby community, and forty-six carbines had been reported missing. Five days after the outbreak of the Plainfield "riot," when conditions in the city were nearly back to normal, Governor Hughes authorized the state police to conduct a massive search of the all-black West End Gardens housing project, in the midst of the riot area, to search for the missing rifles. The state police systematically went through at least twenty-six apartments but found none of the missing weapons. The police had no search warrants, and they justified the action on the basis of a declaration of emergency signed by the governor three days earlier during the height of the unrest.

Di Suvero had already spent a Saturday afternoon in Plainfield on the streets around West End Gardens signing up plaintiffs for a civil suit against the governor for illegal searches. He had enlisted sixty-three individuals who said that they had been victims of the search and wanted to join in the suit. Hank had also approached an old Bergen County colleague from the Hughes campaign, Lenny Weinglass, about working on the case. Lenny had recently resigned as a deputy attorney general and as counsel to the New Jersey National

Guard and had opened a law office in Newark. He was already representing Tom Hayden's NCUP. Lenny and I both had some reservations about suing our old friend Dick Hughes, but we found the case so exciting that we agreed to undertake it as cocounsel. I handled most of the briefwriting, and Len, an outstanding courtroom lawyer, did the bulk of the trial preparation.

The primary legal issue was the constitutionality of the search. The Fourth Amendment to the U.S. Constitution forbids government agents from entering and searching a person's home without a warrant issued by a judicial officer unless there are some kind of exigent circumstances. The state claimed that a declaration of emergency signed by the state's chief executive could substitute for a judicial warrant. We contended that even if a real emergency might justify a search, there was no emergency at the time of this search and the governor's declaration of such was stale. The law at the time was unsettled as to whether a state's chief executive could be sued for damages for violation of constitutional rights.

Our litigation position was undermined by what I assume was a fortuitous occurrence. After we filed suit in federal court against Governor Hughes personally, he filed a third-party complaint against the state of New Jersey, seeking indemnification from the state should he be held liable to pay damages to the plaintiffs. The attorney general's office assigned William J. Brennan III, son of the Supreme Court justice, to represent the state. Len and I were particularly nervous about the issue of executive immunity from suits for damages. The Warren Court had been in the process of stripping public officials of immunity in various circumstances, but those decisions were often five to four, with Justice Brennan invariably a member of the pro–civil rights majority. We immediately recognized that because of his son's involvement in the case, Brennan would be forced to recuse himself if it ever reached the Supreme Court, and we would be deprived of his possibly decisive vote. As a consequence, the defendants had some unusual leverage against us if they were of a mind to settle out of court. And that is what eventually occurred.

We had some leverage of our own, however. Dick Hughes was completing his second term as governor and was ineligible to run for reelection. He did not want to leave office with the threat of personal liability hanging over his head and little bargaining power *vis-à-vis* the state legislature. So when his counsel suggested a monetary settlement during the waning days of the Hughes administration, both sides were in a mood to bargain. We agreed on a figure of $40,000 to be divided between the ACLU, for fees and costs, and the plaintiffs. Each of the sixty-three plaintiffs received a minimum payment of $100, and the remainder of the damages was apportioned according to individual loss, such as property damage and infliction of mental distress. The largest payment went to a woman who was nursing her baby when the troopers burst in on her. In one of his final acts before leaving office, Governor Hughes got the state legislature to approve the settlement and appropriate the money from the state treasury.

In 1974, the U.S. Supreme Court finally ruled, in a case involving the governor of Ohio, that a state's chief executive is not entitled to absolute immunity from damages for violation of constitutional rights but does have a qualified immunity for acts committed in "good faith." Knowing Hughes's commitment to constitutional principles, I have always assumed that he recognized that he had behaved questionably in authorizing the Plainfield searches without a warrant, did not want to have to justify his action at a trial, and was happy to have the search victims compensated for the injustice done to them—as long as the $40,000 did not come out of his own pocket.

* * *

Civil rights was a particularly hot topic at Rutgers Law School in the late 1960s. One of my senior faculty colleagues, Al Blumrosen, had a long history of involvement in legislative efforts to combat racial discrimination in housing and employment. He had been an official with the federal Equal Employment Opportunity Commission (EEOC) as well as an adviser to the New Jersey Division on Civil Rights. He asked me and another junior colleague, Dick Chused (who later moved on to Georgetown Law School), to help establish, under a grant from the EEOC, an academic enterprise designed to streamline the state agency's administrative practices related to enforcing antidiscrimination laws.

The Rutgers Administrative Process Project lasted for two years and succeeded in restructuring the state division's processes for dealing with discriminatory practices in both employment and housing. We issued two thick publications that became models for state antidiscrimination agencies: *Enforcing Fair Housing Laws: Apartments in White Suburbia* and *Enforcing Equality in Housing and Employment Through State Civil Rights Laws*. The project was also a model in the newly emerging field of clinical legal education. The activism of the 1960s was reflected in the law school world by a new enthusiasm for hands-on student education to supplement the traditional Socratic classroom method of case analysis as portrayed a few years later in the book and movie *The Paper Chase*. Activist students agitated for a chance to learn through doing while providing representation for socially worthwhile causes.

The major thrust of our work was to devise methods for exposing and eliminating discriminatory practices without the necessity of case-by-case adjudication. Typically, housing discrimination cases involved the tedious and time-consuming process of finding a specific victim and then proving that the same dwelling would have been rented or sold to a person of a different racial or ethnic background under conditions that the rejected applicant had been prepared to satisfy. We decided to find ways to expose practices that inevitably resulted in discriminatory treatment without having to prove intentional discrimination against any particular individual.

We adopted as our guinea pig the town of Parsippany–Troy Hills, a suburban community about twenty miles west of Newark, which was saturated with relatively low cost garden apartments clearly within the financial means of vast segments of the nonwhite population that resided and worked in the surrounding communities. We determined that there were nineteen separate apartment developments in Parsippany with some fifty-five hundred rental units. Initial visual inspections satisfied us that there were almost no nonwhite families living in eighteen of the nineteen developments; the nineteenth and smallest development was operated by a nonprofit agency that had a specific goal of promoting housing integration. We had the Civil Rights Division issue a joint complaint against the eighteen developments, alleging a pattern and practice of discrimination. We proceeded to prepare for a hearing before an administrative judge. Most of the hearings were conducted in the law school building, thus expanding the educational impact of our program.

The evidence presented at the hearing consisted mainly of objective facts about the rental practices of the eighteen defendants, as set forth in their responses to interrogatories, and expert testimony as to why those practices would inevitably result in the exclusion of nonwhites as tenants. For example, many apartments were rented without public advertising through word of mouth to friends of the already existing white tenant community. When apartment vacancies were advertised, it was invariably in places where the information was unlikely to come to the attention of nonwhite apartment seekers. Additionally, we presented testimony from personnel managers of large local businesses about the difficulties they had recruiting black employees because of the unavailability of housing for them in the area. Inexorably, the case was made that the discriminatory pattern would continue unless the defendants were required to take affirmative steps to publicize their vacancies among the region's nonwhite population. The hearing examiner upheld the complaint of discrimination and ordered remedial action by the defendants, including adoption of our proposal for a tenant referral system, which would guarantee that nonwhites who were seeking housing would be notified of apartment vacancies. This included notification of the local Fair Housing Council, the city of Newark's housing relocation agency, and organizations with large nonwhite memberships.

To assist in exposing other pockets of housing discrimination, we also got the division to adopt a multiple dwelling reporting rule that we had developed requiring landlords throughout the state with more than twenty-five rental units to file annual reports describing the racial composition of their units.

The New Jersey landlord community vigorously contested both our reporting rule and the Parsippany case through the New Jersey court system. In both instances, the courts upheld our program and our legal theories.

*   *   *

During the 1960s, civil rights became politically popular, leading to the passage of important legislation. In the 1970s, civil rights lawyers turned to the courts in an effort to protect and extend the gains achieved through political action. The legal doctrine fueling this movement was *affirmative action*. Civil rights advocates were arguing that it was not enough merely to remove existing barriers to racial equality—that both government and private institutions had a moral and legal obligation to affirmatively assist members of groups that had been the victims of historic discrimination to join the mainstream. Otherwise, the United States would permanently be what the presidentially appointed Kerner Commission described in 1968 as "two nations, one black and one white, separate and unequal."

At Rutgers Law School, we had implemented this principle through our Minority Student Program. The Constitutional Litigation Clinic, which I set up in 1970, devoted much of its energies to cases in which voluntary affirmative action programs were under attack or situations in which reluctant institutions were being sued to implement race-conscious programs to expand educational and employment opportunities for members of racial minority groups.

One such case involved the appointment of African Americans to supervisory positions in the Newark school system. Following the election of a black-led administration in the city, the Newark Board of Education suspended its promotion list for principals and vice principals in order to elevate less senior teachers to supervisory positions in the largely black school system. The action was challenged by the white-dominated supervisors' association. The school board's lawyers, who had prevailed in the federal district court, asked us to take over the case on appeal.

The opinion of the Third Circuit was written by Judge John Gibbons, a Nixon appointee who had headed New Jersey's Advisory Committee on Civil Disorders following the 1967 urban riots and was a strong defender of civil rights. The decision remains to this day one of the most far-reaching federal court pronouncements on the need for affirmative action to overcome the ravages of slavery and racial discrimination. The opinion held that the school board was totally justified in promoting less senior African Americans to positions of supervisory authority in order to provide role models for nonwhite children in the Newark public schools. It completely rejected the claims of the white plaintiffs that they were the victims of racial discrimination.

Unfortunately, in the 1990s, the decision in *Porcelli v. Titus* has become an anachronism. *Reverse discrimination*, not affirmative action, has become the dominant principle in the new race-relations law sculpted by a more conservative federal judiciary fueled by demagogic politicians' appeals to angry white males. In what can only be described as historical irony, legal doctrine created in the 1960s and 1970s to help the victims of discrimination overcome centuries of oppression has now been turned against them and is being used on behalf of the majority population to reinforce its position of social dominance. It is no longer clear that the United States can avoid the fate warned against by the Kerner Commission.

5
The Case of the Long-Haired Travelers

Arthur Kinoy was planning to go on leave for the 1970–71 academic year and asked me to take over his seminar in advanced constitutional problems. With the assistance of David Lubell, a civil rights practitioner from New York, Arthur based the seminar each year on current constitutional issues, usually focusing on cases from the docket of the Center for Constitutional Rights. Students would often have the opportunity to write memos about a case that might be of assistance to the lawyers working on it. Occasionally, Arthur would be handling a case himself, and the students would immerse themselves in it. The landmark case of *Powell v. McCormack*, the suit challenging Congress's power to refuse to seat Representative Adam Clayton Powell, was litigated by Arthur with the assistance of his seminar students.

I was honored that Arthur had asked me to do his seminar. I was very busy with the cases I was handling for the ACLU and was interested in transforming my extracurricular practice into part of my teaching load. I almost always had student volunteers assisting me, and now that I considered myself an experienced litigator, I thought that it would be appropriate to give the students academic credit for their work.

With the support and encouragement of Professor Kinoy and Dean Heckel, I obtained a grant to establish a law office at the law school called the Constitutional Litigation Clinic. The university found us some office space in an old building behind the law school that housed the campus police, and I was able to hire a secretary with the grant funds as well as pay a stipend to David Lubell to work with me part-time. In the late 1960s, many activist students had come to Rutgers, often attracted by Arthur Kinoy's presence. These students flocked to the clinic. The following year, Arthur resumed his seminar, and David Lubell and I continued to operate the clinic, which we expanded by hiring Bill Bender, a Rutgers Law School graduate who had been working for the Center for Constitutional Rights, as the administrative director.

Since 1970, the Constitutional Litigation Clinic has been home base to me—

the place I return to when I am not off doing something else, like running for Congress or working for a congressional committee. I had found the best of all possible worlds for a public lawyer—being paid as a law professor to handle exciting constitutional cases that I would have gladly taken for free.

When we started the clinic in the fall of 1970, I had several pending ACLU cases that I made part of the clinic's initial docket. David Lubell brought in a couple of cases he had been handling pro bono, including a suit against the CIA for death and injury resulting from LSD experiments it had carried out on unsuspecting individuals after World War II.

On assignment from the federal district court, I was also appealing the conviction of a Black Muslim who had refused to report for induction into the army after his application for conscientious objector status had been refused. That case involved both a challenge to the composition of grand and petit juries in the federal court and a claim that it was unconstitutional for the classifications of predominantly black draft registrants from the city of Newark to be judged by all-white suburban draft boards.

That case, *United States v. Nunnally*, ended in the clinic's first major victory when the U.S. Court of Appeals for the Third Circuit ruled that it was illegal for the jury commissioner to fill the jury wheels with two male names for each female name. The jury commissioner had claimed that overloading the jury wheel was necessary to get gender-balanced juries, since more men asked to be excused from jury service than women. However, our students checked newspaper files to determine the composition of the previous ten grand juries and found that every one of those juries had more persons with masculine first names and that the average male-female ratio was about two to one. When the U.S. attorney also claimed that a male criminal defendant was not harmed by having women partially excluded from his jury, we submitted to the court of appeals voluminous data on public-opinion surveys that indicated that women had much more dovish views about the Vietnam War and tended to be more religious than men, thus demonstrating that a religious conscientious objector would indeed be prejudiced by the exclusion of women from his jury.

It was the first in a long string of Third Circuit victories for the clinic. But that came to an end when judges appointed to the court by President Reagan became a majority. Even those Republican judges appointed by the conservative Richard Nixon had been sympathetic to the kinds of civil liberties cases we tended to bring. Generally nominated by liberal Republican Senators Clifford Case of New Jersey or Hugh Scott of Pennsylvania, the Nixon appointees continued a long line of high-caliber judges who made the federal appellate court in Philadelphia a judicial model. The court was changed dramatically by the Reagan and Bush appointees—becoming both more bureaucratic and less sensitive to individual rights—leading civil rights lawyers in New Jersey to shift much of their practice to the state courts.

* * *

The first major new case added to the clinic docket was the New Jersey Turnpike case, or what came to be popularly known as "the case of the long-haired travelers." Steve Nagler, the ACLU state director, had been talking to me for some time about the large number of complaints his office was receiving from drivers who had been stopped and searched by state troopers for no apparent reason. An overwhelming number of such complaints came from college-age individuals, often young men and women who met the description of "hippies," especially males with long hair and beards. Usually these individuals were sent on their way after their cars and trunks had been searched, but sometimes the police would turn up a marijuana joint or seeds and make an arrest.

Such defendants usually pleaded guilty, and if it was their first offense, they generally got off with a fine, which might be less than the cost of hiring a lawyer and fighting the case on the grounds that the evidence had been illegally seized. Even if an accused hired a lawyer, it was only the defendant's word against the police officer's as to the events leading up to the search, and the defendant was likely to be convicted anyway. It was possible, however, for the victim of an unconstitutional search to sue the offending officers for damages under the federal Civil Rights Act; but again, it would be the claimant's word against the cop's, and even if the plaintiff was believed, the measure of damages was likely to be small. And since this was prior to the enactment of the federal statute that authorizes courts to order defendants to pay reasonable attorneys' fees to prevailing plaintiffs in federal civil rights cases, such cases were unappealing to private lawyers.

I suggested to Steve that we consider a civil suit in federal court against the attorney general of New Jersey and the state police department for encouraging or condoning a pattern and practice of illegal searches by the troopers. My idea was to ask the federal court for a mandatory injunction requiring state police officials to properly train their troops to respect motorists' rights and to punish troopers who carried out unconstitutional stops and searches. In this country, courts of equity are empowered to issue injunctions (legal orders) when a legal remedy (usually money damages) would provide insufficient redress. Our federal courts are courts of both law and equity. There is no right to a jury trial in cases brought on the equity side of the court.

The law of search and seizure on the highways was reasonably clear. In order to search a stopped car, police had to have probable cause that a crime had been committed or that contraband would be found. Alternatively, they needed the driver's voluntary consent to the search. There was no clear law at the time prohibiting highway police from stopping a vehicle for documentary inspection. The only precedent that might have authorized a federal court to issue such an injunction against the state police was a recent decision from the Fourth Circuit Court of Appeals upholding an injunction against the Baltimore city police that prohibited them from searching homes in Baltimore's black neighborhoods without search warrants.

The ACLU office contacted the people who had filed complaints about illegal stops and put an ad in Rutgers' undergraduate newspaper soliciting anyone who felt that he or she had been illegally stopped and searched by the state highway police to volunteer to be a plaintiff in the suit. We wound up with thirty-some plaintiffs, including a number of young lawyers, all of whom fit the description of "long-haired travelers or other persons of distinctive personal appearance." Most of our plaintiffs had been totally innocent and had been let go by the police after being searched. I thought that these would be our most credible witnesses, and so much the better if they happened to be lawyers or other professionals. The fact that they could all tell their stories in the same case and corroborate one another would also make their testimony more compelling.

The first named plaintiff in the case of *George Lewis et al. v. George Kugler, Attorney General of New Jersey*, was the son of old family friends, Danny and Barbara Lewis. Barbara was a former colleague at the *Bergen Record*, and Danny, who subsequently became a Hollywood columnist, had been the publisher of the weekly newspaper chain I had edited before entering law school. George's case was typical of our plaintiffs. He was a Rutgers student who had been stopped, searched, and verbally abused by troopers on the Turnpike on his way to school. His angry parents had called me soon after the incident. By the time the case finally completed its odyssey in the federal courts, George had gone to law school and was practicing law.

The theory of the case was that individual troopers, looking for rewards and advancement in the department, picked out "hippie" drivers in the hopes that they might be carrying drugs. The state police regularly bragged about the number of drug arrests made and the amount of illegal drugs confiscated. Since it seemed that no troopers were ever sanctioned for making illegal searches, stopping and searching vehicles was a no-lose activity for them. We were not even sure that our class of long-haired travelers was the main target of police stops. There was reason to believe that African Americans and other people of color were even more victimized by this police practice, but we discovered that such victims were less likely to file formal complaints than the generally white and middle-class members of our plaintiff class. Nonwhites tended to take police harassment as routine and were just happy to escape without being arrested or physically abused.

We filed our complaint in the fall of 1970, and the hearing on our application for a preliminary injunction took place shortly before Christmas. The case had been assigned to Judge Robert Shaw, a judicial troglodyte who seemed to have even less respect for our clients than the state troopers did. My faculty colleague Dick Chused had volunteered to serve as cocounsel, and as I began to question our first witness, Dick, whose hair and beard were longer and thicker than those of most of our clients, was in the back of the courtroom quietly preparing our next witness. Judge Shaw, who had been introduced to Chused a little while earlier, admonished me to have my "client" sit down and shut up or he would remove him from the courtroom. It was not an auspicious beginning. Judge Shaw listened to our first three witnesses describe their run-ins with state troopers, said he had heard enough, and dismissed our case. He ruled that a federal court had no business hearing such a case and told us to go to a state court.

About a year later, the Third Circuit reversed Judge Shaw's decision and sent the case back to him for trial. The opinion was unequivocal in upholding our right to sue in a federal court:

> If the plaintiffs can establish that they are subjected to a deliberate pattern and practice of constitutional violations by the New Jersey State Troopers, we believe that they are entitled to appropriate injunctive relief. Persons who can establish that they are denied their constitutional rights are entitled to relief, and it can no longer be seriously contended that an action for money damages will serve adequately to remedy unconstitutional searches and seizures.

A year after our initial hearing, we were back before a hostile Judge Shaw. When he asked me how many witnesses I intended to call, I replied that it depended on how many he thought it would take to prove a "pattern and practice." He said that I should just start calling witnesses. Six months and sixty-seven witnesses later, we rested our case. The trial did not go on continuously for those six months. After about two weeks, the judge declared a Christmas recess, and then he heard witnesses intermittently for only a day or two a month until the testimony was completed. Our witnesses were mainly plaintiffs and others who matched the description of our long-haired traveler class and had been subjected to illegal searches. Many of our witnesses had been stopped and searched on multiple occasions.

My favorite witness was a young man named Ron from Teaneck, New Jersey. He had been stopped and searched about thirteen times during his junior year at Rutgers College in New Brunswick as he traveled back and forth from his home. Ron had flowing brown hair down to his hips, a full beard, and deep, sensitive eyes. In his senior year, Ron went to study at Hebrew University in Jerusalem. While in Israel, he answered an ad placed by an American documentary filmmaker seeking extras for a movie about the life of Christ. The producer was mainly interested in finding actors to portray Roman soldiers. As he moved down the line of applicants, the producer came to Ron, looked at his full beard and flowing hair, and announced: "You are Jesus." Ron was given the title role in the documentary *Time of the Crucifixion*, which was shown on U.S. network television the following Easter.

When Ron came back to the country to promote the film that spring, we arranged for him to come to court to testify. The New York tabloids had a field day, front-paging the testimony of "Jesus Christ, Superstar" against the New Jersey state police. After leading Ron through his testimony about the thirteen occasions on which the state police had stopped and searched him, I asked him whether his experiences had left him with any animus toward the troopers. Before the defense attorneys could object to the question, he very evenly responded, "I forgive them, for they know not what they do."

The other major evidence we introduced involved the service records of certain state troopers who were notorious for stopping and searching motorists. The evidence showed that these troopers were given citations and commendations for making occasional drug busts, but there were never any adverse consequences when they engaged in unconstitutional searches. The conclusion was obvious: by this pattern of rewards and nonsanctions, the state police officialdom was encouraging troopers to make as many searches as possible in the hope of finding drugs, without regard for the constitutional rights of motorists.

Before Judge Shaw could render a decision, he died of a heart attack. The case was then transferred to Judge John J. Kitchen, sitting in Camden in southern New Jersey. Since Judge Shaw had never made any findings as to the testimony he had heard, the attorney general insisted that the entire case be retried. I disagreed, urging Judge Kitchen to decide the case based on the printed transcript. The judge agreed with me. At a status conference in his chambers, Kitchen told the lawyer representing the attorney general's office: "This case killed Judge Shaw; it's not going to kill me."

Two weeks later, I picked up a newspaper and read that Judge Kitchen had dropped dead. The third judge to whom the case was assigned took sick and retired before reaching a decision. Finally, the case was sent back to Newark and assigned to a young, vigorous judge, Curtiss Meanor, who happily reported in a footnote when he finally issued a ruling that he was still alive and well.

By the time Judge Meanor decided the case, it was 1975. Richard Nixon had put his stamp on the Supreme Court, and much water had flowed over the constitutional dam. The worst of the new doctrine was a case out of Philadelphia entitled *Rizzo v. Goode*. Based on the Third Circuit's earlier ruling in our case, a federal district judge had enjoined the Philadelphia police department from harassing and arresting black citizens on the street of Philadelphia without cause. The decision had been upheld by the court of appeals. However, a Supreme Court opinion decided five-to-four and written by Justice Rehnquist set aside the injunction and held that principles of "federalism" precluded a federal court from supervising the operations of a local police department, even as a remedy for a pattern of unconstitutional police conduct. Judge Meanor therefore held that he was powerless to provide injunctive relief to the plaintiffs in our case, despite the earlier ruling of the Third Circuit authorizing such relief. So it was back to Philadelphia, where the court of appeals noted that times had changed since our original appearance in 1971:

> When this case was initially before us, we determined that the complaint set forth facts which, if proved, would justify a federal equitable remedy. Plaintiffs have now substantiated (and, indeed, augmented) their initial allegations. The district court's extensive findings of fact reveal what can only be described as callous indifference by the New Jersey State Police for the rights of citizens using New Jersey roads. Were it not for the Supreme Court's opinion in *Rizzo v. Goode*, which was announced after the district court proceedings had been concluded, our original mandate in this case would have required that we reverse the district court's denial of injunctive relief in light of plaintiffs' demonstration of numerous violations of their constitutional rights. The Supreme Court, however, has recently given expression to the doctrine of federal equitable abstention as it related to federal court intervention in local police operations.

In other words, Justice Rehnquist had stripped the plaintiffs of their constitutional rights—or, at least, of their right to a judicial remedy.

We filed a petition with the U.S. Supreme Court asking for review, but the petition was denied, with Justices Brennan and Marshall dissenting. (Almost all the jurisdiction of the U.S. Supreme Court is discretionary. When a litigant asks the Court to review a lower court decision, four of the nine justices must vote to hear the case.)

After six years, our efforts to stop police harassment of motorists on New Jersey highways had come up empty.

* * *

About a year later, the U.S. Supreme Court, at the request of the state of Delaware, agreed to review a state judge's ruling that it was unconstitutional for a highway patrol to stop a motorist without reason to believe that some legal infraction had occurred. The case involved a motorist who had been stopped for a "routine" document inspection on a slow night. The cop spotted a marijuana cigarette in plain view on the floor of the car and arrested the driver. At trial, the cop testified honestly that he had no particular reason to stop the car: "I saw the car in the area and wasn't answering any complaints, so I decided to pull them off." The trial judge decided, in a precedent-setting ruling, that the stop violated the Fourth Amendment. When the Supreme Court agreed to hear the appeal, the natural reaction was that the Court intended to reverse the Delaware court. The Supreme Court seldom agrees to hear an appeal in order to affirm a lower court.

The Delaware public defender's office, which had been representing the defendant, asked the ACLU to serve as cocounsel in the Supreme Court. The ACLU asked the clinic if it wanted to write the brief, since it had just been through the turnpike case involving some of the same issues. My clinic law partner Eric Neisser and I agreed to put together a team of students.

The brief we wrote made extensive use of the record from our recent trial. We called to the Supreme Court's attention the findings of Judge Meanor that New Jersey state troopers had consistently used a profile of "long-haired travelers" to stop cars and search for drugs. We argued that if highway police had unrestricted discretion to pick on motorists, some would abuse it by stopping only pretty young women, some would single out people of color, and others would focus on "hippies." We said that in order to protect motorists' constitutional right to be free from unreasonable seizures and searches, it was essential that police be required to have specific and articulable reasons for stopping a moving vehicle.

After extensive internal debate, we mildly suggested in our brief that it would be preferable to make police stop all vehicles—à la roadblocks—than to allow them the right to target specific vehicles. If the entire driving public had to suffer together, police would be less likely to resort to the practice; and if it did get out of hand, voters could complain to their elected representatives, who could restrain such police practices legislatively. Disfavored minority groups targeted by police lacked the political muscle to bring about legislative change.

Eric and I accompanied the Delaware public defender to the Supreme Court hearing and were quite disturbed at how poorly the argument went. The justices seemed hostile to our position, and we were convinced that our side would lose. It was a pleasant surprise several months later when the Court not only ruled in our favor but did so by an eight to one vote, with only Rehnquist dissenting. The opinion adopted our argument concerning the danger of allowing police unlimited discretion to select targets. The Court held that to justify stopping a car, police needed at least "articulable and reasonable suspicion that a motorist is unlicensed or that an automobile is not registered, or that either the vehicle or an occupant is otherwise subject to seizure for violation of law."

The Court then opened the door for other types of spot checks "that involve less intrusion or that do not involve the unconstrained exercise of discretion" and offered the suggestion that "roadblock-type stops is one possible alternative." In subsequent years, friends caught up in police roadblocks took to blaming me for their inconvenience.

*   *   *

About six months after the decision in *Delaware v. Prouse*, I was driving along a back road in New Jersey when I was pulled over by a state trooper. I am still not sure whether he had "articulable suspicion" that I was violating some traffic law—but any cop with half a brain can always articulate a legitimate reason for a highway stop. Anyway, this officer discovered that I was a law professor and asked me what I thought "of the recent decision that we can't stop you without reason."

It was a deserted country road, and I wasn't about to confess my involvement in the case. I merely said, "Oh, I didn't think that was such a bad decision."

He responded, "I ought to give you a ticket for that." But he didn't.

6
Challenging "Big Brother"

There are lots of advantages to being a law professor if you love public law and do not particularly care about making the big bucks. Most importantly, it provides an opportunity to pick your clients and causes and the time to give thought to new legal theories.

Even before I went to law school, I was deeply offended that in a democratic country, agencies such as the FBI could follow me around and compile records on my activities on behalf of peace and civil rights. People who complain about *political correctness* in the 1990s have no idea what it was like in the 1950s. Some people were actually put in jail because they opposed the politically correct line on the Cold War or racial discrimination in the United States. The great singer and actor Paul Robeson was exiled from his native land. Thousands lost their jobs and had careers destroyed. A number were driven to suicide as a result. Government (and sometimes private) agencies such as the FBI and the House Un-American Activities Committee compiled records and dossiers on the politically incorrect views and associations of activists and dissidents and disseminated the information in a deliberate effort to inflict punishment. It was as if the United States had become a parody of the totalitarian society George Orwell portrayed in his classic anticommunist novel *1984*. Uncle Sam was turning into "Big Brother."

I was one of the fortunate ones who suffered no discernible long-term consequences. But my brother Stan, for one, was not so lucky. What the government did to this decorated war hero was disgraceful. After Stan had spent five years risking his life for his country on the battlefields of Europe, his government went about systematically destroying his efforts to establish a career and earn a livelihood. Stan had enlisted in the army even before Pearl Harbor and the United States' involvement in World War II. After completing Officer Candidate School and being commissioned as a second lieutenant, he volunteered to join the Rangers, the forerunner of the Green Berets. He led a platoon at Normandy on D day and spent much of the war leading raids behind German lines. He was wounded twice and was awarded two Purple Hearts and two Bronze Stars. After the war, he wouldn't even apply for the disability pension he was entitled to because he considered his wounds his patriotic duty.

But after the war, he disagreed with U.S. foreign policy that was leading to the Cold War. Despite his public political position, his Ranger comrades honored him in 1948 by electing him the first president of their veterans' association. The federal government was not so forgiving. When the pall of McCarthyism descended in the early 1950s, Stan was employed as a radio and TV scriptwriter in New York City. One day he was unceremoniously fired and given some lame excuse. This was a common experience for writers and artists associated with left-wing dissent. Each time he was offered a new job, the offer would mysteriously be withdrawn by the time he was to report for work. It was obvious that he was on the blacklist. Years later, it was revealed that the FBI had systematically visited employers of suspect individuals—especially those in the entertainment industry—and got them fired. By the time the Red scare receded, Stan had been unemployed for a decade and had been effectively excluded from his chosen profession. He spent the rest of his life, until his death in late 1993, doing odd jobs. The only unifying theme in his entire adult life was his connection to his three sons and to his Ranger comrades in arms, who, in 1990, honored him with the Darby Medal, awarded in memory of Colonel Bill Darby, who was immortalized in the Hollywood film "Darby's Rangers." It wasn't until his death that he was officially rehabilitated in the eyes of his government. He was finally given a proper hero's burial in Arlington National Cemetery, with a twenty-one-gun salute and six white horses drawing the caisson that carried his funeral urn to its final resting place in the shadow of the Pentagon.

*   *   *

In the spring of 1968, I taught a course in civil liberties in which I gave my students a set of constitutional problems to be argued out in the classroom, with two students assigned to each side of an issue. One of the problems had to do with the FBI's authority to compile dossiers on peace activists on the basis of information gathered from otherwise legal sources—that is, without resorting to burglary or other independently illegal activities. The issue was whether the targets of such government surveillance had a legal right to object. The constitutional precedents were not directly helpful, although there was some developing doctrine from the Warren Court condemning actions of governmental agencies that had the effect of intimidating third parties from engaging in speech or associations protected by the First Amendment— the so-called chilling-effect doctrine. One of the leading precedents was Professor Kinoy's *Dombrowski* case. The difficulty was that no court had ever held that "chill" alone, without some other adverse consequence to a particular litigant—such as loss of a job or denial of a benefit—gave rise to a claim for legal redress.

At the end of the semester, an incident in New Jersey provided an ideal opportunity to test the theories we had debated in my civil liberties course. Attorney General Arthur Sills distributed a memorandum to local police and sheriffs' offices instructing them to conduct intelligence that would alert them to the possibility of future civil disorders. All departments were asked to file regular reports with the state police concerning local "protest" activities, including the names of leaders and organizations involved. It was a clear invitation to gather information and create dossiers on perfectly legal political activities and activists. I recruited one of my students, Jeff Fogel, who had written an excellent paper on the issue (and some years later would become director of the New Jersey ACLU), to assist me in preparing a court challenge to the Sills memorandum. I convinced the local ACLU branch to sponsor the case. The ACLU also helped me locate some civil rights and peace activists who agreed to be the plaintiffs in the suit.

Since I knew that such a challenge was unprecedented, I gave careful thought to the selection of a court where I might find a sympathetic judge. In 1968, the federal judiciary sitting in Newark was not particularly hospitable to free-speech litigation. However, state courts also have jurisdiction to hear claims brought under the federal Constitution, and I was aware of a very smart and constitutionally sensitive judge sitting in the Hudson County Chancery Division, a bench once occupied by William Brennan Jr. before his elevation to the New Jersey Supreme Court and then the U.S. Supreme Court. Robert Matthews was the only chancery judge sitting in Hudson County, and since I would be seeking an injunction against the attorney general, if I filed the suit in Hudson, it was just about certain that the case would be heard by him. To stack the deck even further, I convinced a former schoolmate of mine, a bright young lawyer named Mickey Stern, who had been Judge Matthews's clerk after law school, to join me as cocounsel and argue the case, which was filed under the name *Andersen v. Sills*.

Meanwhile, I had written a lengthy article entitled "Police Dossiers and Emerging Principles of Constitutional Adjudication," which set forth our entire constitutional theory. The article had been accepted for publication in the prestigious *Stanford Law Review*, which was doubly important to me. It would provide academic acceptability for the novel legal theory we were espousing, and it was critical to my quest for tenure in the "publish or perish" world of legal academe. When Judge Matthews issued his ruling in our favor, I was in Chapel Hill, North Carolina, attending a summer seminar for new law teachers. I learned of the opinion from the *New York Times*, which found the decision of such significance that it reported it on the front page. Judge Matthews completely agreed with our arguments, found that the Sills memorandum violated the First Amendment, and ordered the state police to destroy all the information that had been reported pursuant to it. For someone who had been the personal target of such political surveillance during an earlier era, it was an especially sweet victory.

The Matthews opinion was short-lived. A year later, the state supreme court reversed it, holding that Judge Matthews had acted precipitously, without an adequate evidentiary record, and remanded the case for further proceedings. Several years after that, following a similarly hostile decision by the U.S. Supreme Court in a parallel federal case that I handled for the ACLU, *Andersen v. Sills* was dismissed by one of Judge Matthews's successors in Hudson.

It is one of the ironies of the legal process that, despite this history of ultimate failure, the case of *Andersen v. Sills* is a litigation landmark. The mere existence of a reported opinion by a highly respected jurist holding that the collection of First Amendment information by a government agency is unconstitutional has created a cottage industry in what is now commonly referred to as "police surveillance" litigation. The fact that few of these cases ever result in a judicially ordered remedy has done little to curtail the proliferation of surveillance lawsuits. The truth is, although courts have been reluctant to order police agencies to desist from such activity—in the absence of clear evidence of independently illegal collection practices—public exposure and public ridicule have given police spying such a bad name that when caught in the act, few public agencies are willing to defend such *Big Brother* practices. I found it particularly ironic when, after the collapse of communism in Eastern Europe, U.S. officials cheered when outraged citizens in those countries invaded the former secret police offices and destroyed the intelligence files maintained by those governments. Under the circumstances, it is difficult for such public officials to justify similar activities by agencies under their own control.

*   *   *

The interplay of the judicial and legislative processes is well illustrated by the second ACLU surveillance case I handled, *Tatum v. Laird*. It was a suit against the U.S. Army and Defense Department to enjoin the operation of the army's domestic intelligence program, which involved the collection of dossiers on civilian political activists by army intelligence. The practice had been exposed by some former intelligence agents shortly after Judge Matthews issued his opinion in the *Andersen* case. ACLU national legal director Mel Wulf asked me to bring a suit in the federal district court in Washington, D.C. The ACLU recruited as plaintiffs a number of civil rights and peace movement leaders whose names had shown up in the army's database.

Shortly after the suit was filed in early 1970, I found myself before conservative Chief Judge George Hart in the U.S. district court in Washington opposing the government's motion to dismiss. I had been speaking for about twenty minutes about the "chilling effect" on Americans caused by army intelligence agents roaming the country and gathering information about lawful protest activities to feed back to the military computers at Fort Holabird.

The judge was obviously unimpressed. He said, "Why would anybody care? Tom Paine wasn't afraid of British spies. Jefferson wasn't afraid."

In frustration, I replied, "Your Honor, I teach a class every day on the first floor in a building in Newark. It doesn't bother me if strangers walk in off the street and sit in my classroom, but I wouldn't want an army intelligence agent sitting there day after day taking notes to send back to the military computers."

Suddenly, Judge Hart got interested in what I was saying. He leaned forward and asked, "Why not? What do you teach, anyway?"

After being taken aback for a moment, I came up with one of those inspired, ad-libbed replies that you usually don't think of until four o'clock the next morning when you're in bed replaying the courtroom colloquy. I said, "I teach that the army can't do that sort of thing." Judge Hart was no more impressed with my teaching than he was with my argument. He granted the government's motion to dismiss.

The following February, I argued the appeal before an extraordinarily conservative and hostile panel of the U.S. Court of Appeals for the District of Columbia. When the government lawyer claimed that the case was actually moot, since the army had practically disbanded its domestic intelligence program, one of the judges, George MacKinnon (father of future self-identified feminist scholar Catherine MacKinnon), got very upset and insisted that the spy program was essential to national security. I was actually worried that the court would issue an order requiring reconstitution of the program in its full glory.

But in between that argument in February and the issuance of the court's decision several months later, the Senate Subcommittee on Constitutional Rights conducted two weeks of televised hearings into the army's domestic intelligence program. Under the sharp attack of committee chairman Sam Ervin of North Carolina, the Justice Department's spokesperson was kept on the public defensive in an effort to justify the program, while at the same time insisting that it had been all but dismantled. That spokesperson, Assistant Attorney General William Rehnquist, publicly argued with Senator Ervin about the justiciability of the case of *Tatum v. Laird* then pending before the D.C. courts. He further insisted that the army's domestic intelligence computer system was "defunct" and that the only remaining printout of the army's database had been deposited into his personal custody for safekeeping. Since I had no doubt after the argument before the appellate panel that it would unanimously affirm Judge Hart's opinion, I can only assume that its two-to-one decision (MacKinnon dissenting) in our favor was a response to the public scorn heaped upon the army's surveillance program by the Ervin hearings.

I must confess that the argument of the case before the U.S. Supreme Court was one of the high points of my life. It is an awesome experience for any lawyer to argue a case before the high court, but on that occasion, my adversary was the eminent Erwin Griswold, solicitor general of the United States and former dean of Harvard Law School. My cocounsel was the legendary Sam Ervin of Watergate hearings fame. Senator Ervin had submitted a friend-of-the-court brief and agreed to share the oral argument with me.

Unfortunately for the cause of justice and democracy, William Rehnquist was appointed a Supreme Court justice by Richard Nixon before the case could be heard. In the weeks prior to argument, there was much public speculation in the press and legal circles as to whether Rehnquist would actually sit on the case in light of his role as government spokesperson on the issue in the Senate hearings. Rehnquist's participation was particularly crucial, because if the Court split four-to-four, our victory would be affirmed. We felt certain that we could count on the votes of Justices Douglas, Marshall, and Brennan, and we hoped for the support of either Potter Stewart or Byron White. If Rehnquist participated, we would need both Stewart and White.

I had proposed to my ACLU colleagues that we file a formal motion to exclude Rehnquist from the case because of his conflict of interest as an active participant on the side of the defendants, but my proposal was rejected as unseemly. There was an unwritten rule that justices of the Supreme Court knew when it was inappropriate for them to hear a case, and there was no record of a formal motion of recusal having ever been filed in the Supreme Court by a litigant.

On the Friday before the Monday argument, I met with Senator Ervin in his Senate office. As I was leaving, I mentioned that there was still time to file a recusal motion.

Senator Ervin said, "Don't worry. I know Justice Rehnquist. He is very conservative, but he's a very honorable man. He will not sit on this case."

Monday morning when our case was called and we approached the bench, I whispered to the senator that Justice Rehnquist had not left his seat.

Ervin replied, "He just wants to listen; he will not participate in the decision."

Senator Ervin may have been partially correct. Uncharacteristically Justice Rehnquist remained silent throughout the argument. It is quite possible that he intended to absent himself from the decision if his vote were not needed. As it was, he provided the fifth vote for an opinion by Chief Justice Burger reversing the court of appeals and dismissing the case. The opinion read as if it had been copied from Rehnquist's testimony before the Senate committee.

After the decision, the ACLU agreed that we should file a motion requesting the Court to withdraw its opinion and asking that Rehnquist be excluded from participation because of his conflict of interest. The Court denied the motion, and Rehnquist wrote an unprecedented sixteen-page opinion justifying his action, although acknowledging that it was a close question. As part of his rationale, he came up with the astounding argument that because his exclusion would have left the Court divided four to four, he had a special duty to participate. That claim turned judicial ethics on its head by suggesting that judges should disqualify themselves only when their votes don't matter. It is precisely when their votes are decisive that judges have a clear duty not to rule on a case in which a conflict exists.

About a year after the decision, I was attending a conference in Washington. During a reception, Senator Ervin came striding toward me and said loudly in his inimitable drawl, "Frank, I sure was wrong about Justice Rehnquist, wasn't I!"

I repeated that story some years later to the Senate Judiciary Committee when I testified against Rehnquist's appointment as chief justice. I told the committee that in my view, Rehnquist was a result-oriented judge who lacked the judicial temperament to be chief justice. I said that he had violated the most fundamental canon of judicial ethics—that no one can be both an advocate and a judge in the same case.

I then told the committee, "It was as if Billy Martin had resigned as manager of the New York Yankees after the sixth game of the World Series and accepted the job as umpire in the seventh game."

*   *   *

Although technically both *Anderson v. Sills* and *Tatum v. Laird* resulted in defeat in the courts, they focused immense public attention on the issue and had substantial impact on the surveillance practices of police agencies. In 1976, the U.S. Department of Justice issued the Levi guidelines (named after Attorney General Edward Levi), restricting the FBI from investigating political organizations in the absence of evidence of criminal involvement. No longer were the FBI and other federal agencies authorized to infiltrate such groups merely because of their opposition to government policy or the militant rhetoric of their members. Those restrictions were eased during the Reagan administration in 1983 but retained the requirement of a criminal predicate for the infiltration of political associations. Although sometimes frequently ignored, those regulations made police agencies all over the country more respectful of the constitutional right of political dissent.

In the wake of the bombing of the Oklahoma City federal building in April 1995, the guidelines came under sharp attack from those who thought that they handcuffed the FBI in the war against domestic terrorism. Proposals for reform were opposed by civil libertarians who argued that Americans should not have to surrender their political freedoms to all-powerful police agencies. However, the counterterrorism bill passed by Congress and signed by President Clinton in the spring of 1996 assigns broad new powers to federal agencies to investigate political activists in the name of combatting terrorists.

Ironically, the misuse of FBI files came under sharp attack by Republicans in 1996 when it was revealed that the Clinton Administration had obtained the files of some 300 persons associated with the Bush White House. Maybe this "filegate" episode will finally convince GOP congressional leaders that they should support legislation controlling the collection and dissemination of such personal records.

7
Putting the FBI on Trial

Normally, the Constitutional Litigation Clinic doesn't accept new cases during the summer months when the students aren't around. But once in a while we get an offer we simply can't refuse.

In the summer of 1972, shortly after the Supreme Court had decided the *Tatum* case, I got a call from the local ACLU office about a case that was right up my alley. An FBI agent had gone to West Morris–Mendham High School in a wealthy suburban community and made inquiries in the principal's office about a student, Lori Paton, who had written a letter to some socialist organization. The principal immediately recognized that the letter had probably been inspired by the political science course taught by Bill Gabrielson and asked the teacher to speak to the agent. Gabrielson, who taught a course entitled Left to Right about the U.S. political spectrum, confirmed that Lori had been in his class and that his students had sent for information in order to write reports about various political sects. The agent seemed satisfied and left, but Gabrielson was concerned that his student's letter had come to the attention of the FBI and feared that the FBI might have established a file on her. He notified Lori's parents.

The Patons and Gabrielson contacted the ACLU office to seek advice. In my first interview with Lori, she confirmed that she had written a letter to the Socialist Labor Party and had received some material that she had since discarded. As a result of my own background, I knew that the Socialist Labor Party was a harmless, moribund sect and could not imagine why the FBI would have any interest in it.

I wrote a letter to the local FBI director on behalf of the Patons, inquiring whether the FBI had been monitoring the mail of the Socialist Labor Party, why it was investigating Lori, and whether it had created any files pertaining to her. Several weeks later I got a reply signed by J. Wallace La Prade, local agent in charge, assuring me that it maintained no mail cover on the Socialist Labor Party, that it knew nothing about any letter Lori had written to the party, and that Lori was "not the subject of investigation by this Bureau." The response ignored my question about the maintenance of records about

Lori. Confused and dissatisfied with that response, the Patons asked us to initiate a lawsuit.

The Supreme Court had only recently ruled in *Bivens v. Six Agents of the Federal Bureau of Narcotics* that federal officials could be sued for damages for violating an individual's Fourth Amendment right to be free from unconstitutional searches. I figured that the same principle should apply to violations of rights protected by the First Amendment. We argued that intercepting a letter to a lawful political party and making a field investigation of the letter writer without further justification was an abridgment of free speech. In addition to damages, we sought the production and destruction of any files concerning Lori and her letter.

The Paton case is a prime example of what lawyers mean when they sometimes talk about litigation as "Russian roulette." As I finally reveal to my students after a full semester of civil procedure, the single most important procedural event in the history of any case is the assignment of the judge. One of the first cases I ever handled—at the height of the Vietnam War protests—involved a suit against the commandant of Fort Dix. I was seeking an order permitting the Committee to Free the Fort Dix 38 to hold a parade and rally near the stockade along the public highway bisecting the military base. Since time was of the essence and I needed a temporary restraining order, as soon as I filed the suit, I asked the court clerk to take me directly to the judge so that I could seek an emergency writ. The clerk led me down the corridor with a big grin on his face. When he took me through the door of Judge Wortendyke's chambers, I knew why he was smiling. Before I could reach the judge's desk, Wortendyke said, "Counselor, I am denying your order and dismissing your complaint."

I said, "Judge, how can you dismiss my complaint?"

He responded, "I was once a military commander, and if any federal judge ever issued me an order, I would have had him shot."

The Paton case was assigned to Judge James Coolahan, who was of the same ilk as Wortendyke and Judge Shaw, my nemesis in the long-haired travelers' case. Coolahan was unconcerned with constitutional rights and fiercely protective of government bureaucrats, especially if they were associated with the FBI. The case was dismissed as soon as the government got around to filing a motion; all our applications to compel discovery from the defendants were still pending. By time we had to file our appeal with the Third Circuit, we were still pretty much in the dark as to what was really behind the FBI's actions. The one new fact we had uncovered was that Lori had inadvertently written not to the Socialist Labor Party but to the Socialist Workers Party (SWP), a left-wing Trotskyist group that had been active in the opposition to the Vietnam War.

The Third Circuit continued the clinic's winning appellate record. It agreed that Lori had the right to sue the FBI agents for damages and sent the case back to Newark with instructions to determine whether the government had in fact violated her First Amendment rights. The court took appropriate note of the fact that the material about Lori was maintained in a file with a "100" prefix, denoting that it concerned "subversive matter." The FBI subsequently insisted that the file designation was of no consequence, that it did not imply that Lori was subversive but merely that her name had come up in an investigation of possibly subversive activity by the SWP. In other words, the FBI cataloged both subversives and nonsubversives together. As I later told the court, it reminded me of an old depression-era political cartoon of a cop clubbing a picket who is protesting, "But I'm an *anti*-Communist." And the cop replies, "I don't care what kind of a Communist you are."

Returned to the district court, the case languished for several years as the defendants stonewalled our requests for information, and Judge Coolahan ignored our motions to compel discovery. However, I was able to take the deposition of the chief defendant, agent La Prade. When I asked him why he had initially denied that Lori was the subject of an FBI investigation, he insisted that he had not intended to deceive. "She was not the *subject* of the investigation," he responded. "She was the *object* of the investigation. The Socialist Workers Party was the *subject* of the investigation."

As the case dragged on, I was becoming more and more frustrated. In the fall of 1977, some five years after we had filed suit, I was again in front of Judge Coolahan on our umpteenth discovery motion. Once again, the judge said that he would take the motion "under advisement" and then announced that the trial was going to start in four weeks. I was astounded.

"How can we go to trial, when you have never decided any of our discovery motions?" I asked the judge. Coolahan was adamant about going ahead.

I returned to my office unsure of what to do. I considered going to the court of appeals for a writ of mandamus, which is a way of getting an appellate court to intervene in a case when there is no ruling that can be appealed. However, I knew that the Third Circuit hardly ever granted such writs and that such an application was likely to delay everything for another year. I finally decided on a most unorthodox strategy. I had great respect for the chief judge of the district court. Larry Whipple was a straight-arrow jurist whose fair and impartial judicial behavior totally belied the fact that he had once been police commissioner of Jersey City under the notorious political boss Frank ("I am the law") Hague. I wrote a letter to Judge Whipple, citing his authority as chief judge to control the docket of the district court, and laid out the sorry history of the case. About a week later I got a call from Judge Coolahan's clerk informing me that the trial had been postponed. About three months later I got a letter from the clerk's office announcing that the case had been reassigned to Judge Whipple. It was all downhill from there.

Judge Whipple ordered the FBI to comply with most of our discovery requests, including turning over the excised investigative files of Squad 2, which handled investigations of the SWP in New Jersey. The files contained a cornucopia of information about FBI efforts to punish and harass people who were associated with the party despite the absence of information about any illegal activity. The FBI had gotten one party member fired from a job with a newspaper and had another supporter dismissed as a scoutmaster. The files also contained information about Squad 2's attempts to disrupt the activities of the Black Panther Party, including efforts to plant false information to make it appear that certain members were government informants.

We also received the correspondence exchanged between La Prade and Washington after my original inquiries about the investigation of Lori. Among other comments, there were warnings about the background of the Patons' lawyer, suggesting that I was no friend of the FBI and that they had to be very careful in dealing with me.

Judge Whipple also ordered that former Acting FBI Director L. Patrick Gray appear for deposition, so that we could question him about the reasons for the mail cover on SWP headquarters. By this time, we had determined that this was how Lori's name had come to the FBI's attention. Under the terms of the mail-cover regulation, a postal inspector would photocopy the external markings, including return addresses, on all letters addressed to the SWP prior to delivery. Those records were turned over to the New York FBI headquarters. The New York office routinely informed the Newark FBI that someone named Paton from Chester, New Jersey, had corresponded with the SWP. The Newark office sent an agent to Chester to investigate. After inquiries with the local police chief and credit bureau, the agent was informed that the Paton family had a daughter at the high school.

When I deposed Gray in Connecticut, where he was living at the time, he had little recollection of the reasons for the SWP mail cover. He agreed that he must have signed an authorization containing a statement of why it was needed to protect national security, but he said that it would have been a routine document prepared for his signature by one of his subordinates. Despite the FBI's vigorous objections, Judge Whipple ordered the authorizing document turned over. It turned out to be the smoking gun we were looking for.

It had long been recognized that mail covers intruded on the constitutional right to privacy and required special justification. The mail-cover regulations of the Postal Service authorized three types of mail covers: those aimed at mail fraud, those needed to hunt down fugitives from justice, and those needed for reasons of national security. National-security mail covers were not further defined but required the personal approval of the attorney general or the head of the FBI, together with a statement of why it was necessary for the protection of national security. The document authorizing the mail cover on

SWP headquarters cited the fact that the party had been active in organizing antiwar demonstrations. After five years of hiding behind claims of national security, the defendants stood naked at the bar of justice. No judge would accept that organizing antiwar demonstrations was a threat to national security that justified interference with the mail.

Judge Whipple issued a ruling that the mail cover on the SWP was unconstitutional and could not justify a field investigation of Lori Paton. Thus, he held that Lori was entitled to damages and that all applicable files in the FBI's possession must be expunged. He also ruled that the national-security provision of the Postal Service's mail-cover regulation was unconstitutionally overbroad, in that it permitted such covers without proper justification.

Lori, who was only interested in vindicating a principle and didn't want to get rich off the case, agreed to settle her monetary claim for $1. To my knowledge, Judge Whipple's ruling in *Paton v. La Prade* remains the only reported judicial opinion holding that an FBI field investigation can be a violation of the First Amendment, even though no further action is taken against the individual.

When I first argued the case in the court of appeals after Judge Coolahan's original order of dismissal, one of the judges asked me why it injured Lori's rights if an FBI agent made inquiries about her in her community. He said, "I am sure when I was being considered for appointment to the federal bench, FBI agents went out and made inquiries about me from my neighbors."

I replied, "Your Honor, when the FBI agent went out to Mendham and started asking questions about Lori Paton, no one thought that she was up for appointment to the federal bench." The judge nodded in apparent agreement and seemed to be satisfied by that response.

*   *   *

Lightning doesn't often strike twice, but ten years after the Lori Paton case came the Todd Patterson case.

Todd was a precocious lad of eleven when he decided to compile his own personal world encyclopedia. In order to do so, he wrote letters to most governments asking for catalogs and information. Shortly thereafter, an FBI agent showed up at the family's door wanting to know why a member of the household was corresponding with communist countries. Mrs. Patterson showed the agent Todd's room and his neat files of information about countries all over the world. The agent thanked her and left.

Todd continued his prodigious correspondence with foreign governments, and envelopes continued to arrive from all over the world, often torn and tattered and resealed, and sometimes empty. On one occasion, Todd received a large envelope from the Soviet embassy in New York City and found inside a letter from Sweden addressed to an unrelated individual in a nearby community.

When Todd was fifteen and already contemplating a career in the foreign service, the family recalled the FBI visit and became concerned that the bureau might be maintaining files on him. When his parents filed a request under the Freedom of Information Act for copies of any such files, the FBI responded that there were some files, but they were being withheld in their entirety for reasons of "national security." Now the family was really concerned and contacted the ACLU.

We filed a complaint in federal court in the spring of 1988 that sought relief under the Freedom of Information and Privacy Acts. We wanted disclosure of the entire contents of Todd's files, and we wanted all copies of them destroyed. Although we alleged that the information about Todd's correspondence had been gathered in violation of the Constitution, I considered the case primarily a test of an important section of the Privacy Act, which had been enacted by Congress in the mid-1970s partly as a result of the extensive publicity generated by the *Tatum* and *Paton* cases about government maintenance of personal data banks. I had even accompanied Lori Paton to testify before two separate congressional committees that were considering the legislation at the time.

The Privacy Act prohibits federal agencies from collecting or maintaining any records describing how individuals exercise rights guaranteed by the First Amendment, except in narrowly defined situations—the most relevant being when it is "pertinent to and within the scope of an authorized law enforcement activity." After more than a dozen years on the books, there was no clear judicial interpretation of that provision. The FBI's position was that anything it did was an authorized law-enforcement activity—in effect, nullifying the act as far as the FBI was concerned. It was our position that since the FBI's political surveillance activity under J. Edgar Hoover had been a major inspiration for the act in the first place, Congress certainly never intended to exempt the bureau from its coverage.

As a result of our lawsuit filed in May 1988, the FBI ultimately released thirteen documents, consisting of thirty pages, concerning Todd. However, most of the contents of those pages were blacked out. One document was a clipping from the *New York Daily News* about our lawsuit. The clipping was stamped "secret."

A major problem with the case was that we had no idea which agency had actually intercepted Todd's mail, and the FBI refused to tell us, on grounds of national security. Thus, there was absolutely no way for us to demonstrate that the information might have been collected without legal authorization. It was most likely that the letters *from* Todd had been intercepted by a mail cover maintained by one of our counterintelligence agencies, such as the CIA or the Defense Information Agency, and we would have little chance of challenging the constitutionality of such a mail surveillance operation directed at a foreign power. However, it also appeared that mail addressed *to* Todd was being intercepted prior to delivery to him. In the absence of a warrant issued by a court, such a mail cover would almost surely have been violative of Judge Whipple's ruling in the *Paton* case.

However, because the federal court upheld the defendants' claim of national-security privilege, we were foreclosed from efforts to prove illegal interference with Todd's mail. We focused, instead, on continued maintenance of a file on Todd after it was obvious that Todd was no threat to national security. Since the only information in Todd's file had to do with his correspondence, which indisputably qualified as First Amendment activity, we insisted that the Privacy Act forbade the FBI to maintain a permanent file.

The only public justification the FBI ever asserted was bureaucratic efficiency. The contention was that unless there were a permanent record of Todd's activities, each time the FBI received information that he had corresponded with a "hostile" foreign power, it might go out and reinvestigate him. We suggested an alternative: the maintenance of a general file of "innocent" correspondents that could be reviewed under such circumstances. The danger of a permanent file indexed under Todd's name was that it would surface every time a government agency sought information about "Todd Patterson." Who knew what the consequences might be if Todd were someday to apply for a government job and it was confidentially disclosed that he had once been investigated for corresponding with communist governments. His application might be rejected without his ever knowing why or having a chance to explain. That was why the Privacy Act provision had been enacted in the first place.

At the hearing before the district court, Judge Alfred Wolin appeared to agree with our theory of the case. At the conclusion of the argument, he announced that he was "not satisfied that the F.B.I. has demonstrated that the files maintained on a claim of exercise of First Amendment rights were pertinent to an authorized law enforcement activity as required by the Privacy Act." He therefore ordered the defendants to submit an additional affidavit "detailing how the records maintained on Mr. Patterson were pertinent and related to a specific law enforcement activity of the F.B.I." Unfortunately, over our objections, Judge Wolin ruled that the new material was to be submitted in camera and ex parte, that is, neither the plaintiff nor his attorney were allowed to see it. After reviewing the government's secret evidence, the judge that said he was satisfied with the government's explanation and dismissed the case.

The court of appeals continued the game of "blindman's bluff." The three members of the appellate panel reviewed the secret government submissions and denied my application to examine the new evidence. The appellate argument was like dancing in the dark. In the discussion among the court, the lawyers from the Department of Justice, and myself, I was the only one not allowed to know the alleged facts on which the case was to be decided. It felt like a scene from Franz Kafka's classic novel *The Trial*, in which protagonist Joseph K is denied knowledge of the reason he was brought before the court.

To no one's great surprise, the court upheld the district court's ruling. The court advised the Pattersons not to be concerned—that there was nothing derogatory about Todd in the files—but in the name of "national security," it was all right for the FBI to continue to maintain the files. Most astounding about the opinion was the court's failure to even acknowledge its ten-year-old decision in the *Paton* case. It was as though the earlier case, which had so many similarities, had been purged from the circuit's collective memory. In truth, the major difference between the *Paton* and *Patterson* cases was the wholesale change in judicial personnel—and judicial mind-set—as a result of the appointments made by Ronald Reagan and George Bush.

The main reliance of the *Patterson* opinion was a group of cases tracing their ancestry to an opinion by conservative Justice Antonin Scalia while sitting on the court of appeals. That opinion authorized the use of secret evidence in so-called national-security cases.

I dutifully filed a petition for certiorari with the Supreme Court, and it was routinely denied. My only remaining recourse was to write an article denouncing the Scalia doctrine titled "Secret Justice and the Adversary System," which appeared in the *Hastings Constitutional Law Quarterly* in the summer of 1991.

8

The Scam Called Abscam

Late one night in the spring of 1980, my wife called me in to the living room where she was watching television. "There's something on about Tompy, and it doesn't look good," she said. "He seems to be involved in some kind of congressional bribery scandal." It was the first announcement of Abscam, an FBI sting operation directed at catching politicians on the take. On that particular evening, reporters were camped outside the Alexandria, Virginia, home of Rep. Frank Thompson Jr., chairman of the House Labor Management Subcommittee, seeking comment on reports that he was about to be indicted for alleged bribe taking.

* * *

I first met Tompy, as he was known to his thousands of friends and admirers, because I had once taught labor law and was considered to be pro-labor. At the suggestion of a mutual friend, Dan Pollitt of the University of North Carolina law faculty, Tompy invited me to serve as the "visiting professor" on the staff of the labor subcommittee during the first session of the 95th Congress, beginning in January 1977.

Since the academic year and the congressional year were not in sync, I actually began my Capitol Hill stint in September 1976. It did not take me long to become a loyal member of "Tompy's people," a small band of Capitol Hill drones who recognized Frank Thompson as one of the true servants of the country's working stiffs and loved him for it. He was responsible for much legislation protecting workers' rights and played a leading role in the establishment of the Peace Corps. He had also been the floor manager of the first federal aid to education act, from which he had blocked a provision to provide aid to parochial schools. This latter achievement, together with his support for abortion rights, won him the eternal enmity of the bishop in his Trenton diocese, who, Tompy would brag, gave a sermon prior to each election day about the need to defeat this heretic. He loved to tell the story about the time he had received a dressing down from his religious leader and he had replied, "I only have to kiss your *ring*."

Tompy had grown up in Trenton, the son of Teddy Roosevelt Bull Moosers. He was a decorated naval officer during World War II, served in the New Jersey legislature, and finally got elected to Congress in 1956. He had been a close friend of Jack Kennedy until, rumor has it, Jackie barred him from the White House because she thought that he encouraged Jack's carousing. Kennedy called Tompy "Topper," because whenever somebody had a story to relate, Tompy could always top it. In New Jersey, Tompy was often mentioned as a gubernatorial candidate by the party's liberal wing, but I am sure he enjoyed life in Washington too much to seriously consider going back to "Tren-ton," as he liked to call it.

Although he took politics seriously and spent his life wheeling and dealing in an effort to pass legislation that he felt would benefit working people, Tompy— unlike most politicians—never took himself seriously. Nor did he ever miss an opportunity to play a practical joke. He loved a good joke of any sort, the raunchier the better. He was a wonderful mimic and had a great gift for story-telling. One of the bonds among "Tompy's people" was that each had a nickname that Tompy had personally bestowed, based on some physical characteristic or idiosyncracy he had discovered. Once Tompy dubbed you, you knew you were a member of the club. The nicknames were sort of like a secret handshake or code words, and club members generally referred to one another by their aliases. There were some members of this club whose real names I never did learn—such as "Irons," which I later learned was actually short for "Iron Balls." I had been working for Tompy for several months when I discovered that he had dubbed me "Aay" or "Aye" or maybe it was "I-I-I." These things were not written down anywhere. When asked to explain its derivation, he referred to my low-key, nonchalant way of responding to issues and problems. He said, "Whenever I ask Askin if he can do something or solve a problem, he shrugs his shoulders and says, 'Aay, I'll take care of it.'" On one occasion, I heard someone compliment Tompy on a speech he had given and ask him who had written it. He responded, with a twinkle in his eye, "I-I-I did."

Tompy's "liberalism" or "radicalism" or call it what you will was not totally consistent. He was certainly not what would now be called "politically correct." He was a terrible sexist. Several years later, I talked him into hiring a former female student of mine as counsel to the Pension Task Force of the labor subcommittee, and he immediately dubbed her "Gams." Nor did she ever find the same professional rapport with him that his male aides did. He also loved ethnic and racist jokes. He believed that his egalitarianism was so well known that he had special dispensation to talk that way. He particularly enjoyed saying such things in my presence, because he knew that I disapproved and often chided him for it. I'm sure he belatedly appreciated my concerns when he was caught making untoward comments for the candid cameras of Abscam.

Tompy also had a reputation as a drinker. When I first asked Dan Pollitt about that, Dan replied, "A drunk Tompy is better than almost any other member of Congress cold sober." He did suggest, however, that serious business be conducted in the mornings.

* * *

As the Abscam story unfolded, it was revealed that Tompy was one of half a dozen members of Congress who had allegedly agreed to accept cash gifts from FBI agents posing as Arab sheiks in exchange for promises of future assistance. In each instance, the accused public official was videotaped in a compromising situation, usually with his hand out as large batches of bills were waved in front of him. In a few instances, the cameras actually showed members of Congress greedily stuffing the cash into their pockets. The television networks began to play excerpts from the grainy surveillance tapes depicting unwitting and venal politicians eager to barter the public trust for a share of the Arabs' oil millions, and the public was outraged. Tom Puccio, the special U.S. attorney in charge of the Abscam investigation, was all over the media taking credit for having exposed political corruption.

At first, I did not know what to think. I knew Tompy as a good public servant dedicated to the interests of working people. But I couldn't swear that he hadn't been tempted to accept $50,000 in exchange for a vague promise that if these ersatz sheiks ever needed political asylum in the United States he would try to help them. That was the allegation against him. Tompy swore that he never took a cent, and I was prepared to believe him until the government proved him guilty beyond a reasonable doubt.

His trial was postponed until just after the 1982 congressional election so that he could campaign without the distraction of a trial. I joined others of "Tompy's people" in Trenton on election day to try to save him from being found guilty by the voters before his case could get to a jury. We were unsuccessful. He was defeated by an unknown and undistinguished Republican whose only campaign issue—other than Tompy's indictment and pending trial—was that he was a spokesman for the antiabortion movement. Tompy's long career of distinguished public service was over no matter what the outcome in court.

Tompy's trial began the Monday after election day in a Brooklyn courtroom. One of the counts against him was conspiracy, and he was being tried together with Rep. John Murphy of Staten Island. Since Murphy had allegedly accepted a payoff on Long Island, the government had obtained its indictment against Murphy and Thompson in the Eastern District of New York. Apparently, Puccio thought that he could find a friendlier jury there than in either New Jersey or Washington, D.C.

The case against Tompy was circumstantial but, as carefully structured by the FBI, believable by a jury. Unlike most of the Abscam cases, there was no tape of Tompy accepting cash or anything else of value or saying that he was willing to accept anything. In fact, the only time money was mentioned on tape, Tompy said that he didn't want any.

Tompy had been approached by a Philadelphia lawyer named Howard Criden, who claimed that he represented some Arabs who wanted to invest money in Tompy's economically depressed district. Criden was an unwitting dupe who thought that he could parlay his familiarity with some area politicians into quick money. When Tompy made inquiries about Criden from acquaintances in Philadelphia, including a judge, the reports were positive. After canceling an earlier meeting in Tompy's Capitol Hill office, Criden convinced him to meet with his "clients" in a town house in Washington's Georgetown section.

The main evidence against Tompy consisted of videotapes of two meetings in the town house that day. The entire scenario had been crafted by Melvin Weinberg, an experienced con man with a criminal record who had convinced the FBI that he could trap some corrupt politicians in exchange for leniency on pending criminal charges. Weinberg enlisted Criden to turn up some politicians willing to do business with the sheiks. During the morning meeting in Georgetown, the alleged representative of the sheiks, an FBI agent named Anthony Amoroso, told Tompy that his clients had lots of money to invest in his district, but they were afraid that a future revolution in their homeland would leave them in need of asylum in the United States. Tompy said that he would be willing to do what he could to help people who had invested in his district. At one point, he picked up a telephone and called his office to get one of his aides to do some research on rights of asylum. Meanwhile, Amoroso and Weinberg were plying him with alcohol. The FBI cameras succeeded in portraying a tawdry, locker-room atmosphere, with the four men sitting around a bottle of scotch and Tompy holding forth with his usual lewd stories and obscene comments, including some sexually pejorative remarks about a particular New York congresswoman. However, when Amoroso suggested that he would like to give him some money, Tompy unequivocally replied, "I'm not looking for any money."

The next videotaped scene showed Criden returning to the town house after driving Tompy back to Capitol Hill. Criden asked for the $50,000 Weinberg had promised if he could get Thompson to work with the Arabs and accept their money. During a two-hour argument, Criden insisted that Thompson was in on the deal and wanted to take their money, but that he (Criden) would have to give Thompson his share. Amoroso accused Criden of trying to rip them off, pointing out that Thompson specifically said that he didn't want any money. He said that the deal was off unless Thompson would openly accept money. Criden told them that Thompson was just being cautious and would not accept their money openly.

Weinberg finally told Criden how to get Thompson to change his position: "The shittin' guy's a boozer.... Give him another drink." After some more pleading by Criden and an unexplained phone call for Amoroso (presumably from his Justice Department superiors watching on the hidden camera), the agent finally agreed that if Criden brought Thompson back to the town house, Thompson would not have to accept the cash or even acknowledge it. He agreed to hand over the money in a briefcase. (That agreement violated the prevailing FBI guidelines for sting operations, which required that bribes be up front, that cash be delivered directly and by hand, and that the quid pro quo be spelled out in plain English.)

Criden brought Thompson back to the town house at about 7 P.M., and after some banter in which neither cash nor payoffs were mentioned, the agents pushed in Thompson's direction a closed briefcase (which viewers knew contained $50,000 in cash). Thompson then pushed the briefcase toward Criden and said, "Howard, look at that for me, will you." When Amoroso then suggested that Criden should be "good for a $10,000 campaign contribution," Thompson again cut him off and said, "No, no. I wouldn't take a ten thousand . . ." At trial, Tompy testified that prior to returning to the town house, Criden had told him that the Arabs had some papers and other documents they wanted him to see having to do with their finances and proposed investments.

The other major pieces of evidence against Thompson were Criden's claim that several weeks later he met Tompy for breakfast at a New Jersey restaurant and gave him half of the payoff money, and the testimony of Pennsylvania Rep. John Murtha, who testified that Thompson had approached him on the House floor and told him about some rich Arabs who had money to invest and that "there was walking-around money available" for cooperative congressmen. Murtha met with the "Arabs" but was not indicted. There was disagreement with the prosecution over whether Murtha's testimony against Thompson was in exchange for a promise of immunity for himself. The jury found both Murphy and Thompson guilty.

*   *   *

Tompy was represented from his indictment through the trial by the prestigious Washington law firm of Arnold & Porter, along with an experienced New York criminal trial lawyer named Steve Kaufman. By the end of the trial, the firm claimed that Tompy still owed it half a million dollars in fees and expenses. There was only a few thousand dollars left in the Thompson Defense Fund, which had been organized by Tompy's friends, and Arnold & Porter declined to handle the appeal until it was paid at least a substantial part of what was due. I agreed to handle the appeal through the Constitutional Litigation Clinic, with the assistance of Dan Pollitt, as long as the out-of-pocket expenses would be covered by the defense fund. The case presented a number of extraordinarily complex constitutional issues relating to congressional speech and debate immunity, entrapment, and the right of the government to videotape public officials without probable cause. My students were excited at the opportunity to work on such a significant and high-profile case.

The first thing we had to do was master the entire transcript of the trial and pretrial proceedings. Dan Rezneck, who had been Tompy's chief counsel and had handled most of the pre- and posttrial motions, was extremely cooperative. A half dozen students joined me for a day-long briefing in the Arnold & Porter offices in D.C., including a viewing of the videotapes. After viewing the tapes for the first time, the thing that struck me most vividly about the defense strategy was that nothing had been made of the fact that by the second meeting, Tompy was obviously drunk and oblivious to most of what was going on around him—obvious, anyway, to someone who had long social experience with Tompy. He was never a falling-down drunk. He would just begin to fade out and become unfocused.

I questioned Rezneck about the trial strategy and why the defense had never brought this to the jury's attention. He said that it had been Tompy's decision. Tompy was embarrassed about his drinking habits, and since it was originally believed that the trial would take place before the election, he was afraid that such an emphasis would be politically disastrous. Apparently, when the trial was postponed until after election day, that decision had not been reconsidered.

In studying the transcripts, I came across a startling discrepancy. During the second crucial meeting at the town house, when the closed briefcase was pushed in Tompy's direction and he pushed it over to Criden, Tompy uttered words that were a matter of dispute between the prosecution and the defense. The government had prepared written transcripts of all the dialogue for distribution to the jurors, so that they could follow the sometimes garbled words being spoken as they viewed the videotapes. In the government's transcript, Tompy's comment is translated as "Howard, look *after* that for me, will you."

The defense argued that the transcript was inaccurate, that what he had really said was, "Howard, look *at* that for me, will you." Obviously, the government's translation supported its theory that Thompson knew that there was money in the briefcase; the defense version was consistent with Tompy's testimony that he thought that the briefcase contained documents. The judge had instructed the jury to decide for itself what had been said. My students and I carefully reviewed the videotape, and it was absolutely clear to all of us that the defense translation was accurate and that the government's version was nothing more than wishful thinking.

I considered this distinction to be crucial to our appeal. The appellate judges were much less likely to take our legal arguments seriously if they were convinced that Thompson was a knowing crook. The appeal was heard by a three-judge panel of the U.S. Court of Appeals for the Second Circuit headed by Judge Jon O. Newman, a well-respected jurist with a reputation as a fair-minded and liberal man. Indeed, when Newman was appointed to the federal bench by Jimmy Carter, I had attended a reception in his honor at the New York apartment of Norman Dorsen, who was then president of the American Civil Liberties Union.

In our brief to the appellate court, I carefully pointed out the disagreement over the translation of the crucial comment as the briefcase was transferred. Since the government's brief would surely rely on its version to emphasize its claim of Thompson's cupidity, I told the court that it was absolutely essential that it view the tape itself. I was shocked when the court handed down a ninety-page opinion written by Newman that not only upheld the conviction but in three separate and unrelated sections quoted the government's version of the disputed statement to bolster its conclusion that Thompson had no sound legal objections to his prosecution and was obviously as guilty as hell. It was clear that the court was oblivious to the heated debate over the crucial evidence, which could only mean that the court had not only ignored the videotape but had not even read our brief! I could hardly believe my eyes.

I decided to file a petition for rehearing focusing solely on the disputed language. Although the words were eminently clear to anyone who bothered to view the tape, I retained an audio engineer to analyze the videotape. He thought that I was crazy. Since the words were clear, why did I need an engineer? I got him to remove all background noise and do a reexamination. He signed an affidavit, which I submitted along with the petition for rehearing, that there was absolutely no doubt that Thompson's words were "Howard, look at that for me, will you." Stripped of the flowery legal verbiage, the petition for rehearing essentially said: Look, I don't know why you guys are so eager to railroad Frank Thompson, but I carefully explained to you that you could not decide this case without listening to the crucial tape and recognizing that the government's translation of what you obviously believe to be the critical piece of evidence is inaccurate. But you apparently never read my brief at all. Now please look at the tape and get it right!

In denying rehearing, Judge Newman, who authored the opinions in all the Abscam cases tried in the Second Circuit, wrote that the panel had now viewed the tape and was uncertain about what the actual words were, but it really didn't matter. In other words, after placing so much reliance on those words in its original opinion, it now didn't care what Thompson had actually said.

*   *   *

Unless you are the solicitor general of the United states, trying to get the U.S. Supreme Court to review a lower court decision is always a long shot. But we harbored hopes that Abscam in general, and the Thompson case in particular, raised issues so important to our constitutional structure that maybe we had a chance. My petition to the Supreme Court explained the significance of the case as follows:

> Abscam is *sui generis* [unique]. Little in our jurisprudence precisely prepares us for the issues it presents—especially as they are framed by the conviction of former Congressman Frank Thompson, Jr., a much honored public servant who had never been tainted with the hint of corruption during a long and distinguished military and political career until he was lured before the secret cameras of Abscam.
>
> As a test of our criminal jurisprudence, the outcome of this case will decide whether law enforcement in this country is to be transformed from a system of crime prevention and detection to one of creation and inducement.
>
> Equally far-reaching is the potential impact of this case upon the political and legislative process and upon fundamental rights of privacy of all Americans. As one Court of Appeals observed in regard to Abscam: "The Executive Branch of the government of the United States has carried out a plan to determine whether members of the Legislative Branch and others would commit bribery offenses if presented with the opportunity to do so. In a constitutional democracy, this maneuver inevitably raises sensitive issues of public policy and public law."

Aside from Tompy's case, I always thought that the fundamental problem with Abscam was that it allowed the FBI—through unscrupulous middlemen like Weinberg and Criden—to roam at large and try to ensnare public officials about whom there was no cause to believe that they were otherwise corrupt. It may be true that everyone has his or her price—as Robert Redford's movie *Indecent Proposal* attempted to demonstrate. Even if Frank Thompson could not be tempted to promise some fairly innocuous future assistance to an Arab sheik for $50,000, would he have succumbed for $250,000? $500,000? $1 million? Shouldn't the FBI be required to obtain a judicial warrant on the basis of some kind of evidence that the target was independently corrupt before dragging an unsuspecting public official before their hidden candid cameras? And shouldn't they be required to produce more than circumstantial evidence and self-serving testimony that a guy they had been plying with booze all day was aware that he was being handed a case full of money, before destroying his public career and carting him off to Lewisberg federal penitentiary? As I stated in my petition to the Supreme Court:

It will not go down as one of law enforcement's finest hours when Weinberg instructed Criden on how to get Thompson to accept their offer before the camera: "The shittin' guy's a boozer; Give him another drink."

All my concerns and efforts notwithstanding, Tompy wound up serving twenty-six months in prison, an ordeal that clearly aggravated a preexisting heart condition and could only have hastened his death several years after his release into political obscurity. I was privileged to be one of his honorary pallbearers when he was finally laid to rest in Arlington National Cemetery with a naval honor guard firing the traditional salute to one of its fallen heroes.

9
The Rosenberg Trial Revisited

When Julius and Ethel Rosenberg were executed at Sing Sing on June 19, 1953, I was picketing for clemency in front of the White House. The Rosenberg trial was one of the traumatic events of the McCarthy era. Avowed Communist Party members who had been accused of turning over the secret of the atom bomb to the Russians, the Rosenbergs had both been sentenced to death. They continued to proclaim their innocence all the way to the electric chair. People on the Left fervently believed that the Rosenbergs had been framed, despite the damning testimony of Ethel's brother, David Greenglass, who claimed to have turned over atomic secrets to Julius for transmission to the Russians.

It was clear that the trial had taken place in an atmosphere of anticommunist hysteria in which it would have been possible to convict any admitted Communist of just about anything—even without hard evidence. The U.S. Left had actually distanced itself from the Rosenberg trial and the worldwide protests in its aftermath—apparently for fear that association with the Rosenbergs might taint the entire movement as a group of Russian spies. In retrospect, it is probably not that far-fetched to believe that a committed American Communist who believed that U.S. nuclear power might be turned against a "defenseless" Soviet Union might have assisted "our glorious Russian allies" to defend themselves by helping them gain access to the bomb. What is hard to believe is that such individuals would remain active party members, thus guaranteeing close scrutiny of all their activities by the FBI.

* * *

The Rosenbergs left two small sons, who were adopted by a family named Meeropol. By the early 1970s, Robert and Michael Meeropol had grown into young manhood and dedicated themselves to clearing the names of their birth parents. With the aid of a group of left-wing lawyers headed by Marshall "Mike" Perlin in New York City, they undertook litigation under the Freedom of Information Act (FOIA) to gain access to government files that they hoped would demonstrate their parents' innocence.

The FOIA was one of those pieces of progressive legislation that resulted from the Watergate scandal in an effort to strengthen legal constraints against government corruption. What had become clear in the early 1970s as a result of the exposure of the misdeeds of the Nixon White House, the Hoover FBI, and a cloak-and-dagger CIA was that the U.S. Constitution had been turned on its head. Whereas the system was supposed to make the American people sovereign and government agents accountable to us, it was obvious that things had gone awry. The leaders of the Washington establishment had come to believe that they had a right to spy on the private affairs of the citizenry while keeping their own public acts secret. The Federal Privacy Act and the FOIA were adopted in an effort to put things right again. Under the FOIA, government records were to be presumptively available for public inspection, except for certain categories of exempted documents. Of course, government bureaucrats were constantly trying to expand the exemptions in opposition to citizens seeking information about the behavior of public officials and agencies.

When Robbie and Michael and Mike Perlin appealed to the Constitutional Litigation Clinic for assistance, they were already in the midst of a huge battle with the FBI over the release of hundreds of thousands of pages of documents dealing with the case. After reviewing those documents already released, I found that there were two pieces of information of immense significance.

First, it was absolutely clear that the government had no real case against Ethel and that she had been deliberately used as a hostage in an effort to force Julius to confess. Even as to Julius, it was obvious that the government had viewed the death sentence as leverage for a confession. Whatever information he had or had not passed to the Russians, he had not provided them with the secret of the atomic bomb. Indeed, the government prosecutors were well aware that Klaus Fuchs, a German refugee scientist who had spent the war in England as part of the Allied team working on the bomb, had regularly provided the Soviets with just about everything the West knew about developing nuclear technology. Fuchs had been prosecuted for espionage and had returned to Communist East Germany as the director of its nuclear industry after serving a relatively short sentence in a British jail.

Released documents suggested that the prosecutors had deliberately played a game of chicken with the Rosenbergs—expecting to force a last-minute confession from Julius in exchange for Ethel's life, if not also for his own. Phone lines were kept open between the execution chamber and the White House in the expectation of an eleventh-hour reprieve. Instead, the Rosenbergs both went to their deaths proclaiming their innocence, and President Eisenhower refused to intervene.

Second, the released documents revealed that the trial judge, Irving Kaufman (who later donned the mantle of a liberal eminence in the federal judiciary), appeared to have played an active role in the government's concerted campaign to use the death sentence as a bargaining chip with the Rosenbergs. There was evidence that Judge Kaufman had improperly held private meetings with prosecutors. He seemed to have considered himself not as a neutral adjudicator but as a member of the prosecution team. In fact, these revelations about his ethically questionable conduct created substantial controversy within the liberal legal community after the release of the FOIA documents. There were some who attempted to generate a congressional impeachment investigation; others in the liberal community rushed to the defense of the man who was viewed as a liberal pillar of the legal establishment.

I told the Meeropol brothers that because of our revolving student enrollment, it was impossible for the clinic to involve itself in the document hunt. Such an undertaking, which threatened to go on for many years, required a consistent team of analysts who were knowledgeable about the information that had and had not been released and how each document and piece of information related to all the others.

However, we were interested in trying to figure out a way to reopen the case based on new evidence. We agreed to research two separate routes to take the Rosenberg case back to court.

First, we discovered some arcane and seldom used procedures whereby a criminal prosecution could be reopened even after the sentence had been carried out. However, we could find no precedent for doing so after a defendant had been executed. Moreover, if we followed that route, the burden would be on us to prove the actual innocence of the accused. That appeared to be an insurmountable obstacle in the absence of a full retraction by David Greenglass. Alternatively, we decided that there might be a way for Michael and Robbie to sue members of the prosecution team for the wrongful deaths of their parents. In such a lawsuit, we wouldn't have to prove the Rosenbergs' innocence, only the violation of their rights by government agents leading to their deaths. I figured that we could get around the statute of limitations on the ground that no cause of action had arisen until the misdeeds of the government officials had been revealed in the newly released documents.

The major legal sticking point was the scope of immunity of the various federal officials and agencies involved. The purpose of immunity is both to protect the public treasury and to prevent the disruption of public business by unjustified lawsuits. There are three kinds of immunity. *Sovereign immunity* protects government and its departments from having to respond at all to lawsuits. The United States cannot be sued without its consent although the federal Torts Claims Act waives immunity for certain types of conduct. *Qualified immunity* protects public officials from suits for actions carried out in good faith. Additionally, certain high-level officials have an *absolute immunity*, even for conduct that was undertaken maliciously. For example, it has been decided that judges have absolute immunity for all actions that fall within the judicial orbit. So even if a judge had malicious reasons for sentencing a criminal defendant to be executed, there would be no legal recourse—although if the judge pulled out a gun and carried out the sentence on the spot, that would be outside of judicial authority.

It was therefore clear that the Meeropols had no recourse against Judge Kaufman. However, the full scope of prosecutorial immunity had not yet been settled. My students and I studied the possibility of bringing suit against those members of the Department of Justice and the U.S. attorney's staff who had actively participated in the Rosenberg prosecution.

We had several theories of prosecutorial misconduct. First, it was clear that important exculpatory information had been withheld from the defense. Even back in the 1950s, that denial of due process might have entitled the defendants to a new trial if it had been brought out on appeal. However, it was not clear that it provided their survivors with a civil cause of action for damages. The same was true of the knowing use of false evidence by the prosecution. Indeed, until the *Bivens* case was decided by the Supreme Court in 1970, it had not been established that there was a right to sue federal (as differentiated from state) officials for the violation of constitutional rights.

We ultimately decided that our strongest claim was one growing out of the hostage scenario. We believed that we would have a viable lawsuit if we could prove a conspiracy to hold Ethel hostage and to misuse the threat of capital punishment—and indeed, contriving with the trial judge to do so—for the purpose of forcing a confession from Julius. And the evidence to prove such an allegation seemed quite compelling.

But just when we thought that we had come up with a viable cause of action, the U.S. Supreme Court pulled the rug out from under us. In 1976, the Court decided *Imbler v. Pachman*, a case in which a prosecutor had been sued for damages for knowingly using perjured testimony that resulted in the conviction and incarceration of an innocent person. The Court ruled that the prosecutor was totally immune from a suit for damages under the Constitution. The majority concluded that anything less than absolute immunity risked "harassment by unfounded litigation that would cause a deflection of the prosecutor's energies from his public duties, and the possibility that he would shade his decisions instead of exercising the independence of judgment required by his public trust." It was one more in a series of decisions by the post-Warren Court majority denying legal remedies to persons victimized by public officials.

The clinic conceded defeat and abandoned its efforts to reopen the Rosenberg case. Nearly twenty years later, the Meeropols' FOIA litigation continues in an effort to obtain public disclosure of the total Rosenberg file.

It was of more than passing interest when the 1993 American Bar Association convention conducted a simulated retrial of the Rosenbergs before an impartial jury, based on all the evidence that had been made public. The jury voted acquittal of both defendants. Public controversy over the Rosenbergs' guilt has been rekindled more recently by the release of documents from the intelligence files of the former Soviet Union suggesting that Julius had indeed been a Soviet agent.

10
Shopping Malls and Other Public Forums

From the ages of sixteen to twenty-four, my life was largely taken up with what can generally be referred to as grassroots political organizing. In other words, I tried to influence public policy and engage in political action through low-cost methods, generally involving the public distribution of handbills and flyers. The objective may be to convince people what to believe, get them to vote for a particular candidate, or urge them to contact a government official on behalf of some cause. When I was a kid, the preferred means of reproduction was the mimeograph machine. Today, that has been replaced by various kinds of photocopying processes. Today, as then, the most cost-effective means of disseminating a message is having volunteers hand out flyers at places where people congregate or having volunteers walk house to house and deliver them. Some people like to place their printed matter under the windshield wipers of parked cars, but I always thought that this was more likely to annoy recipients than to gain their support. An effective organizer wants to win people over—not antagonize them.

I suppose that my early experiences—as well as two underfinanced political campaigns of my own—have made me particularly sensitive to the needs of grassroots organizations and organizers. I know from firsthand experience how tough it is to communicate a message to the public without the wherewithal to purchase time in the mass media—newspapers, television, radio, billboards—or to engage in massive direct-mail campaigns. That probably explains why I have devoted a lot of my legal attention to protecting the rights of such groups to spread their messages. This has largely involved providing legal protection for the right to hand out advocacy literature at shopping malls and the right to canvass door-to-door during hours when people are at home and can be personally solicited. To me, such activities are the very essence of the constitutional guarantee of freedom of speech. As I told one court: "If Paul Revere had to get out the word in a hurry today that the British—or the Russians or the Martians—were coming, where would he go? Clearly, to the shopping malls."

For a long time, the U.S. Supreme Court agreed with me on the importance of protecting the right of grassroots organizing. Back in 1941, in a case that involved door-to-door solicitation, Justice Hugo Black observed that the First Amendment provides special solicitude for "the poorly financed causes of little people." That was one in a series of cases in which the Court extended constitutional protection to leafleteers and other political and religious proselytizers who distributed their printed materials on public streets, in parks, door-to-door, and even on the streets of privately owned company towns. That progression of free-speech cases reached its high point in 1968, when the Court ruled five to four, that the First Amendment protected the exercise of free speech at privately owned shopping malls. The Court's opinion noted that in many areas those shopping enclaves had replaced the old town squares and village greens where people had once congregated and discussed the issues of the day.

Then came the change in the composition of the Supreme Court following the election of Richard Nixon as president. The Republican Nixon had campaigned as an opponent of the Warren Court's liberalism, focusing his wrath on the Court's decisions expanding the rights of criminal defendants. Directing that charge against the Democratic Party was somewhat anomalous, since the main architects of the Warren Court decisions—Chief Justice Earl Warren and William Brennan—had both been appointed by Republican President Dwight Eisenhower. Warren himself was a former Republican governor of California and had been the GOP's vice presidential candidate in 1948. Nevertheless, Nixon promised to appoint to the Court what he referred to as "strict constructionists" who would stop expanding constitutional rights.

Of course, one of the first rights the new majority stopped expanding—and began retracting—was freedom of speech. By 1974, the Court had overruled the earlier decision involving shopping malls. The new majority invoked the principle of "state action," which holds generally that constitutional rights operate only against governmental conduct. Since shopping malls were privately owned, the U.S. Constitution did not stop them from prohibiting the exercise of free speech, no matter that they were performing functions previously fulfilled by public space. That decision left open the possibility that the free-speech provisions of various state constitutions might protect free speech within specific jurisdictions. (The protections of the U.S. Constitution are a floor, not a ceiling.) So it was that in 1980, the California Supreme Court held that the California Constitution reached beyond the acts of state agents and protected speech at public gathering places such as shopping malls.

*   *   *

I took up the issue in New Jersey in 1983. The New Jersey Supreme Court had demonstrated a strong commitment to free speech, and the language of the New Jersey Constitution in that regard was quite similar to California's. The clinic's first shopping center case involved the Bergen Mall, one of half a dozen such enclaves along Route 4 in Paramus, about six miles from the George Washington Bridge. My client, Eric Gerstmann, was an eighteen-year-old college student who was running as an independent candidate for the board of freeholders, the county's legislative body. He had been arrested for handing out political flyers at a public bus stop located on mall property. We had a two-day show trial in the Paramus municipal court in which we created a record to show that the mall, in addition to being a shopping mecca, was a community gathering place.

The magistrate found my client guilty, and we appealed to the county court, where the judge decided in our favor and reversed the conviction for trespassing. He based his ruling on a 1980 decision by the New Jersey Supreme Court involving the distribution of political pamphlets at Princeton University. In that case, *State v. Schmid*, the court agreed with the California decision that once owners opened their property to public use, they gave up their right of total dominion over activities conducted on that property. The court said that such property owners could *regulate* the distribution of noncommercial literature but could not prohibit it altogether.

The prosecution was represented throughout by Andrew Napolitano, who agreed with me that this important constitutional issue needed judicial resolution—which required an opinion from an appellate court. Although we had won an acquittal, my client agreed to risk further appellate review and the possibility of reinstatement of the conviction. I suggested to the prosecutor that he appeal the decision to the New Jersey Appellate Division, which he agreed to do. It was a disappointment when the court refused to decide the case and dismissed the appeal on jurisdictional grounds, ruling that my client could not waive his constitutional right against "double jeopardy"—that is, his right not to be tried twice for the same offense.

After the first Bergen Mall case, it was back to the drawing board. The week that the antinuclear play *The Day After*—about the outbreak of a fictional nuclear war—was to be shown on network television, members of the peace movement wanted to distribute flyers at the Bergen Mall promoting the show. The mall had by then issued regulations governing leaflet distribution, but the rules were so restrictive that the group could not comply. The major impediment was a requirement that the leafleteers obtain insurance coverage for any remote harm that might occur as a result of the literature distribution. Because of the nature of the insurance industry, there were no companies even interested in selling such a policy, and if there had been, the cost would have been prohibitive. Other rules unnecessarily restricted the number of distributors, their location, and the frequency of access. The judge ruled for us on all counts. Unfortunately, the defendants did not appeal, so we were again denied the opportunity to obtain a binding appellate opinion.

When members of the peace movement were denied the right to hand out materials at the huge Willowbrook Mall in Wayne, I again brought suit. This time, Willowbrook backed down and offered my clients space at a community booth in the center of the mall. Again, I was denied a definitive legal ruling.

When I ran for Congress in 1986, I personally greeted voters and handed out my campaign literature at Livingston Mall in my congressional district. When ordered to leave by security guards on pain of arrest, I asked the ACLU to represent me. When my lawyer sought a restraining order against the mall, the judge convinced the owners to agree to allow me access for the remainder of the campaign. For the fourth time I had prevailed in a shopping center suit, but the law of New Jersey remained unresolved.

In the meantime, courts in many other states had ruled on similar arguments under their respective constitutions, most of them coming down on the side of private property.

*　*　*

The Persian Gulf War finally provided the opportunity I had been looking for. Soon after President Bush announced Operation Desert Storm to oppose Iraq's invasion of Kuwait, an ad hoc coalition of peace and religious organizations sprang up under the title of the New Jersey Coalition Against War in the Middle East. The organizers planned a statewide mobilization of their volunteers to hand out literature in opposition to Persian Gulf hostilities over the Veterans Day weekend in November 1990. The plan was to send their volunteers to commuter hubs during the Friday rush hours and to shopping malls all over the state on Saturday and Sunday. I instructed them to ask mall management to allow small groups of volunteers to pass out leaflets somewhere in the malls' common areas. When the malls all denied permission, I agreed to bring suit.

When reporters asked me why my clients wanted to go to the shopping malls to spread their message, I replied: "It's like when Willie Sutton was asked, 'Why do you rob banks?' and he answered 'Because that's where the money is.' The malls are where the people are."

We sued ten of the largest malls across the state in the superior court in Hackensack, where the case was heard by the county assignment judge, Peter Ciolino. Ciolino has a reputation among lawyers as a fair-minded judge, but I sensed hostility to our cause from the start. Ignoring the previous rulings by his Bergen County judicial colleagues, he denied us a temporary restraining order. He even delayed setting a date for a hearing on a preliminary injunction, despite the imminence of armed conflict in the Middle East. The state supreme court denied our emergency appeal.

We wound up with an eleven-day trial in June 1991. The ten defendants were represented by six different law firms. Two of the defendants were represented by a former attorney general of the United States, Nicholas Katzenbach. The defendants' lead counsel was a law firm from Michigan that represented the Taubman Company, one of the nation's leading shopping center developers. The same firm had successfully defended bans on shopping center leafleting in Connecticut, Michigan, and Wisconsin. Its experience in Connecticut was clearly now being used as the model for defending such cases.

In Connecticut, a lower court had granted a temporary injunction to permit the National Organization for Women (NOW) to collect petitions in support of the equal rights amendment at West Farms Mall. While the case was on appeal, the Ku Klux Klan announced that it wanted to hold a demonstration at the mall in Klan regalia. Permission was denied, but the application was widely publicized—by the shopping center, I suspect. When three Klansmen in white sheets showed up, hundreds of anti-Klan demonstrators also gathered. By the time the police intervened, a near riot had ensued. The Connecticut Supreme Court—apparently properly impressed by the mischief that had resulted from the trial court's order—reversed the lower court and held that the state constitution did not protect leafleting and petitioning at shopping centers. In our case, defense counsel missed no opportunity to remind the court what had happened in Connecticut and to predict that the same thing would happen in New Jersey if the plaintiffs prevailed. They conveniently ignored the fact that leafleting had been going on at California shopping malls for a dozen years without a single untoward incident.

*   *   *

It is sometimes difficult to convey even to law students how idiosyncratic our seemingly highly structured trials are and why lawyers go to such great lengths to avoid them. Nor is it easy to explain how much real power is wielded by trial judges, whose errors are technically subject to review by an appellate court. First of all, the right to appeal is akin to the right to a second operation if the first surgeon messes up. In our case, I firmly believe that Judge Ciolino excluded 75 percent of our relevant evidence. Of course, after the trial was over and he had ruled against us, I had every right to appeal those errors and have an appellate court tell him two years later that he had been wrong and to try the case all over again. I'm sure you get the point.

It was not entirely clear why we needed a trial at all, let alone eleven days of testimony. It was pretty clear that the judge had made up his mind from the outset that shopping centers were different from a private university and that the state supreme court's Princeton decision was inapplicable. But since the judge refused to dismiss our case outright and we were going to have a trial, we figured that we would do it right.

In the Princeton case, the supreme court had set forth a three-part test to determine when private property owners who had opened their property to public use were required by the New Jersey Constitution to allow others to engage in expressive activity. That test required a court to examine (1) the normal use of the property, (2) the nature of the public invitation to use the property, and (3) whether the stranger's use would disrupt the normal use of the property. In effect, the legal test set forth elements to be considered but did not clearly state how each element was to be evaluated. But most importantly, the case had resolved that, unlike the federal Constitution, New Jersey's provisions guaranteeing free speech operated against private entities as well as government agencies.

Our case consisted of three main types of evidence: (1) information about the range of noncommercial activities officially allowed and encouraged at the various malls—ranging from health fairs and seminars arranged by the malls themselves to mall-walker programs that encouraged senior citizens and others to utilize the corridors as aerobic tracks; (2) evidence of the public amenities offered on the properties, such as public bus stops, municipal police patrols, and public lounges where visitors could hang out, snack, and greet and meet friends; and (3) testimony that the peaceful and orderly distribution of printed materials would not adversely affect commercial activity at the malls.

Much of our evidence was documentary and had been submitted to the court in advance of the trial. Through discovery, we had established the events, activities, and amenities at each of the ten malls, as well as the types of commercial and public entities located at each one. One mall provided space for a police substation, one had a post office on the premises, and one had a public auditorium for rent to community groups. Many of these amenities were portrayed in several hundred photographs taken by our photographer and submitted as evidence. Although the defendants all claimed that they were politically neutral and took no position on U.S. policy in the Persian Gulf, our photos included shots of posters supporting the war and other public displays of official support for government policy.

My favorite piece of evidence was a photograph of a dedication stone in front of the main entrance to one of the malls that proclaimed:

Monmouth Shopping Center
Dedicated to the Famous Americans of Monmouth County
Past—Present—Future

When I cross-examined the mall manager as to the consequences if one of those famous Americans to whom the mall was dedicated were to stand by the plaque and hand out her printed credo, the manager conceded that she would be arrested for trespass.

Taken together, our evidence left little room for doubt that New Jersey's ubiquitous shopping malls had indeed become the new town squares and village greens in many parts of the state. We even introduced the writings of James Rouse, the country's premier shopping center developer (two of his malls were defendants). Rouse had written long ago that it was the intent of mall architectural design and theory to make them into the new "Main Streets" of a region.

In an effort to refute the defendants' claims that handing out leaflets would disrupt normal mall operations, we attempted to present a number of witnesses to testify that distributing politically opinionated literature in places of public congregation—such as public streets and commuter terminals—did not cause disruption or confrontation. For reasons that remain a mystery to me, the judge ruled most of this testimony irrelevant. He would allow only evidence concerning events at the defendant malls, which was severely limited, since such activity was not permitted there. He finally relented and permitted us to present the testimony of one peace activist who had regularly been distributing handbills at the Bergen Mall under the injunction I had obtained half a dozen years earlier. And the court allowed us to present the testimony of an expert witness from the Citizen Action movement about the best methods of grassroots organizing and why it was economically essential to such groups to be able to spread their messages at shopping centers.

Although Judge Ciolino also blocked our efforts to introduce evidence of the experience in California over the previous decade, we had already introduced, by stipulation of the defendants, two affidavits that conclusively demonstrated that such activity was both common and benign.

The defendants' case consisted primarily of testimony by mall designers and architects who claimed that leafleting in the common corridors would be disruptive to the soothing ambience carefully created to encourage shopping and, especially, impulse buying. They were at a loss to explain how jazz concerts, health fairs, and the general hustle and bustle of the arcades contributed to that soothing and relaxed atmosphere. Nor did the defense witnesses ever attempt to explain how permitting leafleting on the exterior sidewalks—the walkways between the parking areas and the enclosed malls—would adversely affect commercial activities.

The defendants' major piece of evidence was a Gallup poll that they had commissioned to demonstrate that people would avoid going to shopping malls if they thought that they might be confronted by partisan advocacy. Of course, the poll did not explain to respondents that if they might be confronted by leafleteers at one mall, the same thing would be true at competitor malls and shopping centers. In other words, there would be no place to hide—even if shoppers really wished to avoid proselytizers. We put a rebuttal expert on the stand to testify that the poll was not a reliable predictor of how individuals would actually behave should New Jersey courts rule that citizens had a constitutional right to hand out printed materials at shopping centers.

It was not a great surprise when Judge Ciolino ruled in favor of the malls. In a pedestrian opinion, he held that the primary purpose of the defendant property owners was commercial (no one had ever suggested otherwise), therefore, they did not have to accommodate expressive activity. The Appellate Division panel that heard our appeal seemed interested and engaged in the case, allowing the usual forty-minute oral argument to go on for almost two and a half hours. I was somewhat disappointed when it issued a pro forma opinion affirming Judge Ciolino without discussing any of the underlying issues.

The New Jersey Supreme Court, like the U.S. Supreme Court, controls its own docket. Although technically the court is obligated to hear appeals involving substantial constitutional issues, it can choose not to decide an issue by merely dismissing the appeal without a hearing. Therefore, when the court certified our appeal on October 26, 1993, I figured that we were at least halfway home.

My optimism was shaken when I showed up for arguments in the supreme court's chamber in Trenton on March 14, 1994. The first blow was a notice that Justice Stewart Pollock had recused himself from hearing the case and was being replaced by Judge Herman Michels of the Appellate Division. Justice Pollock had spoken and written extensively and positively about the *Schmid* case, and I had been counting on his vote. Judge Michels had a reputation as one of the most conservative members of the Appellate Division. I was sure that I had lost one vote right off the top. The other concern had to do with the participation of Chief Justice Robert Wilentz. Wilentz had recently undergone surgery, so his absence from the bench was not a surprise. What was disconcerting was the fact that the presiding judge, Justice Robert Clifford, made no reference to the chief's absence and did not ask counsel if there was any objection to Wilentz's listening to the tapes of the arguments and participating in the decision, which, in my experience, was the normal procedure.

I thought that the argument itself went quite well. I had assumed in advance that Justices Alan Handler and Daniel O'Hern would be sympathetic to my argument, and their questions and reactions solidified that view. Indeed, O'Hern made one of the most cogent observations of the day when one of my adversaries stated that my position that the shopping malls had replaced the old town squares was "ridiculous." O'Hern deftly pointed out that the attorney should think more carefully about his argument in view of the identity of his client: Rockaway Townsquare Mall. Although a judge's comments at oral argument are not always a reliable indicator of a subsequent vote, Justice Gary Stein also seemed to be articulating strong arguments in favor of our position and appeared extremely unsympathetic to the defendants' case. In contrast, the court's lone female member, Marie Garibaldi, whom I had always found to be a kind and warm-hearted human being off the bench, indicated total hostility to my position. Justice Clifford, known as the court's unpredictable curmudgeon, was his usual enigmatic self. Based on judicial attitudes that morning, it seemed that the sitting judges might split three to three. If so, the opinion below would be affirmed, and we would lose. I was therefore quite disturbed when the *New Jersey Law Journal* reported in the following week's edition that Chief Justice Wilentz was not planning to participate in any of the cases heard during the week. However, when I called the court clerk, Steve Townsend, to confirm that fact, he said that the chief had taken the tapes of all the arguments and had made no final decisions as to which ones he would skip. I took heart from a gut feeling that the chief justice would not let such an important issue be resolved by a split vote. I even mentioned to Townsend that *Court TV* had taped the entire argument and that the chief could watch the rebroadcast.

Robert Wilentz is a brilliant jurist who evokes strong, but quite mixed, reactions from New Jersey lawyers. Under the New Jersey Constitution, the chief justice is an extremely powerful figure, and many accuse Wilentz of exercising his powers in an arbitrary and autocratic manner—partly because he insists on high standards of ethical behavior by members of the bar. To many New Jersey attorneys, Wilentz is antilawyer. Those who dislike Wilentz insist that his only credential for his job is his political lineage. His father was the Democratic political boss and former attorney general David Wilentz, prosecutor of Lindbergh baby kidnapper Bruno Hauptmann. His brother Warren, senior partner of the major law firm that bears the family name, was a one-time Democratic candidate for the U.S. Senate.

No matter how he came to the job, I have always considered Wilentz to be a pioneer legal thinker who made the New Jersey Supreme Court one of the most respected and forward-looking judicial institutions in the country. Under Wilentz's leadership, the New Jersey judicial system has pioneered in dealing with frontier issues such as exclusionary zoning, racial discrimination and affirmative action, rights of privacy (including abortion), and educational funding—as well as free speech. Although many accuse Wilentz of being aloof and autocratic, my son Jonathan, who spent a year as his law clerk, attributes this reputation to the chief justice's shyness and reserve. In personal relationships, Jonny found him to be warm and considerate.

It took more than nine months from the date of argument—an unusually long time—for the court to issue its opinion. When the supreme court clerk's office called on the morning of December 19 to inform me that the opinion would be released at 10 A.M. the following day, this began one of the longest days of my life. I had invested more than ten years in this issue, and I had a personal stake in the outcome, as well as an objective concern about the issue itself. The ACLU office in Newark had arranged for someone to pick up the opinion at the clerk's office and fax it to Newark. I paced my office like an expectant father on the morning of the twentieth. At 10:35, I picked up the phone and Marsha Wenk, the New Jersey ACLU's legal director, was shouting joyously. She read me the operative sentence from the syllabus to the court's opinion:

> HELD: The right of free speech embodied in our State Constitution requires that regional shopping centers must permit the distribution of leaflets on societal issues, subject to reasonable conditions set by the centers.

My shouts of "Hallelujah," which reverberated through the offices of the Constitutional Litigation Clinic, brought colleagues and students running. It was a wild and joyous celebration.

Seldom had my instincts about a decision turned out so right. The vote was four to three, with the chief justice writing the majority opinion for the court. It was a seventy-five-page opus celebrating the right of free speech in our democratic society. Most satisfying was that Wilentz had adopted nearly our entire line of argument. He had obviously been impressed by our evidence about the role of shopping malls in the social and cultural life of New Jersey in the latter part of the twentieth century and had completely endorsed our argument that "Main Street" had moved to suburban malls. The opinion stated:

> We look back and we look ahead in an effort to determine what a constitutional provision means. If free speech is to mean anything in the future, it must be exercised at these [shopping] centers. Our constitutional right encompasses more than leafleting and associated speech on sidewalks located in empty downtown business districts. It means communicating with the people in the new commercial and social centers; if the people have left for the shopping centers, our constitutional right includes the right to go there too, to follow them, and to talk to them.

Justice Garibaldi wrote the dissent, which Michels and Clifford joined. I was especially disappointed that I had lost the vote of Clifford, who had retired from the court the previous weekend at the age of seventy. Justice Clifford was a thoughtful, intelligent man for whom I had great respect. Yet in the only two cases I ever argued in the New Jersey Supreme Court—both of which I won by four-to-three votes—Clifford had been part of the dissent. Interestingly, in my earlier supreme court case, Justice Garibaldi had provided a decisive vote for the majority, and Justice Stein, who was crucial to victory this time around, had dissented.

* * *

The Citizen Action movement was born in Ohio and spread outward toward both coasts. In an earlier incarnation, it was a homegrown product of Chicago's venerable community organizer Saul Alinsky. The purpose of such populist movements is to organize people in their communities to try to influence the way government deals with the issues that affect their daily lives—the environment, local taxes, tenant rights, and so forth. They are in some ways akin to neighborhood trade unions.

The founders of the Citizen Action organizations discovered that it was possible to finance their operations on a pay-as-you-go basis by hiring young organizers to go house to house with their ideological message and solicit contributions at the door. If the canvassing took place when adult members of the household were at home, the solicitors could raise enough money from those small contributions to pay their own minimal salaries and turn over the excess to support the other educational and lobbying activities of the organization. The program turned out to be so successful that other grassroots nonprofit groups began to emulate it. There was even a training school, the Midwest Academy, established in Chicago to instruct members of the local affiliates in organizing techniques. That's why in communities across the country, on any given evening, there are young men and women knocking on doors, handing out literature, and collecting signatures on petitions dealing with a variety of public policy issues from cleaning up toxic waste to educational reform. On occasion, the solicitation may include support for candidates for public office.

I became Citizen Action's turf lawyer in New Jersey. As the movement developed, a number of New Jersey municipalities, sometimes under pressure from home owners who did not like people ringing their doorbells at night, adopted ordinances restricting house-to-house solicitation. Since it was clear that the U.S. Constitution protected some type of door-to-door solicitation, towns restricted the activity only during certain hours. The restrictions ranged from a firm 5 P.M. cutoff to sunset. They were justified as crime-prevention measures or for the protection of privacy in the home.

The problem for the movement was that it could not survive on daytime canvassing. As more and more women entered the workforce, there were not enough adults at home during the day to make canvassing prior to 4 P.M. economically viable. At the time we went to trial in federal court in Newark, the break-even point for a canvasser (payment of the canvasser's own salary and organizational overhead) was $85 a night, or $17 an hour for five hours of actual canvassing. Experience had proved that it was not possible to collect that much in contributions during the middle of the day. It was the organization's practice to canvass from 4 to 9 P.M. From 1 to 4, the canvassers received training and carried out other organizational chores.

We initially brought suit against ten municipalities that had cutoff times for door-to-door solicitation earlier than 9 P.M. However, four of them quickly agreed to rescind their ordinances, and we proceeded against the remaining six, the largest of which were Paramus, Woodbridge, and Edison Township. The case was assigned to Harold Ackerman, a Carter appointee who had a reputation for being sympathetic to constitutional rights. Even before the actual trial got under way, Judge Ackerman decided that on the basis of precedent, the plaintiffs were likely to win and issued restraining orders allowing the canvassing to proceed temporarily in several of the defendant municipalities.

The trial consisted of five full days of hearings over a period of several months. Our witnesses were mainly Citizen Action canvassers and supervisors who testified about the basic structure and operations of the organization and the economics of grassroots organizing. A member of the faculty of the Rutgers School of Criminal Justice testified that prohibiting nighttime canvassing was unlikely to reduce the incidence of crime in the defendant communities. The defense witnesses were mainly police officials from the defendant towns.

The trial had ended, and we were waiting for Judge Ackerman to issue a final ruling in our favor when the court of appeals in Philadelphia pulled the rug out from under us. In a case involving almost identical ordinances in four towns in western Pennsylvania, the circuit court ruled, two to one, that the restrictions were not unconstitutional. It upheld a lower court determination that the ordinances *did* reduce crime and protect privacy and that nonprofit organizations had "alternative means" of exercising their rights of freedom of expression, such as direct mail, telephone solicitation, and handbilling on the streets and in shopping centers. Judge Ackerman summoned the lawyers back to court and asked me why, based on the appellate court ruling, he wasn't bound to dismiss our case. I argued that no matter what had been found in the Pennsylvania case, our evidentiary record demonstrated that such ordinances would not reduce crime and that the plaintiff organization would be put out of business unless it could conduct evening solicitation. Indeed, we had carefully established through testimony that there were no "alternative means" for Citizen Action to carry out its mission. Direct mail or media advertising required an up-front outlay of capital that was unavailable to it; telephone solicitation provided neither the economic return nor the interpersonal communication of face-to-face contact; and solicitation at shopping centers was invariably prohibited by the property owners. (This was prior to our shopping mall victory.) Furthermore, the organization's mission was dependent on face-to-face interchange with constituents. Judge Ackerman was not impressed. He said that he was bound by the ruling of his superiors in Philadelphia that these types of ordinances passed muster under the First Amendment.

Going to the court of appeals is like playing Russian roulette. When I argued the Citizen Action appeal, the system prevented lawyers from finding out until the morning of the argument which three judges would be hearing a case (the process has recently been changed so that a lawyer can find out in advance). It was a great relief when I looked at the docket sheet posted in the clerk's office and saw the panel I had been assigned. It included one judge who had approved the earlier Pennsylvania canvassing decision, one who had dissented, and a district judge sitting temporarily on the appeals court—Louis Pollak, a First Amendment scholar who had been a former dean at both Yale and Penn Law Schools.

I had actually prepared two separate arguments. If I had drawn an unsympathetic panel, I was prepared to tell the court that it should refer the case to an en banc hearing, which is a hearing before all the active judges of the Third Circuit. Such a hearing was required for the court to overrule a decision of an earlier panel. However, in light of the panel I had drawn, when the presiding judge asked me, "Mr. Askin, do we have to en banc this case," I replied, "No, Your Honor. This case is distinguishable from the Pennsylvania case."

It was surely one of the most enjoyable appellate arguments I ever had. Judge Pollak was especially interested in discussing the intricacies of constitutional litigation and the difference between constitutional *law* and constitutional *fact*, which I argued was at the heart of the case. It was my position that since the constitutional standard was fact based, it was possible to have identical ordinances that could be held constitutional in one case and not in another. Most importantly, the earlier case had been decided under a legal standard that focused on the "availability of alternative channels of communication." The Pennsylvania court may have found as a fact that such "alternative channels" existed in western Pennsylvania, but Judge Ackerman had found that there were no "alternative channels" in the northern New Jersey communities involved in our case. Indeed, Judge Ackerman had essentially ruled that although there were no "alternative channels" as a matter of *fact*, he was bound by the circuit's ruling that there were "alternative channels" as a matter of *law*. I argued that Judge Ackerman was wrong on the latter point and that he should have heeded his own factual findings.

I had little doubt when we left the courtroom that we had won. Oral arguments can often be misleading as to the leanings of a judge or a panel of judges, but there was little room for doubt in this case. What surprised me when we received the court's opinion was that it had ruled not only that the curfew provisions of the ordinances were unconstitutional but also that the fingerprinting requirements imposed by a few of the defendant towns also were unconstitutional. It was the first case in which the fingerprint provisions of a licensing regulation had been found unconstitutional. We had argued that other cases were different because they had always been litigated under a Fourth Amendment privacy theory—that it was different when fingerprinting was required to engage in speech-related activities protected by the First Amendment. And we had introduced evidence that some of the young Citizen Action canvassers associated fingerprinting with criminality and refused to canvass in towns where fingerprinting was required. The court adopted our argument.

Then we held our breath waiting to see if the U.S. Supreme Court would accept the defendants' petition for review. It was denied, with two justices noting their disagreement.

The case went back to Judge Ackerman's court to determine the amount of damages the defendant municipalities would have to pay the plaintiffs to compensate them for the times they were forbidden to canvass and the amount of attorney's fees the ACLU would receive under the Civil Rights Attorneys Fees Act. After substantial negotiations that dragged on for about a year, the defendants agreed to pay a total of nearly $200,000 to be divided between damages and fees.

One consequence of our victory is that my doorbell is now frequently rung in the evening by solicitors for one good cause or another. On such occasions, my wife, who was never really fond of this particular case of mine, usually calls out in disgust, "Frank, it's *your* friends at the door."

11

Homeless in Morristown

Richard Kreimer was certainly one of my most interesting clients, if not one of the most lovable. I recall Jules Pfeiffer once writing that the ACLU needed a better class of clients, and the truth is, people who become the centers of landmark legal battles are often not the people you want to invite to your dinner parties. They tend to be obsessive, self-absorbed, and self-righteous. Meet Richard Kreimer.

Richard came from an upper-middle-class Morristown family that had fallen to bickering after the death of the parents. For reasons I never quite got straight, Richard lost whatever share of the inheritance he had received, including his home. He suffered both physical and emotional problems that seemed to make him unemployable, and he had been ruled eligible for Social Security disability payments. His meager income was insufficient to obtain housing in the affluent Morristown area, but Richard was unwilling to leave the community where his dwindling supply of friends lived. So he lived on the streets.

As a homeless person, Richard spent large chunks of his time at the Morristown library. Although not well educated, he was reasonably literate and made extensive use of library resources. As long as the former chief librarian remained, Richard was welcome at the library, although there was apparently some grumbling about his body odor, appearance, and allegedly obnoxious behavior from library staff members. In fact, Richard would be ideal to illustrate the definition of *disheveled*, and he bathed irregularly. He was also a bit cross-eyed, and library patrons sometimes complained that he stared at them in peculiar ways. Allegedly, he sometimes dozed off while reading. He was also very argumentative.

The library staff used the appointment of a new director to escalate their campaign against Richard. On a number of occasions he was asked to leave; if he refused to do so, the police were called. Some of the local cops had grown up with him and refused to persecute him. Others thought that he was obnoxious and fair game. Those who pushed him around became defendants in one of the federal civil rights suits he brought on his own behalf. The library trustees were also sued when they passed regulations authorizing the librarians to exclude him upon complaints of his body odor, staring, or dozing off.

Richard was lucky enough to have his case assigned to Judge Lee Sarokin, who decided that Kreimer needed a lawyer to represent him. He assigned a former law clerk of his, Bruce Rosen. I had known Bruce since the days when he had covered the federal courts for the *Bergen Record* while attending law school. After his clerkship, Bruce became the editor of the *New Jersey Law Journal*. Bruce invited me and the clinic to be cocounsel. The students expressed a great deal of interest in the case. Part of the clinic's pedagogy is to involve students in cases that appeal to them and will motivate them. Thus, for the clinic to take on a case, there must be interest and commitment on the part of at least one faculty member and a sufficient number of students.

*   *   *

We jumped in and began preparing legal memoranda concerning homeless individuals' right to library access and the conditions under which such access might be denied. It turned out that there was almost no law on point. Although there was a good bit of law on the First Amendment rights of libraries not to be censored by other public officials, there was no precedent involving the duty of public libraries to be open and accessible to members of the public. However, it seemed clear to me that such a right existed and could be restricted only for weighty and compelling reasons.

At the same time, Bruce was attempting to negotiate a settlement with the defendants, as was Denise Reinhardt, a former student of mine who had been assigned to represent Richard in his suit against the police department. But it became obvious that we had a vendetta on our hands. Richard was unquestionably the most hated man in the Morristown area. Not only did most of the public officials have it in for Richard, but their affluent constituents did not want a penny of tax money paid over to this pariah, whose unkempt likeness showed up regularly on the front pages of the local papers. Since he had nothing else to do all day but hang out on the streets, Richard had taken to holding almost daily press conferences in front of city hall. Whatever money he had seemed to be in dimes and quarters, which he fed into a public phone to announce to one and all the time of his next public statement. To the reporters, he was something of an antihero.

There were two things militating in our favor to force a favorable settlement. One was the fact that everyone assumed that Judge Sarokin would rule in our favor. Second, the town's insurance company wanted out as the attorneys' fees piled up. Because we had sought punitive damages in both suits and had named numerous local officials as defendants, it had been decided at some point that each defendant was entitled to a separate lawyer. The insurance company and the town attorney were at odds over the responsibility for payment of those fees. We would hold status conferences on Richard's cases with as many as twenty-five attorneys in attendance. However, the local elected officials were so adamant about not paying Richard off that we could not reach an agreement, even though we kept reminding them that it would be much cheaper for the library to build a public shower facility for Richard's use than to continue the litigation.

Both sides proceeded to file motions for summary judgment with the court. Judge Sarokin agreed with our legal analysis. He ruled that individuals had a fundamental constitutional right to receive information and that a public library was a quintessential public forum for providing access to information. As such, he ruled that regulations that restricted access to such a facility had to withstand the strictest scrutiny. He found that the library was unable to justify its regulations under that tough standard. If the homeless were unable to comply with the hygiene standards, Judge Sarokin said in his ringing statement, it was the duty of government agencies to revoke their conditions of life, not their library cards. (Several years later, conservative Senate Republicans cited this opinion in their unsuccessful efforts to block Sarokin's elevation to the court of appeals.)

When the case went to the court of appeals in Philadelphia, the U.S. library community was split. The New Jersey Library Association fully supported Morristown and argued that librarians should have discretion to expel what it called "problem patrons" whenever they were bothering other users. However, the Freedom to Read Foundation, an arm of the American Library Association, filed an amicus brief agreeing with Judge Sarokin that the right of access to library materials could be restricted only for compelling reasons, although it took no position on whether Richard himself was expellable.

* * *

The decision of the three-judge panel of the court of appeals was schizophrenic, to say the least. It reflected a split, which had been apparent during oral argument, between Judges Morton Greenberg and Robert Cowan. The first two-thirds of the opinion appeared to reflect Cowan's views and was devoted to rejecting the Morristown library's argument that it was *not* a public forum. Siding with the plaintiff, the court announced:

> Our review of the Supreme Court decisions confirms that the First Amendment does not merely prohibit the government from enacting laws that censor information, but additionally encompasses the positive right of public access to information and ideas.... [T]his right ... includes some level of access to a public library, the quintessential locus of the receipt of information.

Thus, the Court of Appeals agreed with Judge Sarokin that the hygiene rule was to be given exacting scrutiny by a federal court, and could be upheld only if it were "narrowly tailored to serve a significant government interest and . . . leaves *ample alternative channels of communication.*" It was on that latter question—the availability of alternative channels of communication—that the appellate court differed with Judge Sarokin and the plaintiff.

It was the plaintiff's position that there were no alternative channels of information available to a homeless person in Kreimer's situation and that denying him access to the library left him without access to the information he needed to be a knowledgeable citizen. The essence of the argument was that Kreimer was unable to comply with the hygiene regulation because of his homelessness; thus it was up to the library to provide him with either some means of access to its materials or the means to comply with its hygiene regulation. When I told the Court of Appeals in oral argument that the library's minimum duty was to provide a separate reading area for persons unable to comply with the hygiene rule, Judge Greenberg asked whether I was advocating segregation. I replied that I was not, but if that were the only alternative, it was preferable to total banishment. Judge Greenberg signed the opinion for the court and responded to this argument with an extraordinary leap of faith, which was the key to its decision:

> [W]e find that this rule leaves open alternative channels for communication in the sense that so long as a patron complies with the rules, he or she may use the library's facilities.

It was the ultimate catch-22! If compliance—ignoring the plaintiff's inability to do so—provides the alternative, no rule or regulation could ever run afoul of the First Amendment. It essentially abolishes the legal requirement of "alternative channels of communication." The court did not explain how a person in Kreimer's situation was supposed to comply with the hygiene requirement in the absence of public bathing facilities in the Morristown area.

Richard was insistent that we ask the U.S. Supreme Court to review the case, but we talked him out of it. We told him that there was no chance we would do any better with Rehnquist and company and that they might overrule the positive parts of the opinion.

*   *   *

Prior to the decision in the Court of Appeals, we actually settled the damages parts of both cases. The insurance company finally prevailed in its arguments with local officials, and the town agreed that Richard should be paid off. I take it that the insurance company saw a rising tide of attorneys' bills and realized that even victory in the Court of Appeals could not prevent a trial before Judge Sarokin on Richard's claims of deliberate harassment. So even though the appellate decision confirmed the library's authority to enforce its rules, it did not affect a generous financial settlement for Richard, the amount of which I am not at liberty to reveal because of a confidentiality clause in the settlement agreement.

Despite the substantial financial settlement, Richard remained homeless. With the help of a social worker, Richard made an extensive search for an apartment in the Morristown area but was unable to find a permanent place to live. Although I tended to take Richard's reports with a grain of salt, his social worker confirmed that no one wanted to rent to him—either because he was so notorious or because he had no housing or employment references. So, for an indefinite period after his big payday, Richard was renting motel rooms by the night and occasionally returning to his favorite Morristown park for an evening when the weather permitted. By day, he continued to hang out in the middle of Morristown, commenting on the passing scene and meeting with the various television producers and literary agents who were always trying to figure out how to market Richard's story.

*   *   *

I also became Richard's voting rights lawyer. In that regard, we established legal precedents of even greater significance than those in his library case.

It was early in my representation that Richard mentioned that he wanted to register to vote, but the board of elections wouldn't accept his registration because he had no mailing address. There was a homeless shelter in town, but Richard refused to stay there because of its religious affiliations. I asked the director if he could receive mail there anyway, but the director refused because of Richard's notoriety and the director's unwillingness to antagonize the shelter's local financial contributors. The post office said that he could not rent a post office box unless he had a permanent mailing address, and that general delivery was good for only thirty days.

I contacted the board of elections and took the position that the constitutional right to vote could not be dependent on the availability of a mailing address. I threatened to sue. The superintendent of elections requested an opinion from the attorney general of New Jersey. In fact, there were a few reported opinions around the country involving the right of the homeless to vote. They all upheld that right, but the cases assumed that there was a place such as a church or homeless shelter to which the election board could direct nonforwardable mail to verify the registrant's status before each election. By the time Attorney General Robert Del Tufo issued his opinion, the Morristown postmaster had agreed to accept on an indefinite basis any mail addressed to Richard from the board of elections. However, he warned me that if word got out and other homeless persons tried to take advantage of it, he would rescind his agreement.

Del Tufo's far-reaching opinion affirmed the right of the homeless to vote and the duty of boards of elections to facilitate that right. Although it was issued in response to the Morris County board of elections' request for guidance on the Kreimer case, it was circulated as an official attorney general's opinion to election officials throughout the state. It was such a precedent-setting ruling that it became the lead story on page one of the *Newark Star-Ledger* on the day after it was issued. The opinion made it clear that it was the duty of election officials to figure out how to communicate with registrants. For example, I had suggested that the board of elections send Richard his mail in care of itself and hold it for him to pick up prior to each election.

Shortly thereafter, my Constitutional Litigation Clinic colleague Eric Neisser used the precedent to establish the right of a battered woman who did not want her former husband to have access to her address from a public voter list to register to vote from a post office box.

* * *

Since he had little else to do with his time, Richard decided to run for mayor of Morristown. Actually, he also planned to run for governor of New Jersey, but he couldn't collect the required eight hundred signatures on a nominating petition. He did manage to gather the fifty-odd signatures he needed to run for mayor. When he filed the petitions, a local councilman challenged them on the ground that Richard did not reside in Morristown, since by that time, he was sleeping most nights at a motel in a nearby community. I told the board of elections that it was my position that until he could find a permanent residence (which a nightly motel room was not), he was entitled to continue to vote from his former address, which was "the streets of Morristown." I also argued that his voting residence determined his eligibility to run for office. The county clerk agreed, and the challenger appealed to the superior court. But before there was even a formal hearing, the judge dismissed the appeal.

Let it be noted that Richard was not elected.

PART III

TALES OF POLITICS

12
Doing Battle with J. P. Stevens and Friends

For the first thirty-five years of my life, I suppose I viewed the U.S. Congress as part of the problem. And based on our past run-ins, I am sure that the feeling was mutual. So it took me aback when I got a phone call in the spring of 1976 inviting me to spend a year as special counsel to a congressional committee.

The phone call was from Dan Pollitt, a prominent teacher of labor law at the University of North Carolina in Chapel Hill who was also associated with the ACLU. Dan explained that he had a long-standing relationship with Congressman Frank Thompson Jr., chairman of the House Labor Management Subcommittee. Thompson had turned the subcommittee's counsel position into a sort of visiting professorship, and Pollitt was the first visitor. Since Pollitt had to return to Chapel Hill the following semester, Thompson told him to find another "radical" labor law teacher to succeed him. Dan had picked up the law teachers' directory, come across my name near the top of the alphabetical list, and recognized me as an ACLU lawyer. I told Dan that I would love to spend a year on Capitol Hill, but explained that I had taught labor law only once, about eight years before, and was no expert in the subject. Dan said that I would still know more than almost anybody else on the Hill. He said that if I was interested, he would arrange for me to come down and meet Thompson, who represented the Trenton area in south Jersey and was known to me by reputation as one of the most liberal members of the New Jersey delegation.

At that time, about four months before the New Jersey presidential primary, I was serving as treasurer of the Fred Harris campaign in New Jersey. Harris was a populist senator from Oklahoma who was running a low-budget grassroots campaign for the Democratic nomination eventually captured by Jimmy Carter. The morning I got on the plane for Washington, I picked up the *New York Times* and discovered that Frank Thompson was heading the New Jersey presidential campaign of Mo Udall. After Dan introduced me to

107

Thompson, the first thing I said was, "Mr. Chairman, you should understand that I may be running against you for national convention delegate on the New Jersey ballot in June," and explained that I was a leader of the Harris slate.

Tompy, which was what everybody called him, shrugged off my announcement. "Don't worry," he said, "we're both backing losers. Mo's a friend of mine, and I have to do this, but Fred Harris is a great guy."

Tompy and I hit it off instantly. I arrived on Capitol Hill the following September in time for Congress to close down and go home for the November elections. At least I had plenty of time to study up on labor law. As I soon realized, nothing much was going to happen on Capitol Hill before the following March. Dan had already set the agenda for the committee in the event a Democrat was elected president. We had to reform the National Labor Relations Act to streamline the procedures of the National Labor Relations Board so that employers couldn't use the law as a shield for unfair labor practices and to delay union bargaining elections. As things stood, companies were quite willing to pay insubstantial fines in order to frustrate labor organization and harass union activists. Carter's victory that November, after eight years of Republican control of the White House, assured a meaningful congressional session for labor legislation.

* * *

In many ways, Tompy was a Capitol Hill anomaly. As the Democratic chairman of the House labor subcommittee, he was the trade union movement's "rabbi" in Congress. There was a steady stream of labor leaders in and out of his office, and the major strategy sessions to figure out how to advance labor's interests took place there. But the major AFL-CIO leaders really did not like Tompy's overall politics, and the feeling was mutual. George Meany's crowd never forgave him for having been an outspoken critic of the Vietnam War, and he detested their hawkish attitudes. (Tompy once told me that President Kennedy had promised him shortly before his assassination that he was planning to withdraw our "advisers" from Vietnam in 1964.) Tompy also had vastly more liberal views on most social and lifestyle issues than the socially conservative minions on 16th Street, headquarters of the AFL-CIO. But since Tompy relished being the champion of the working class and they were the official labor leadership, they tolerated each other.

No one ever doubted Tompy's devotion to the interests of the labor movement and working people. One day in the midst of our efforts to redraft the Labor Relations Act, I got a call to come down to the chairman's personal office. When I walked in, I saw sitting with him the lobbyists for the National Association of Manufacturers and the Chamber of Commerce, the major representatives of business interests in Washington. Tompy very sternly informed me that these gentlemen had been complaining that I was not accessible to them, that I didn't return their phone calls and wouldn't meet with them to hear their ideas for labor law reform. The irony of the situation flabbergasted me. Here were two of the most influential men in Washington griping that they were being excluded from the political process by insignificant me, who ran one of the few offices in the entire U.S. government in which they weren't welcome with open arms. Of course, their complaints were reasonably accurate. I knew that Tompy was interested in revising the labor laws to accommodate the needs of unions, not management, so I didn't waste my time listening to the suggestions of the business community. In any event, I played it straight and agreed that I would be more hospitable to his visitors. As the two men headed for the door, Tompy winked at me, and when they were out of ear-shot he said, "Don't give those sons of bitches the right time."

Tompy once explained to me that after all his years in politics he was a bit bored with the day-to-day grind and could no longer focus on details. He hired knowledgeable staff whose political views paralleled his own and allowed them to exercise his power and authority to help out the poor and working people. If you walked into his office and said, "Tompy, the textile workers are getting screwed because the Department of Labor isn't doing enough about brown-lung disease," he'd say, "Well, get me Ray Marshall [secretary of labor] on the phone, and write down what I should say to him." I would provide him a script about the need for new brown-lung regulations, and he would deliver it like the seasoned political actor he was.

In the spring of 1977, a few days before Jimmy Carter's famous energy address to the nation, I was chatting with Tompy when he got a call from Frank Moore, the president's congressional liaison. Moore was obviously sounding out congressional leaders about various aspects of the president's energy proposals—gas-guzzler tax, alternative energy, synthetic fuels. The conversation had being going on for a few minutes, and Tompy was being noncommittal, with an occasional "uh-huh." Finally, I walked over to him and handed him a note that said "nationalization of energy resources." Tompy nodded, smiled, and finally said to Moore, "Why doesn't the president propose nationalization of our energy resources." There was obviously a long pause on the other end, and when Moore regained his composure, he apparently rejoined, "Can you get that through the House?" Tompy, who at the time was furious with the White House and especially the presidential counsel for having sabotaged his effort to pass a situs-picketing bill to aid the construction trades, answered, "Well, maybe if the White House would muzzle that son of a bitch Burt Lance, I could pass something over here."

* * *

We worked on the labor law reform package throughout the spring and into the summer. After the labor lobbyists and House and Senate staffers had finally agreed on a set of eleven proposals, the draft was sent to the White House for review. Everyone knew that labor law reform would precipitate a knock-down-drag-out fight with the corporate community, and it was agreed that the final bill needed the enthusiastic support of the president if there was to be any chance of passage. The strategy was for the president to send the final bill to Congress as his own proposal.

Finally, we got a call to meet at the Department of Labor to receive the administration's version of the bill. As we sat around a table comparing the new draft with our original, I noted that one section had been changed in a way that made no practical sense. A provision intended to make a specific change in the operation of the law to respond to an antilabor judicial decision had been edited so as to be legally unintelligible and meaningless. I pointed that out to the White House representative, who nodded in agreement. When I started to suggest a revision, she stated, "Can't be done."

"Why not?" I asked in puzzlement.

"The president himself drafted the new language. This is the bill, take it or leave it."

That moment was my epiphany about the Carter administration and the president's politically fatal attempt to micromanage every aspect of government policy. Obviously the president had received various conflicting comments about provisions of the bill and had sat down in the Oval Office to personally resolve disputes over arcane issues of labor legislation that someone of his background could not possibly comprehend fully—as smart as this former nuclear sub commander unquestionably was. As a result, he had written a provision of would-be law that made no sense whatsoever to anybody. But when you are a member of the president's team and the president says take it or leave it, you take it.

By the time the actual bill was introduced, it was just about time for the summer congressional recess. I had to figure out some way to dramatize the issue and pave the way for success on the House floor in the fall. The J. P. Stevens Company had been battling with the textile union throughout the South for a decade and was the model scofflaw against which labor law reform was directed. Some people referred to the reform proposal as the "J. P. Stevens Bill." No matter how many times the company was found guilty of unfair labor practices or how many fines it paid, its workers still labored under the most oppressive conditions, and its lawyers successfully blocked and delayed union organization.

I suggested to Tompy that in order to attract media and public attention to the bill, we hold public hearings in the heart of J. P. Stevens country, in Roanoke Rapids, North Carolina. Tompy greeted the idea enthusiastically and told me to make the arrangements. When I discovered that there was no convenient airport, I arranged for the committee to charter a bus from Washington and invited the press to ride along. We labeled it a "rolling press conference on labor law reform." The media ate it up, and the event was a huge success. It may have been the first and last time all three television networks covered a congressional hearing on a subject as mundane as labor law.

Tompy was in his glory. When we arrived back at the Holiday Inn after dinner, every member of our group discovered in his or her room a packet of materials from J. P. Stevens welcoming us to town and describing what a model company it was. In opening the hearings the next day, Tompy commented on those intrusions, saying, "Back in New Jersey, we call that breaking and entering."

By the time the bill actually went to the House floor, I was already back at Rutgers beginning a new semester. However, I continued to travel down to Washington every week and was on the floor when the time came for final action at the beginning of October. It was a heady experience to sit at the floor manager's table and help guide the daylong debate on this important piece of legislation.

The House results exceeded our wildest dreams. Despite furious lobbying by the business community, the bill passed by nearly a hundred-vote majority. The wine and liquor flowed unsparingly at the Democratic Club that evening, with the labor lobbyists picking up the tab.

*   *   *

It was the original strategy of the labor movement to bring the bill to a Senate vote early in 1978, before the business community had time to frighten and mobilize local chambers of commerce all over the country. Senator Harrison (Pete) Williams, chair of the Senate Human Resources Committee, had agreed to go along. However, the Carter administration intervened. The president was fearful that a Republican-Dixiecrat filibuster against the bill would delay his efforts to win Senate approval of the Panama Canal treaty. He insisted that Panama go first. That decision was the undoing of labor law reform.

By the time the Senate was ready to take up the measure, my academic year was just about over. I got a call from one of the AFL-CIO lobbyists I had worked with on the House side informing me that they would like my help in the Senate fight. The bill was scheduled to reach the Senate floor in mid-May. I told him that since classes would be out by then, I could be available. A few days later, he called and told me that Senator Pat Moynihan of New York was willing to hire a temporary labor consultant for the duration of the anticipated filibuster and debate over labor law reform, and I should send him a résumé. When Moynihan's aide interviewed me, she noted that my ACLU involvements (I had recently been elected one of the general counsel of the national organization) and other activities indicated that there might be many issues on which the senator and I had divergent views. I said, "If the senator can tolerate me for a few weeks, I am sure I can tolerate him." A bargain was struck.

Working for Moynihan was as different from working for Tompy as night from day. Although they were both pro-labor Irish Democrats widely noted for their love of the sauce, the similarities ended there. At the time, Moynihan was in his neoconservative phase, and his staff reflected it. They were still fighting the Vietnam War and constantly railed against the "pinko" Mondale advisers the vice president had installed in the State Department. The Moynihan staff talked about Carter foreign policy staffers as if they were referring to Kremlin bureaucrats. The office was also considerably more stuffy than Tompy's informal crew. The political and social tone of the office was set by Moynihan's administrative assistant Eliot Abrams, later an official in the Reagan administration who pleaded guilty to lying to Congress during the Iran-Contra scandal. When Abrams formally introduced me to the senator, Moynihan mused, "What shall we call you, Dr. Askin or Professor Askin?" I suggested that "Frank" would do (not daring to suggest "Aay"), when Abrams chimed in, "Not in this office."

I spent the next six weeks on the floor of the U.S. Senate while Republican and southern Democratic senators exercised their vocal cords in opposition to fundamental changes in the nation's labor laws. Meanwhile, local chambers of commerce and other business associations around the country flooded the senators with millions of letters and postcards objecting to legislation that would make it easier for workers to organize and enforce their rights under federal law.

The Senate is alleged to be a great deliberative body, and unlike in the House, the rules make it difficult to cut off debate. Once a group of willful members makes up its collective mind to obstruct a particular proposal, it takes a supermajority of the one hundred members to shut it up. Once upon a time, it took a two-thirds vote, which, in the days before the Federal Voting Rights Act and the registration of massive numbers of black voters, gave the southern Dixiecrats an almost total stranglehold. Modern reforms reduced the requirement to 60 percent, and a substantial body of rules has grown up to regulate this ritual known as a filibuster. If the active filibusterers are few in number, the Senate leadership can force them to keep talking around the clock—as long as it can keep a majority of members on hand to answer quorum calls whenever demanded. If a substantial number of senators actively support the filibuster, about the only thing the majority leaders can do is wait them out until sixty members are sufficiently disgusted to vote cloture. Thus, forty-one determined members can stop any legislative business. There are rules that permit interruption of the talkathon to permit the consideration of emergency matters when all sides agree.

As the opponents of labor law reform droned on, the novelty of spending my days on the floor of the Senate wore off, and tedium began to set in. Moynihan was one of a group of pro-labor Democrats who would take the floor to respond to the occasionally lucid arguments put forward by the filibusterers, so I kept having to turn out materials for him. But the truth is that little of what I wrote ever made it into the record. Whenever Moynihan got up to speak about labor law reform, he would point out that we needed this legislation to combat communism and stop the Russians. Since I worked cooperatively with other Democratic staffers and union lobbyists, I would feed speech material that Moynihan had rejected to my colleagues in the hope that it wouldn't go to waste.

About once a week after the second week of the filibuster, the Democratic leadership would schedule a cloture vote. The first few were mere formalities, with no special pressure applied to wavering members. Starting about the fourth week, the labor movement's lobbyists began to twist arms, reminding undecided members about past financial support and attempting to increase pressure from constituents back home. On June 14, cloture gained fifty-four votes. We always knew that when push came to shove, we could count on about fifty-seven or fifty-eight votes. We still held out some hope for liberals Lawton Chiles of Florida and Dale Bumpers of Arkansas, although we knew that they were under tremendous pressure from the business communities in their conservative states. Both were afraid that it would be political suicide to provide the decisive vote for the bill. The labor lobbyists were frantically trying to convince a few more moderate Republicans to agree to vote to close debate, even if they intended to vote against the bill itself. There were already half a dozen liberal Republicans solidly in support of the bill, including Jacob Javits of New York, Clifford Case of New Jersey, and Lowell Weicker of Connecticut. There were constant rumors that Russell Long, Democrat of Louisiana, was bargaining with the White House over his vote. One rumor had it that he would support cloture in exchange for an increase in sugar tariffs.

Then Bobby Byrd, the Democratic majority leader, announced that he thought that he could deliver the vote of John Sparkman of Alabama, an old-line Dixiecrat who was in both his dotage and his final term. As the pressure grew for the Senate to move on to the other business backed up on its calendar, the leadership decided to make one last-ditch try for the magic sixty. The showdown came on June 22. As the dramatic moment neared, Sparkman entered the chamber with Byrd holding one arm and Hollings of South Carolina holding the other. Everyone held their breath as we waited to see who would get Sparkman's vote. Hollings prevailed, and the majority leader agreed to send the bill back to committee in the faint hope that further compromises might produce the additional votes needed. The bill was never heard from again, and the U.S. trade union movement has continued in a state of decline ever since.

*   *   *

Once a member of Tompy's club, always a member. He had loyal former staffers all over the land who were ready to give advice and comfort to the chairman whenever called upon. Shortly after the battle over labor law reform, a national emergency was created by a nationwide coal strike. President Carter was threatening to invoke the Taft-Hartley Act, which the unions referred to as the slave-labor law, and order the strikers back into the mines. Tompy invited Dan Pollitt and me to Washington to consult with him and his subcommittee counsel Fred Feinstein, whom Tompy had dubbed "Harpo" because of his head of curly hair. Fred had been a student of mine at Rutgers and had gone to work for the National Labor Relations Board after law school. When a position on the subcommittee opened up while I was there, I had arranged for Fred to join the staff. Fred remained as counsel to the subcommittee until 1994, when President Clinton appointed him general counsel of the National Labor Relations Board. That position allowed Fred to become the hero of baseball fans all over the country when he forced an end to the baseball strike by suing the club owners for refusal to bargain in good faith just before the scheduled opening of the 1995 season.

Fred, Dan, and I put our heads together for several days and came up with a fresh strategy to deal with the coal industry impasse. Instead of invoking Taft-Hartley and forcing the miners to work for the mine owners under the preexisting conditions they were striking against, we proposed that the president seize the mines as Harry Truman had seized the steel mills in a labor dispute during World War II. And we proposed that the profits earned during the seizure be placed in a fund to compensate victims of black-lung disease, which was plaguing the mining communities. Tompy liked the idea and promised to present it at a White House meeting called by the president to discuss the situation with congressional leaders. On the morning of the meeting, the three of us waited anxiously in Tompy's office with his administrative assistant Billy Deitz. Finally Tompy returned, looking a bit downcast.

"What happened?" we asked.

"Well, we were seated in the East Room, and Fritz [Tompy's good buddy Vice President Walter Mondale] passed me a note that said, 'No questions please, just support.' After that, I just couldn't say anything."

13

No Nukes Are Good Nukes

In 1969, I was driving near our apartment in the city of Newark with my son Jonny, who was then five years old. It was during the frenetic mayoral campaign between the incumbent Hugh Addonizio and the nominee of Newark's first Black Political Convention, Ken Gibson. Jonny looked up at a billboard and recognized the face of television personality Bill Cosby.

"Dad, why is Bill Cosby's picture on that sign?" he asked. I explained that Cosby was asking people to vote for Ken Gibson for mayor. "Is Ken Gibson a good man?" Jonny came back.

I told him that I thought he was. After a few more moments of reflection on the criteria he had just established for the job, Jonny said, "You're a good man, Dad. Why don't you run for mayor?"

I went through a detailed explanation of the difficulties of running for mayor—of having to raise lots of money, and running around making speeches, and trying to get lots of people to vote for you. Jonny was not deterred, insisting that he and his sister and mother and grandma would help. Then, after further reflection, he asked, "What's bigger—mayor or president?"

Informed that the president was more important, he decided that I should run for that office. Not willing to ignore my son's serious and sincere thoughts, I carefully explained what would be involved in a presidential campaign, ending with the observation that a presidential candidate is kept so busy that he wouldn't even have time to come home and play with his children.

That latter revelation gave Jonny pause, and he finally inquired, "Does the mayor have time to play with his children?"

I responded in the negative. Jonny sighed and ended my first political foray with, "Never mind, Dad. You be the man who stays home and plays with his children."

* * *

I finally did get bitten by the candidate bug—or, as they say, succumbed to Potomac fever—somewhere in the middle of my stint with Tompy. As a person who spent his life trying to influence public policy, I loved working on Capitol Hill. However, I decided that what I really wanted was to be a member of Congress with a voting card and not just a staffer carrying out others' agendas. I also figured that congressman was about the only job in the world that would be even more fun than the one I already had.

Since I had also become a regular reader of the *Congressional Record*, I began to watch the activities of my own representative, a longtime Democratic incumbent named Joe Minish. I knew that Minish had a background in the trade union movement and was considered a friend of the labor community and the consumer movement. What I came to realize as I tracked his voting record was that he was a George Meany labor Democrat in every sense of the term. He was a hawk on war and peace issues, voting to finance every useless weapons system the Pentagon and defense contractors could dream up; he was antichoice on abortion; he had voted to prohibit affirmative action programs to assist people of color achieve full equality; and he had a dreadful record on issues relating to basic civil liberties. A member of the House Banking Committee, he had a reputation for being in the hip pocket of the banking lobby. However, he had also done some good work as the sponsor of something called the Renegotiation Board, which had achieved some success in recouping overpayments from inflated defense contracts.

The idea of running against him in a Democratic primary began to take shape. Our voting residences were less than a mile apart in the same town, West Orange, which was the largest municipality in what was then the Eleventh Congressional District of New Jersey. At the time, the Eleventh District encompassed a number of relatively small suburban and industrial municipalities to the north and west of Newark.

Up to that time, I had had only marginal involvement in Democratic politics since moving from Bergen County. West Orange was in Essex County, which included the city of Newark and was a major Democratic stronghold in the state. I had been part of the Essex County McGovern slate for convention delegates in 1972, and I had been part of the fringe Fred Harris campaign in 1976 before heading off to Washington. While I was away, a liberal reform movement had taken control of the Democratic Party in Essex County. After a bitter political battle, a charter reform campaign had succeeded in changing the form of county government to provide for an elected county executive. Peter Shapiro, a young, liberal reformer who had earlier upset the party bosses to become the youngest member of the state legislature, was elected the first county executive. I had voted for charter reform and Shapiro by absentee ballot.

When I returned to New Jersey, I began to involve myself in Democratic politics, and especially the Essex County Democratic Coalition (ECDC), which served as a sort of reform club for Shapiro's liberal inner circle. I also increased my activities in the peace and disarmament movement spearheaded by New Jersey SANE (originally the Committee for a Sane Nuclear Policy), which I had long been a member of, and I began taking a leadership role in coalition movements to refocus national priorities away from military spending and toward domestic needs. I paid particular attention to building bridges between the black Democrats of the inner cities of Newark and East Orange and the liberal suburban Democrats who were the core of the Shapiro organization. With Newark city councilman Donald Tucker, a veteran of the civil rights movement, I had organized the Coalition for Human Priorities, which ran conferences and conducted other kinds of educational and lobbying campaigns challenging the federal government's budget priorities.

I was seriously considering running against Minish for the congressional nomination in the 1980 Democratic primary and made no secret of my political aspirations. I had discussed it with Tompy, and he had given me mild encouragement while warning me that there was little he could do to help me. Although he was no fan of Minish, Tompy was in no position to antagonize his colleague. Tompy had recently become chairman of the House Administration Committee as a result of a scandal involving the former chairman, Wayne Hayes of Ohio, who had put his paramour on the committee payroll. Minish was a member of the committee, and Tompy had need of his vote on occasion.

I also discussed my plans with Peter Shuchter, Shapiro's chief of staff, who warned me that Shapiro would be unable to give me direct support because of his own need to maintain cordial relations with the congressman. Wherever I went and to whomever I spoke, I found little real regard for Minish but much fear of his power. That fear was compounded by Minish's reputation for being ruthless toward those who crossed him. Indeed, when my name was finally mentioned in the press as a possible challenger, Tompy told me that Minish had approached him on the floor of the House and angrily accused him of putting me up to it. As Tompy quoted him, Minish said, "Who is this fuckin' urban guerrilla you're running against me?"

It was my plan to build a left-liberal coalition to support me in the Democratic primary against Minish—the peaceniks, feminists, abortion rights proponents, gays, academics, civil libertarians, civil rights activists, and environmentalists. This was not just a political strategy to advance my own personal political ambitions. This was who I was. I supported all those social causes, and I wanted to be elected to Congress to advocate their interests. My model was New York Congresswoman Bella Abzug. I was also seeking support from the more progressive trade unions in the area, but I realized that this would be difficult in light of Minish's long-standing connections to the labor movement. I also knew that some of my natural allies would be reluctant to openly support me in the face of labor's commitment to Minish.

A primary is not like a general election. In a Democratic primary, one is dealing with a much smaller and more targeted electorate, and social interest groups can be much more influential. If the environmental movement or the gay community decides to throw all its resources into a primary election, it can be a significant force, whereas in a general election, such a constituency may be more like a pebble thrown in the ocean. It was always my view that I could win a primary from Joe Minish with no more than twenty thousand votes, a figure that I believed was reachable under the right combination of circumstances.

In addition to my base among the social activists, I was counting on strong support, financial and otherwise, from the many hundreds of my former students who were now practicing law in and around the district.

Toward the end of 1979, I sent out a letter to friends, colleagues, community activists, and former students explaining that I was "testing the waters" for a possible congressional race and soliciting their comments and financial contributions. The letter had just gone into the mail when Iran took the American hostages. The hostages quickly became the major political issue of the time, and, like the Cuban Missile Crisis back in 1962, it relegated other issues to the back burner.

The Democratic politics of 1980 was further complicated by Ted Kennedy's announcement that he was going to challenge Jimmy Carter for the Democratic nomination. Since I knew that I could not raise enough money to run a high-profile race, it seemed clear that a campaign of my own would be lost in the shadows of a Carter-Kennedy primary fight. I decided to postpone my own political aspirations, enlist in the Kennedy campaign, and use the approximately $10,000 I had raised to publicize myself and build a political base for 1982. My main effort in this regard was to begin publishing and distributing an occasional four-page newsletter called *The Frank Askin Report*. The first issue, dated April 1980, included a "Message to Voters of the 11th District," which explained:

> It had been my intention to seek the Democratic nomination for Congress from the 11th District in the June 3 primary. I was encouraged to do so by friends and colleagues who share my view that the 11th District deserves far better representation in our national legislature. That plan has been temporarily diverted by the realities of American politics: It is exceedingly difficult for a person not independently wealthy and without the support of powerful special interests to raise the enormous sum that is required to wage a successful campaign against an entrenched incumbent, irrespective of his shortcomings.

*   *   *

I've always thought that Jimmy Carter was a much better human being than he was a president. He has certainly demonstrated that since leaving public office. As president, he was something of a bumbler. If I had thought that he could actually be reelected, I probably would have been less enthusiastic about Ted Kennedy. But between viewing Carter as a loser and seeing Kennedy as the embodiment of the progressive wing of the Democratic Party, the choice was clear. I had never been a fan of Jack Kennedy's politics, but I did have great admiration for Bobby in the last stages of his life. Indeed, I was supporting Robert Kennedy when most of my friends were being "clean for Gene" McCarthy. And I thought that Ted probably had the best political attributes of both of his brothers—Jack's charisma and Bobby's compassion. He clearly had some character flaws, but I was willing (I concede maybe *too* willing) to overlook them in the interest of larger issues.

If I was going to support Ted Kennedy, I decided that I should go all out and try to use it to my own future political advantage. I wanted not only to go to the national convention as a delegate but also to carve out a role for myself that would bring me some public recognition. In 1980, convention delegates were being chosen by local district caucuses. Would-be delegates submitted their names to their preferred candidate's organization; if approved, they could place themselves in nomination among that candidate's supporters at a Democratic district caucus.

About three hundred Kennedy supporters showed up at our district caucus at Verona High School, and some thirty or forty candidates placed themselves in nomination for the eight slots on the Kennedy district slate. Although eight names would be selected to go on the primary ballot, it was clear that, at most, only five delegates would be able to go to the convention, because of party rules guaranteeing proportional representation for the losing slate in the June primary. And because of gender-balance rules requiring an equal number of men and women, the male convention delegates would be restricted to the top two or three finishers at the caucuses, even assuming that Kennedy carried the district on primary day. Fortunately, I worked hard in advance of the caucus convincing friends and supporters to show up that Saturday afternoon in Verona. I finished second in the balloting to a young man who brought out some 130 relatives to vote for him.

Having come that far, I was determined not to be an anonymous convention delegate. Each of the major presidential candidates was eligible to place supporters on the three convention committees—platform, rules, and credentials. I decided that I wanted to be on the Platform Committee and began to contact those political friends who might have some influence with the Kennedy campaign in getting me appointed. I thought that my best boosters would be Tompy, Peter Shapiro, and Victor Kamber, an extremely capable AFL-CIO official in Washington whom I had worked with during the campaign for labor law reform.

There were to be five delegates from New Jersey on the committee, with the winner of the June primary naming three and the loser two. Because of affirmative action considerations, I realized that the Kennedy campaign would be able to select only one white male. I don't know which of my "rabbis" was most influential—they all claimed credit. Maybe it required all of their efforts for me to be selected. In any event, at the state delegate convention held a few days after the primary, which Kennedy swept, I was informed that I was one of the Kennedy nominees to the Platform Committee, which was to hold a four-day meeting in Washington, D.C., at the end of June. I was also told that my main competition for the committee slot had been Senator Bill Bradley. However, Bradley insisted on remaining neutral in the presidential contest, and Kennedy would not choose him without a formal endorsement. So Bradley would end up being appointed a committee member by the Carter campaign, which controlled a majority of the Platform Committee and could afford to be magnanimous. The Carter campaign appointed New Jersey Governor Brendan Byrne as its other delegate.

*　　*　　*

Once my name was publicly listed as a member of the Platform Committee, I was inundated with propaganda from special-interest groups that wanted their concerns reflected in the 1980 Democratic platform—issues ranging from saving the whales to choosing a new national anthem to legalizing marijuana. Many voters may believe that political platforms are not worth the paper they are printed on, but organizations engaged in efforts to influence public policy consider them important documents in their continuing struggles to change things in this country and the world. For probably the first time in my life, I was being "lobbied" for my vote.

It was on the train to Washington that I began to screen my mountain of mail. One pamphlet caught my special attention. It was an appeal from a Quaker-based group in New York City for an international moratorium on the testing, production, and deployment of nuclear weapons. It rested on the simple proposition that the United States and Soviet Union already had enough nuclear warheads stockpiled to destroy each other many times over. Despite that unassailable fact, the Carter administration had been reluctant to propose such a moratorium to the Soviets—apparently fearing that the Republicans would attack it for being "soft on communism." During the last year of his administration, Jimmy Carter seemed intent on demonstrating that he was just as much a hawk as Ronald Reagan when it came to dealing with the Russians. I decided to make the nuclear freeze campaign my pet project and to try to incorporate the idea into the Democratic Party platform.

The deliberations of the Platform Committee were scheduled to run from Thursday morning, June 21, through midday on Sunday, June 24. The Kennedy forces had scheduled a caucus for Wednesday evening, the twentieth. There were some sixty-odd Kennedy delegates among the 150 committee members. The honchos of the Kennedy campaign had prepared a number of alternative planks to challenge the draft platform that would be offered by the Carter majority. The centerpiece of Kennedy's alternative platform was a plan for national health insurance. The Kennedy proposals also called for strengthening the platform in areas dealing with abortion rights, housing, job training, services for the elderly, child care, environmental protection, alternative energy, and discrimination because of sexual orientation. The Kennedy staff, headed by Paul Tully and Susan Estrich, solicited our support for its proposals but emphasized that we were not obligated to support any issues that we could not in good conscience accept.

During an open discussion period following the briefing, I acknowledged my obligation to Senator Kennedy for having selected me for the committee and said that I was happy to support his entire domestic agenda. However, I expressed concern that the Kennedy foreign policy proposals, like Carter's, were "too jingoistic and militaristic, with insufficient emphasis on the quest for peace and disarmament." I was told that I was free to propose my own amendments to the foreign policy plank but that the Kennedy campaign apparatus would not be available to support them.

As the formal part of the meeting broke up, several other delegates expressed agreement with my comments, and we decided to form our own informal peace caucus within the Kennedy delegation and to reach out to like-minded Carter delegates as well. Among our mini-caucus were Gloria Steinem, the feminist leader; Ted Sorenson, President Kennedy's former aide and speechwriter; and Esther Smith, a leader of reform Democrats in Manhattan whom I had worked with in the past. They all agreed with my idea to make the inclusion of a nuclear-freeze plank our primary goal. The committee members had been broken into four task forces. Sorenson had been assigned to the foreign policy task force, and Steinem, Smith, and I were all on the human needs task force. Sorenson agreed to sponsor the freeze proposal.

Meanwhile, the Kennedy delegates put up a struggle in the human needs task force in support of the Kennedy planks, and we won some concessions. On my own initiative, I got included in the platform a statement that federal police agencies should never investigate individuals merely because of their political beliefs and associations. I considered it personal vindication to get such a plank included in the platform of a major political party. However, when the Carter campaign drew the line and forced votes, our side routinely lost by margins of about 60 percent to 40 percent. Such was the fate of the Kennedy health care proposal, which the Carter forces argued would be too expensive.

In the meantime, Sorenson had reported to our mini-caucus that the nuclear-freeze proposal had been defeated in the task force, but since many of the

Kennedy delegates had voted for it, it had received enough votes to be eligible for a minority report at the plenary. However, when I arrived on Sunday morning, Sorenson informed me that he had compromised the issue. He had agreed to abandon the minority report in exchange for a plank committing a Democratic administration to abide by the provisions contained in the Strategic Arms Limitation Talks (SALT) II treaty with the Russians, even in the absence of U.S. Senate ratification. I strenuously objected on the ground that SALT II, although an advance toward arms control, still permitted the regulated expansion of nuclear arsenals. I believed that we had to insist on a freeze, but Sorenson said that he had committed himself to the compromise and that it was out of his hands. I told him that he couldn't speak for me, and if necessary, I would take the minority report to the floor of the plenary session.

The nuclear-freeze minority report was one of the final items to come before the committee. My report was defeated seventy-eight to fifty-one. Under the committee's rules, a minority report could be presented to the national convention only if 25 percent of the members of the Platform Committee formally signed a petition of support. That was a simple matter for those minority reports that had the official backing of the Kennedy campaign. Indeed, the necessary petitions were circulated by the Kennedy staffers prior to formal voting by the committee. I faced the problem of having to gather a minimum of thirty-nine signatures without staff support as the committee session was adjourning and delegates were heading for the door and the airports. Fortunately, a couple of the Kennedy aides volunteered to assist me, and we were able to gather the requisite number of signatures. That meant that I was going to have the opportunity to address the Democratic National Convention at Madison Square Garden in July.

* * *

My colleagues in the SANE organization, both in New Jersey and nationally, were ecstatic that I was going to be able to present the nuclear-freeze proposal as a minority report at the national convention. They immediately began a nationwide campaign to line up support among both convention delegates and the public at large. In some states, such as New York and New Jersey, the Kennedy delegations organized public forums around platform issues, and freeze advocates made sure to attend and urge support for my minority report. A nationwide coalition, headquartered at the Massachusetts Institute of Technology and headed by a political scientist and armaments expert named Randall Forsberg, sprang up to support the nuclear moratorium. Letters were sent out to every convention delegate explaining the proposal and soliciting support.

As the sponsor of an official minority report, I was eligible to choose two seconding speakers, who did not have to be convention delegates. After consultation with Randy Forsberg, I invited the eminent Harvard scholar and former ambassador to India John Kenneth Galbraith and retired U.S. Navy Admiral Eugene LaRocque, chairman of the Center for Defense Information, to be my seconders.

The freeze proposal got a major boost on the morning of the platform fight, which was the third day of the convention, when it was formally endorsed by Senator Kennedy. Kennedy had formally withdrawn as a presidential candidate in a speech the night before, but his endorsement virtually guaranteed the votes of his many delegates for Minority Report 21. The New Jersey delegation, which was headed by Peter Shapiro, had already overwhelmingly endorsed it.

When the debate and vote on Minority Report 20 had been completed, it was a huge thrill for me to stand at the podium in Madison Square Garden and look out over that vast auditorium as a field of placards proclaiming support for a nuclear arms freeze and Minority Report 21 spontaneously blossomed throughout the arena. Of course, the peace movement had been working for weeks to print and circulate the placards and guarantee their distribution throughout the convention floor for unfurling at the crucial moment. I had worked carefully to prepare my three-minute speech, and I still cherish my copy of *The Official Report of the Proceedings of the 1980 Democratic National Convention*, in which it is reprinted at pages 444–45:

Argument in Favor of Platform Minority Report No. 21 by Frank Askin of New Jersey

MR. ASKIN: Mr. Chairman, fellow Democrats, I rise to speak in favor of Minority Report No. 21. This plank, I emphasize, did not originate with any of the presidential campaigns. It is a grass roots proposal supported in the Platform Committee by both Carter and Kennedy delegates.

But it is first and foremost a proposal on behalf of our children and future generations, not to speak of ourselves and present generations. This proposal is quite simple: that the United States and a Democratic Administration remains willing to join in a nuclear arms moratorium whenever the Soviet Union and other nuclear powers will agree to do so.

I find it hard to believe that anyone should be opposed. I can understand people saying that we must continue that nuclear arms race out of necessity, so long as our enemies will not agree to stop. But can anyone truly believe we should want to pursue this deadly contest even if our enemies were willing to call it off? That is all this amendment proposes, that we continue to press the Soviet Union and other nuclear powers for an international freeze on the deployment and testing of weapons of mass destruction.

It does not contemplate any unilateral action by the United States. I realize that some may deride this proposal as visionary, and maybe it is;

but what is wrong with a platform that is visionary? Hubert Humphrey was visionary when he fought for a civil rights plank in 1948, but those visions eventually became reality.

We are surely visionary when we pledge to wipe out poverty, but let us hope that we never abandon that vision. And let us not now abandon the vision of a world which does not have to live in constant dread of nuclear catastrophe, because it is surely inevitable that unless somehow, sometime we find a way to stop expanding and start dismantling the nuclear stockpiles, the nuclear holocaust will occur, by accident if not by design.

That the White House takes this threat seriously is revealed in recent plans to provide shelter for the nation's leaders while we make preparations to fight so-called limited nuclear wars. Of course, no one has explained where the rest of us are to find shelter from the nuclear holocaust.

If there is one commitment the Democratic Party owes to the world and posterity, it is this: that we will bend every effort to make sure that the nuclear holocaust does not occur, especially in view of the militaristic frenzy displayed at our adversary's recent convention.

We must let the world know that at least one party in this country prefers the path of peace to the path of mutual destruction. (Applause).

When Galbraith, LaRocque, and I were through speaking, Chuck Robb, who was then best known as the husband of Linda Bird Johnson but was later to become governor and then senator from Virginia, rose to speak on behalf of the Carter campaign and the Platform Committee majority. Governor Riley of South Carolina, who was chairing the session, then asked for the yeas and nays. A chorus of voices resounded on each side, and the governor proclaimed that the nays had it. Meanwhile, by prearrangement, Peter Shapiro, on behalf of the New Jersey delegation, was attempting to get the chair's attention to demand a roll-call vote by state delegations. Riley was ignoring him. I finally ran to the podium, grabbed Riley by the arm, and told him that the New Jersey delegation was trying to be recognized. He finally acknowledged Shapiro's motion and asked that there be a division of the house as to whether there should be a roll-call vote.

Under the rules, if half the delegates stood up, a roll call was in order. If you have ever witnessed a national convention, you are probably aware that in the midst of such proceedings, 80 percent of the delegates are already on their feet at such times. In addition, less than half the people on the convention floor at that moment were delegates anyway, since the hall was inundated with staff and press. Despite all that, Riley looked out over the sea of humanity milling around below him and announced that the request for a roll call had been defeated. As I headed backstage, whatever dejection I felt at the defeat of the minority report was washed away when Congresswoman Patsy Mink of Hawaii, who had been watching the proceedings on television, looked up as I walked by and said, "That was a wonderful speech."

*   *   *

Despite the outcome, the convention debate on Minority Report 21 was the catalyst for a vast campaign that swept across the country during the next several years. In states and cities throughout the country, grassroots movements sprang up to support a nuclear arms freeze and to call for public referenda on the issue. By 1982, the freeze initiative was the subject of statewide ballot initiatives in ten states and passed in nine of them. In New Jersey, it was approved by a landslide vote. The call for a nuclear moratorium had gained such popular momentum that a proposal that had been a minority report two years before was included without opposition in the Democrats' 1982 midterm platform, even though it was still being denounced by President Reagan and his administration as a "communist trick."

In an extraordinary exercise of political revisionism, the director of the Democratic National Committee was quoted in the *New York Times* on June 14, 1982, to the effect that revision of the party's platform was necessary because the freeze issue had not arisen until after the party's 1980 convention. A few days later, the *New York Times* printed a letter from me recalling my unsuccessful efforts at the 1980 convention:

> It may be politically convenient for the Democratic Party to deny its own complicity in the perpetuation of the nuclear arms race, but there are important political lessons for the country which can only be learned by setting the record straight. . . . This is not meant as sour grapes. At least the Democratic Party, as opposed to the other one, has had the good sense to respond positively to the public outcry for an end to the nuclear arms race—albeit belatedly. What Democratic officials might ponder is how much political grief might have been avoided if the party had been out front on this issue during the 1980 campaign rather than echoing the Reaganites' false cries about a new missile gap.

Several months later, I received in the mail from Senator Kennedy's office a copy of the book *Freeze! How You Can Help Prevent Nuclear War*, written by Senators Kennedy and Mark Hatfield of Oregon. It was inscribed "To Frank Askin, who was there long before anyone else—with warm regards. Ted Kennedy."

By the end of 1982, a majority of the U.S. House of Representatives had actually voted to endorse the proposal for a multilateral nuclear arms freeze. Unfortunately, the Reagan and Bush administrations ignored the demands for a negotiated end to the nuclear buildup, and both the United States and the Soviet Union continued to increase their nuclear stockpiles until the total collapse of the latter. Ever since then, the world has been worrying about the disposition of the thousands of nuclear warheads scattered throughout the former Soviet empire, now dissolved into independent states, some with their own nuclear arsenals. Whether any of those warheads have found their way to third-world terrorists, we may never know until it is too late. Even assuming the best, the nuclear powers still have to figure out how to dismantle and dispose of all the superfluous nuclear weapons created during the runaway nuclear arms race that some of us did our best to halt, with only limited success.

14

Askin' for Votes

Fans of the folk-singing parodist Tom Lehrer may recall a line from his song about the Spanish Civil War that goes, "They won all the battles, but we had the best songs." My 1982 primary fight with Joe Minish can be described along similar lines: my opponent got most of the votes, but we had lots of great parties.

The formal kickoff of the campaign took place in the summer of 1981 at a fund-raising party in the elegant and spacious Montclair home of friends Bob and Connie Van Amberg, with Gloria Steinem as the guest speaker. Congressman Minish had recently received the highest rating of any New Jersey Democrat from Jerry Falwell's Moral Majority organization, and I had decided to make Minish's conservative stance on social issues a major theme of my primary campaign. We titled our event "Stand Up to the Moral Majority."

As a result of our collaboration on the Democratic Platform Committee the year before, the much-in-demand Steinem agreed to come to New Jersey on my behalf. The event was electric. About three hundred people were crowded into the Van Amberg home, and people seemed genuinely excited about trying to elect a progressive Democrat to replace the tired old political warhorse Minish. Gloria was, as usual, charming and brilliant. My son Danny was so caught up in the excitement that as we drove home, he asked me, "Dad, what do you have to do to get elected Speaker of the House?" I suggested to him that we take one election at a time.

One tip-off of the difficult road ahead should have been obvious from that fund-raiser's bottom line. Despite the large and enthusiastic crowd, the campaign netted only about $5,000 after expenses, a drop in the bucket for a serious congressional campaign. The problem, I quickly realized, was that nobody *had* to contribute to my campaign or buy tickets to my events. Since I had no political power, no one owed me anything. And since almost no one thought that I could beat an entrenched incumbent like Minish, no one had any great need to get in my good graces. On the contrary, few people who were truly interested in political favors could even afford to be seen at my events (or be listed in my contributor reports) lest Minish find out and hold it against them.

One thing I am proud of is that in my two political campaigns, the single best source of financial support was my former students out practicing law. But I never became comfortable calling on my friends and colleagues to send me checks. In recent years, when people ask me if I would ever consider running for office again, my stock answer has been, "I'm not going back on a street corner with a tin cup."

*   *   *

If there is one lesson that my two congressional campaigns drove home, it is the almost insurmountable task faced by a nonincumbent who is not independently wealthy. While the incumbent could sit back and pick up large checks from political action committees (PACs) that wanted to curry favor, I was trying to hustle contributions of $25 to $100 from people who liked me and thought that the country would be better served if I were elected in his place but who had no other personal stake in the outcome. Plus, since most of my fund-raising was done by direct mail and consisted of small contributions, it cost my campaigns more than fifty cents for each dollar raised. A $5,000 check from a PAC is practically all net.

On top of all the other advantages, an incumbent member of Congress has the franking privilege and a large staff paid for by the taxpayers. Although the frank is not supposed to be used for political advantage, of course it is. A member of Congress is allowed to send a limited number of free mailings to the entire district in every two-year cycle, and many of those mailings are "banked" until just before election time. The rules actually prohibit mailings within sixty days of an election, but as the rules are interpreted by the House postmaster, as long as the mail is delivered to the House post office within the prescribed time, it can be mailed out right up until election day. It isn't the postmaster's fault that everybody brings their material in just before the deadline and it takes the next two months to process all of it.

Of course, it is also illegal for congressional staffers to go to the boss's district and do political campaigning while on the public payroll. However, there is no rule against those staffers taking a couple of weeks of vacation time just before an election and spending it in the home district and volunteering in the campaign. In fact, it is done all the time. Nor are there any clear rules on how much vacation time a member of a congressional staff is entitled to or any public mechanism for accounting for vacation time.

As I write this, Congress has been deadlocked for years over political campaign finance reform. Because of the inherent advantages that incumbency brings, I am skeptical about the effectiveness of even the best of those proposals. Although a substantial level of public financing and sharing of the franking privilege might equalize things a bit, even that would have slight impact unless it was extended to primary elections. Besides being anathema to the legislators who would have to vote for it, such an extension would probably be so expensive that the general public would balk at the price tag, thus providing incumbents with a legitimate excuse to protect their own hides by voting against it. The fact is that 75 to 80 percent of the congressional districts in this country are one-party districts, where the only possibility for real change takes place in the dominant party's primary. But it is in primary elections where the power of incumbency is at its zenith.

* * *

The real beginning of my 1982 primary campaign was the nuclear-freeze referendum in November 1980. When that election was successfully concluded, I just kept right on campaigning, with the nuclear freeze as a centerpiece of my congressional platform. To save on expenses, I rented part of the New Jersey SANE office in Montclair as my campaign headquarters. In addition, SANE had chosen me as its person of the year in recognition of my role in the nuclear-freeze campaign. As its award, the organization bought me a batch of bumper stickers to get the campaign off the ground and on the road, so to speak.

Since I couldn't afford a full-time professional campaign manager, I hired one of my bright young law students, David Coyne, who had a background in New York politics and was willing to work cheap. My office manager was a tireless volunteer, Pat Sordill, who was deeply committed to peace and an end to the nuclear arms race.

* * *

Most campaigns for national office are waged these days through direct mail and radio and television advertising. I was never able to afford paid media and had to carefully ration my use of the mails. There were about seventy thousand Democratic households in the Eleventh Congressional District. Even with reduced bulk-rate postage and extensive use of volunteer labor, it would cost at least thirty cents apiece to prepare, print, and mail voter appeals. One such mailing to all registered Democrats in the district would have consumed almost half of my entire campaign budget. So the great bulk of my campaign operations consisted of me and volunteers distributing inexpensively repro-duced literature by hand to targeted audiences.

When I was a kid, teachers and fellow students used to make wisecracks that made use of my name, such as "Askin, you're askin' for it." My son Jonny turned it on himself by using "Who's Askin?" as the title of his junior high school newspaper column. When I went out campaigning for votes, I would try to get people to remember me by saying, "Remember, I was the guy who was *askin'* for your vote."

When I could come up with mailing lists of interest groups—environmentalists, feminists, peaceniks, educators, gays and lesbians, civil libertarians—we would send them materials intended to appeal to their special concerns. I also spent time seeking formal endorsements from such organized interest groups and would then try to convince them to contact their own members living in the district to support me.

I always thought that our most effective campaign gimmick, although of fairly limited use, was a flyer about U.S. policy in Central America that volunteers distributed in front of movie theaters as audiences filed out after seeing the film *Missing*. The film, which starred Jack Lemon, was a true story about an American student kidnapped and murdered by the U.S.-backed dictatorship in Chile. It was a powerful indictment of U.S. Latin American policy. Our flyer cited Minish's support in Congress for that policy and my proposals for change.

I also had a special handout for the district's large commuter population. I would station myself and volunteers at busy bus stops and train stations during the morning and evening rush hours. I would walk among the commuters, introducing myself and offering them my prescription for solving the mass-transit crisis being faced in northern New Jersey. They were a great captive audience and were usually starved for reading matter while waiting for a bus or train to arrive. It was exhilarating to look back and see a whole line of people standing at a bus stop reading my proposals for mass transit.

My worst campaign experience occurred during one of those commuter forays. I was at the Port Authority bus terminal in New York during the evening homeward-bound rush and was walking down a line of commuters waiting for buses to the white-ethnic communities in the northern end of the district. At the time, Mario Cuomo was running against Ed Koch for mayor of New York City, and Koch had made Cuomo's opposition to capital punishment a campaign theme. As a result, the newspapers and television news programs were filled with discussions of the issue, despite the fact that it was totally irrelevant to the administration of the city. (It was this kind of political demagoguery that has always made me scornful of Ed Koch.) As I walked down the line of commuters shaking hands, one man asked me how I felt about capital punishment. I replied that it was not really an issue before Congress, but I was opposed to it on philosophical grounds. The man crumpled up my flyer, threw it to the floor, and turned to the person behind him and said, "Hey, this guy wants our votes and he's against capital punishment." That message spread like wildfire up and down the line, and people to whom I had already spoken started to tear up my material and throw it down. I got away from there as fast I could and warned myself to be very careful about getting drawn into discussions of capital punishment in the future.

Although, in general, I was pretty forthright and outspoken in my views, there was another issue about which I expressed my opinion cautiously—the drug problem. For a long time, I have been convinced that the drug epidemic is not curable through the criminal process. (It may be the only issue on which William F. Buckley Jr. and I are in agreement.) The only thing that vigorous prosecution seems to accomplish is to drive up the price. There always seem to be new suppliers ready to take over for those caught and sent off to our bulging prisons and jails. But discussion of decriminalization seems to be off-limits in our political culture, and those who advocate such a drastic position are ridiculed and hardly ever heard from again. So when questioned about the drug problem, I would emphasize the need for more drug-treatment programs and increased drug education, but I stopped short of suggesting that it was time to consider decriminalization.

*   *   *

While I was working feverishly to generate public debate over Minish's record and my competing views on major public issues, he was busy disrupting my campaign. We spent a good deal of time attempting to solicit celebrities identified with liberal social causes to come to the district and campaign for me. Such events were important both because they attracted media attention, which we could not afford to pay for, and because they could be used for raising desperately needed funds.

For several months, I had been attempting, without success, through mutual friends in Los Angeles to contact Ed Asner about making such an appearance. Asner was extremely popular as a result of his Lou Grant role on the award-winning *Mary Tyler Moore Show*. Then I read in the newspaper that Asner was due in New Jersey the following week to campaign on behalf of Andy McGuire, a former liberal congressman from the Bergen County area who was seeking the Democratic nomination for U.S. Senate. I immediately got on the telephone to George Slaff, a personal friend and former mayor of Beverly Hills, and asked him to try to get Asner to broaden his New Jersey itinerary to include helping me. In forty-eight hours, I got word back that Asner had agreed, and my staff began to put together a house party in Montclair. The next day I got a call from a local newspaper reporter asking me to comment on the fact that McGuire had canceled his Asner event because he did not want to be associated with me. I was shocked and immediately called McGuire, who was a friend of mine and shared my views on most political issues. Andy told me that he could not afford to offend Joe Minish by seeming to be allied with my campaign.

Meanwhile, we went ahead with our own plans. Then, about seventy-two hours before the scheduled event, I got a call from Asner's office saying that he had decided to cancel the New Jersey trip altogether. I immediately got back on the phone to George Slaff to see if there was any way to undo the undoing. After another twenty-four hours, George called me and said that it was hopeless. As he pieced things together, Minish had called a leading liberal member of the California congressional delegation—a man whose voting record was much closer to my platform than to Minish's—and imposed on him to intercede with Asner. Asner, who was a leader of the Screen Actors Guild, was told that Minish had strong labor backing. Of course, Asner was not told that Minish was antiabortion, a military hawk, and a strong backer of President Reagan's Central American policy. (I should note here that Asner graciously made it up to me in 1986.)

There were other occasions on which Minish flexed his political muscle to disrupt my efforts. I had prevailed upon Professor Galbraith, on the basis of our relationship at the 1980 Democratic National Convention, to make an appearance on my behalf. Since he was not eager to come to New Jersey, we arranged a cocktail party on Central Park West. Former U.S. Attorney General Ramsey Clark also agreed to attend and make a pitch for contributions. It was a grand event, and Galbraith spoke warmly in praise of my role in initiating the nationwide nuclear-freeze campaign.

As he was getting ready to leave, I mentioned that we had taped his remarks and would like his permission to use them in radio commercials if we could raise enough money to air them. Galbraith said he could not give me such authorization. He explained that one of his sons worked for a friend of his who chaired the House Banking Committee, of which Minish was also a member. He said that he had been placed under tremendous pressure to cancel his appearance altogether. He felt bound to honor the commitment he had made to me, but had agreed to do nothing else in my behalf against Minish.

The only member of Congress who was apparently not concerned about standing up to Joe Minish was Harold Washington, the future mayor of Chicago. My son Steve, who had attended the University of Chicago and had been a journalist in Chicago, was working as Washington's legislative aide at the time. One day Steve tentatively asked his boss, "You know my father is running in the primary against one of your colleagues. You wouldn't want to endorse him, would you?"

Washington replied, "You mean Minish, who votes for the Walker amendments against affirmative action? Of course I'll endorse your father." I heard sometime later that Washington received a rebuke from the Speaker of the House for having publicly endorsed me.

Washington was one of the sponsors of a fund-raiser held at the Capitol Hill town house of Stewart Mott, the liberal philanthropist. The very occurrence of that event was an illustration of the zaniness of the political process. As someone well known for supporting liberal and progressive candidates, Mott was one of the first people I had gone to for financial support. After making some inquiries in New Jersey, Mott's staff told me that he couldn't help me because I couldn't win.

About six months later, Mott's staff learned that the liberally oriented National Committee for an Effective Congress (NCEC) had rated my campaign "marginal," meaning that it was not hopeless. Convinced that maybe I did have a chance, Mott agreed to sponsor the event in my behalf. I then went back to the NCEC, which had also told me that it couldn't help me because I couldn't win. When the NCEC staff heard that Mott was helping me, they were impressed. "He must think you have a chance," one of its directors told me. "We'll have to reconsider our position." I don't know whether the NCEC ever discovered that Mott's support for me was based on its own assessment of my viability. In any event, the NCEC provided my campaign with some demographic and other assistance before it was over.

*   *   *

Their fear of offending Minish also kept me in frequent confrontation with Peter Shapiro and his staff. Shapiro was up for reelection as county executive. I knew that Peter could not allow me to run as part of his slate and appear on the same line on the primary ballot, but I was hoping that he would agree to an "open primary," in which there were no slates and the candidates all ran independently. However, Minish and Peter Rodino, the venerable chairman of the House Judiciary Committee who was facing a primary challenge from an African American opponent in an overwhelmingly black district that included Newark, both wanted to be included on an official party slate headed by Shapiro.

I had another brief confrontation with the Shapiro campaign when my major piece of campaign literature hit the streets. It included a picture of me with Shapiro and John Atlas, a leader of the New Jersey Tenants Organization, taken at the Essex County Jobs Development Conference about a year earlier. The conference had been carried out under a grant from Essex County, and Shapiro had appointed me as chairman. I assume that as soon as Minish saw the piece he raised hell with Shapiro and demanded that he do something about it. I got a phone call from one of Shapiro's aides telling me that I was not authorized to use his photograph in my campaign literature and demanding that I withdraw the piece from circulation. I politely thanked her for the call but told her that the photograph had been taken at a public event and I had every right to reproduce it. I heard no more about the matter.

*   *   *

One of the sweetest happenings of the campaign was an editorial endorsement by the *Bergen Record*, the newspaper that had fired me some twenty years before. The *Record* wrote:

> In the Eleventh District . . . there's a David-Goliath contest worth watching. David is Frank Askin, a Rutgers law professor who is nationally known as civil libertarian and Democratic Party activist. . . . Goliath is Rep. Joseph Minish, a machine politician whose major legislative accomplishment in ten terms in the House . . . was a law establishing credit unions for servicemen based overseas. We're pulling for Mr. Askin.

Unfortunately, neither the *Record* nor anyone else was pulling hard enough. Instead of the twenty thousand votes I was looking for, I received about nine thousand or about 26 percent of the total. In retrospect, it probably wasn't a bad showing for a political neophyte with a shoestring budget against an entrenched incumbent with virtually unlimited financial support and a political machine.

Of the twenty-seven municipalities in the Eleventh District, I carried only one outright. That was Mountain Lakes, a small, affluent Republican community without an organized Democratic organization where the relatively few Democrats tend to be independent and cerebral. I also carried three of the four wards in the cosmopolitan and heterogeneous community of Montclair but lost the predominantly black Fourth Ward, where the voters tended to support the official party line by just enough votes to shift the townwide result. In the ethnic, blue-collar northern end of the district, I lost by margins of seven and eight to one.

My sweetest memento of the campaign is a letter dated June 23, 1982, three weeks after the primary, on Democratic National Committee stationery and signed by the party's national chairman Charles T. Manatt. The letter congratulated me on my primary victory and promised assistance in the upcoming general election. To this day, I wonder whether Minish was sent the condolence letter.

DEMOCRATIC
NATIONAL COMMITTEE   *1625 Massachusetts Ave., N.W.*   *Washington, D.C. 20036*   *(202) 797-5900*

Charles T. Manatt
Chairman

June 23, 1982

Professor Frank Askin
P.O. Box 754
Orange, New Jersey   07051

Dear Frank:

    On behalf of all the Committeemen and women of the Democratic
National Committee, I am very pleased to congratulate you on your
recent primary victory.

    I would like to offer you my personal thanks for seeking
election to Congress from the 11th district of New Jersey. It is
especially heartening, Frank, to know that you have joined an
historic team of Democrats for Congress in 1982, the most important midterm-election year of the past three decades.

    The campaign-services division of the DNC exists to help with
your campaign. Please do not hesitate to contact its director,
Angie Martin, or her assistant, Matthew MacWilliams: they are
ready to supply valuable resources such as a fully up-to-date campaign manual, a consultants' list, help in complying with FEC
regulations, and access to the campaign talent bank. In addition,
they very much look forward to meeting you and your staff to discuss the campaign, if they have not yet had that opportunity.

    May your success thus far continue, and we shall celebrate
victory this November.

               The very best of luck,

               Charles T. Manatt
               Chairman

15

Mission to Moscow: Eluding the KGB

As a result of court-ordered redistricting following the 1982 Congressional election, the Eleventh District was substantially transfigured prior to the 1984 election. The district was moved west into wealthy and conservative Morris County, and the blue-collar communities in the north were eliminated from the district, as was much of the nonwhite population. The Republicans put up one of their state legislative leaders, Dean Gallo, to run against Minish. Gallo was a realtor of no special competence or accomplishment, but he was part of a strong Republican political organization in Morris County. Gallo had the added advantage that it was a presidential election year, and Ronald Reagan was reelected with a landslide victory over Walter Mondale. I made a sort of peace with Minish by publicly endorsing him and even held a house party for him with a group of neighbors. At least on economic issues, I found Minish preferable to Gallo. Minish lost by about twenty-five thousand votes in heavy balloting. Minish also left a lot of angry supporters behind when it was discovered that he had some half a million dollars of unspent funds in his campaign account that he was able to convert to his personal use. I decided that I would try to obtain the Democratic nomination to run against Gallo in 1986.

My West Orange Democratic Party leader, Warren Grover, was also a leader of the Essex County Jewish establishment and shared that group's rather conservative views in the area of foreign policy. Although Warren was a social friend, he found my politics a bit too radical for his liking. He was particularly annoyed that I had traveled to Central America in 1985 and had come back denouncing U.S. support of the Nicaraguan contras in their efforts to overthrow the Sandinista government.

Warren began to prod me about making a trip on behalf of the Conference on Soviet Jewry to visit refuseniks in the Soviet Union—Soviet Jews who had applied for permission to emigrate but had been refused. He didn't have to prod me too hard. I recognized that because of my expressed concern for the civil rights of Palestinians, my commitment to the state of Israel was viewed a bit skeptically in the Jewish community, which played a major role in Democratic politics in Essex County. Gallo, in contrast, had ingratiated himself by wholeheartedly supporting both aid to Israel and freedom for Soviet Jews. I figured that it could not hurt me to follow the path of so many other U.S. politicians and make a pilgrimage to the embattled Jewish communities of Moscow and Leningrad. My wife, Marilyn, was outraged when she discovered that the United Jewish Appeal had paid the expenses for Gallo's trip, whereas we were expected to finance our own.

Not only were we required to pay for our own travel, we were also given a list of items to buy and "smuggle" to Soviet Jews. We were provided with a few special items to deliver to specific leaders of the refusenik community, such as a camera, a sophisticated watch, and some medicines that were unavailable in the Soviet Union. Among the items we were asked to obtain for distribution were several tape recorders with pause buttons to facilitate the teaching of Hebrew to those who were hoping to immigrate to Israel. We were also asked to take a large supply of cigarettes and candy—to be delivered to several families with relatives in Soviet prisons who could use those items to bribe prison guards—as well as technological magazines, because those available in the Soviet Union were outdated.

Marilyn and I were given several days of briefings by conference officials and were provided with a list of about fifteen families we were supposed to try to contact and visit. Some had been on the "refused" list for as long as fifteen years. Many were scientists who had been told that they could not leave because they knew scientific and military secrets. We were provided with background information on each family.

We were given the telephone numbers of our contacts but were warned that they should not be written down in the event we were searched. Marilyn devised a code using our checkbook register. Our subjects were listed cryptically as payees, and a coded system of entries in the amount column represented their phone numbers. We were also advised never to use the phones in our hotel rooms—except to report our arrival and itinerary to the U.S. embassy—but to place our calls from public telephones. We were told to assume that our hotel rooms were bugged and to write notes to each other when discussing sensitive matters.

The worst mistake we made was choosing the dead of winter for our journey, but it was the only time we could both conveniently arrange to be away. Marilyn's presence was essential, since she could speak both Yiddish and Russian; she had been a student at the Russian Institute at Columbia University before going to law school. The Soviet Jewry Conference arranged for us to travel with a couple from Philadelphia whom we had never met. He was a rabbi and had a special mission to conduct religious services and distribute religious materials to Jews in Moscow and Leningrad.

*   *   *

The trip got off to a good beginning when our Pan Am flight from Kennedy airport missed the connection and we had to stay overnight in London, which was certainly preferable to an additional night in Moscow. When we finally arrived in Moscow, we quickly discovered that the trip was fraught with danger. Although we had been whisked through customs without incident, our travelling companions informed us that they had been subjected to a frightening and humiliating strip search and had been detained for five hours. Some of the religious materials they were carrying had been confiscated, and several salamis they were bringing for kosher families had been sliced open. Then when they arrived at the hotel, they were greeted by KGB agents, who warned them that they were to have no contact with Russian citizens during their stay. They were scared to death and had decided that they would attempt no contacts with Russian Jews. Intourist, the Soviet tourist bureau, may have been trying to make amends for the KGB's boorish behavior, since the couple was given the hotel's most luxurious duplex suite.

Marilyn and I were also concerned by these developments but decided not to be deterred from our mission. I figured that it could not possibly hurt my political aspirations to be arrested or publicly harassed by the KGB. We were, however, concerned for the families we were planning to visit. After settling in our room and checking in with the U.S. embassy, we headed off to the bank of public phones near the GUM department store in Red Square, across from our hotel.

We had been provided with several kopek coins for telephone calls. Since Marilyn could converse in both Yiddish and Russian, she made all the calls. Once we found a telephone that worked, things proceeded smoothly. The procedure was always the same. She would identify herself as a friend from the United States who would like to visit. Our hosts would invariably give her instructions as to which subway to take and promise to meet us at the train station. The subways were unbelievably efficient. They were the main means of transportation for six million Muscovites, and trains came along every two or three minutes. Most of the stations were like art galleries. Whereas almost everything else we saw in our travels there was third rate, the subway system was a technological and artistic marvel.

Our hosts would always recognize us as the visiting Americans as we stood on the subway platform looking bewildered. Then we would walk to their apartment or, on occasion, take a local bus. Even if we had only a couple of blocks to walk, the trips were often slow and quite treacherous. It was the last week of December, with the temperature around zero, and the streets and sidewalks in some neighborhoods were sheets of ice.

We always felt quite conspicuous as we trudged through the streets or rode buses with our newfound Russian friends. We feared not so much for ourselves as for them. If they could spot us immediately on a busy subway platform, we must have been equally obvious to anyone who was not disposed to be friendly. However, the Russians put us at ease. They said that we should assume that the KGB was aware of our activities, which was fine as long as we didn't flaunt it. A number of the people we met actually believed that it was to their advantage if the government knew that they were receiving visitors from the United States. The authorities might be inhibited from taking action against them if it was known that they had friends in the United States keeping an eye out for them. As we were told by one of our hosts, a former Red Army colonel and World War II hero who had been demoted to private thirteen years earlier when he had applied for an exit visa: "You do important work for us. Because they know you visit us and care for us, you save us."

There were other indications of official condonation of our activity. For example, we encountered other American Jewish travelers on similar missions. Each morning at breakfast at our Leningrad hotel, we ran into a family with four children from Savannah, Georgia—a typical southern family. On the third morning, we introduced ourselves and realized from their name that they were Jewish. After further conversation, we discovered that they were the leaders of a Jewish congregation in Savannah. Of course, we then found out that while the children were off sightseeing and shopping each day, the parents were bringing succor to local Jews. What we began to suspect was that this entire Soviet Jewry project was being promoted by Intourist, since without us, there would have been practically no tourist business in the Soviet Union in midwinter.

Of course, that theory was inconsistent with the harassment of our Philadelphia traveling companions, who continued to be greeted by KGB agents each time they landed in a new city. We would meet them each morning for breakfast, at which time they would give us a shopping bag full of items they had expected to deliver to their contacts on their now abandoned itinerary. They would then take off for a normal day of sightseeing and theatergoing. Maybe, we speculated, the fact that he was a rabbi who was planning to conduct religious services made him uniquely unwelcome to the government. Meanwhile, Marilyn and I continued on our rounds totally unbothered by Soviet officialdom, even though we would leave our hotel each morning with bulging shopping bags and return home at night empty-handed.

* * *

We visited thirteen families and met thirty-five individuals in Moscow and Leningrad during our week and a half in the Soviet Union. We also spent several days in Kiev but were advised not to visit anybody there because local authorities had been cracking down on dissidents. I had wanted to visit Kiev anyway, because that was where my paternal grandparents had come from. However, when I asked for a local telephone directory on the remote possibility that I might be able to track down some relatives, I was told that none existed.

I was fascinated by the political opinions of the refuseniks. The majority tended to express points of view that in the United States would have been considered conservative, but they were far from monolithic. Understandably, they were not terribly well informed. They believed nothing they read in the Soviet press and tended to accept uncritically whatever they heard over the Voice of America or read in the U.S. magazines that their visitors occasionally brought them. For example, a number of them even opposed U.S. arms limitation talks with the Russians; they distrusted the Soviet government and believed that the Soviets would violate any agreement. They were quite divided and confused about this new man Gorbachev, who had recently arisen as the country's leader. Some were optimistic that a new age was about to dawn; others were convinced that he offered only more of the same. The latter were convinced that it was impossible for anyone with decent motives and instincts to rise through the party hierarchy to a position of such power. They were hungry for any information we could supply about events in their own country.

Almost everyone we met was living in economic distress because they had been fired from their jobs and had to eke out meager livings as best they could. We met with scientists, engineers, and mathematicians who were working as janitors and boiler room attendants because they could not find other employment. We were surprised that the authorities had made no attempt to dispossess them of their state-owned apartments. As near as we could discern, the right to housing was so ingrained in Soviet law that even political dissidents were protected from eviction. So even though most of the apartments we visited were small and overcrowded, our hosts had been able to remain in their homes even after many years of public disgrace and ostracism.

The same seemed to be true of pensions. The government made no effort to cut off whatever pensions the refuseniks were entitled to by law. In fact, there was some concern among the older members of the refusenik population—those past or near retirement age—as to how they would survive economically if they were eventually allowed to emigrate. They could count on their small pensions, low-rent apartments, and free medical care as long as they remained in the Soviet Union but had no idea what kind of economic support would be available if they were to relocate to Israel or the United States. A number of them told us that they no longer had any real personal incentive to leave but still hoped to do so for the sake of their children.

One of the families we visited we met by accident at the Leningrad synagogue.

Lev Shapiro was known to us as an outspoken leader of the refusenik community, but he was not on our list of planned visitations. At the time, Shapiro was in a public battle with Leningrad school officials over their refusal to permit his seven-year-old daughter Naomi to attend the same English-language neighborhood school attended by her older brother. Shapiro had accused the officials of visiting the "sins" of the parents upon his daughter. We also discovered that Lev was a cousin of a friend and legal colleague of ours in New Jersey, Larry Lerner. We were delighted about two years later when we ran into Larry and he reported that cousin Lev had finally been allowed to depart for Israel with his family.

*   *   *

Dealing with the Soviet bureaucracy was a constant nightmare. We became convinced that the two most common words in the Russian vocabulary were "not possible." We had been booked on a flight from Kiev that would get us back to Moscow airport at 8:30 P.M. New Year's Eve. Since we were hoping to be able to attend a New Year's Eve party at the U.S. embassy, we tried every which way to switch to an earlier flight. But wherever we went, the answer was always the same: "not possible." By the time we arrived at the embassy, we were told that no more people could be accommodated. We wound up celebrating New Year's in Red Square, which was filled mostly with foreigners drinking champagne and shattering the bottles on the ground. Marilyn was concerned about the mess they were leaving to be cleaned up the next morning by the old women we would see all over downtown Moscow with their push brooms and scoops.

As impressive as the Moscow subway was, the Russian airplanes were the exact opposite. They were small and crowded and served only dry sausage and stale bread. Most Russian passengers brought their own refreshments. The planes' dinginess and general appearance did not inspire confidence. The cabins resembled old trolley cars. (At least foreign travelers got preferred seating while the Russians had to line up and wait to board.) When we arrived in Kiev at 10 P.M. after one of these dreary flights, we were told that there was not a single restaurant open in the entire city at that hour. We sat in the hotel bar drinking with some Israeli Arabs for several hours, but there was not a bite of food to be had.

Fortunately, we avoided one air flight by taking the night train from Moscow to Leningrad, an eight-hour journey brightened by waiters who served tea in ancient samovars. Unfortunately, I was sick most of the night and spent it running back and forth to the primitive toilet at the end of the corridor.

With the exception of the Moscow subway and the Hermitage Museum in Leningrad, most of what we came across in our travels was as shoddy as the airplanes. Apartment buildings were invariably in total disrepair. The hall-ways were drab, with paint peeling off the walls; stairwells were as dank as any New York tenement; elevators were totally uninviting. The shelves in the groceries and meat markets we passed on the street were usually empty, and the occasional store with a fresh shipment of something invariably had a queue that stretched around the block. Restaurants were impossible. Service was slow, menus were sparse, and food was tasteless.

The people, however, seemed to be well and warmly dressed for the Soviet winter. Fur coats and fur hats abounded. When we inquired about this ap-parent fashion consciousness, we were told that people had little else to do with discretionary income, since there were so few consumer goods available, and saving for big-ticket items such as automobiles was beyond the dreams of the average citizen.

Our overall impression was that the Soviet Union was a backward, third-world country that could not possibly be a serious threat to the mighty United States of America. It was a country that obviously needed international stabil-ity and an end to the arms race—even more than our own country did (as Ronald Reagan geometrically increased our national debt each year to pay for his obsessive desire for larger nuclear arsenals and bigger and better air and sea armadas).

That was one of two messages I repeated over and over again as I lectured throughout northern New Jersey about my trip. The other was the need to keep up the international pressure on the Soviet Union to alleviate the plight of the Russian Jews, because it was quite apparent that pressure was extremely effective.

*　*　*

We had one more official job to perform when we stopped in Paris for a few days on our way home. One of our Russian hosts, a biologist, had asked us to smuggle a manuscript to her publisher in France. The government had denied her permission to either publish it in the Soviet Union or send it abroad. We breathed a sigh of relief when we again passed through Moscow customs without incident and our plane was finally in the sky. The fact was, we had no idea what that manuscript contained. For all we knew, we could have been carrying classified military information.

One of the more whimsical occurrences of our trip took place during that Paris respite. After ten days of communicating in alien tongues, we decided to seek out an English-language film that had not been dubbed into French. Walking along the Left Bank, we were excited to discover a marquee adver-tising an American film *version originale* with French subtitles. Our excite-ment turned to joy when we discovered that it was a Mel Brooks film that, as far as we could tell from its French title, was unfamiliar to us. However, as we settled into our seats, we found that we were viewing *Silent Movie*, Brooks's spoof on silent pictures that conveyed its dialogue solely through its (now French) subtitles. It was an apt end to a topsy-turvy journey into never-never land.

16

Running for Congress Again: Coattails and Albatrosses

The off-year election in 1986 meant that there were no major contests to bring out the Republican voters in Morris County. In Essex County, however, Peter Shapiro was up for reelection as county executive, which I hoped would result in a heavy Democratic vote in Eleventh District towns in Essex. Even though the Morris part of the district accounted for about two-thirds of the district's population, it was quite possible that Essex voters would cast as many as half the votes in such an election. After studying the voting history of the forty-nine towns included in the Eleventh District, I constructed an optimal scenario in which I would lose the Morris end of the district by only eighteen thousand votes while carrying the Essex towns by twenty thousand—Shapiro's margin of victory in those towns during his previous run. In other words, I had a plan to win on Peter Shapiro's coattails. Little did I know that by 1986, Peter would become an albatross.

The first event that disrupted my plan was the 1985 gubernatorial election. In a heated primary contest, Shapiro won the Democratic nomination to run against Tom Kean, the popular Republican incumbent. Shapiro took one of the worst beatings of any Democrat in the state's history. Shortly after that election, Peter got involved in a political brawl with Raymond Durkin, the Essex County Democratic Party chairman and Shapiro's choice for state party chairman after he won the gubernatorial nomination the year before. Durkin was from the old school of patronage politics, not a political reform technocrat like Shapiro. For Shapiro, the alliance with Durkin was one of expediency, and their eventual falling-out was probably inevitable.

The immediate consequence was a bitter Democratic primary fight in June 1986 between a Shapiro slate and a Durkin-backed slate. After much maneuvering, Shapiro agreed to include me on his ticket as the Eleventh District congressional candidate. Durkin was more interested in county offices, and since he didn't think that the Democrats had any chance in the Eleventh District anyway, he never got around to fielding a candidate against me. As a

144

consequence, my only primary opposition came from a follower of Lyndon LaRouche, a perennial candidate who offered only token opposition.

In any event, I had already ingratiated myself with the Morris County Democrats and felt that I could win a real primary fight under any circumstances. In Morris County, where the Democratic Party was weak, the Democrats tended to be more cerebral, more liberal, and more issue oriented. This is a common occurrence in Democratic Party politics. In the large cities and urban areas, which Democrats tend to dominate, the party has strong machines fueled by nonideological politicians who are more interested in patronage and the other perks of political power. In more conservative rural and suburban areas dominated by Republicans, where there is little advantage to being a Democrat, the Democrats are generally more intellectual and idealistic, interested in issues and government more than personal aggrandizement. (That generality gets more skewed in black-dominated urban areas, where grasping politicians have to compete with issue-oriented civil rights leaders who see political power as a mechanism for achieving social change.)

The pseudo–primary contest with a LaRouchite gave me an opportunity to solidify my support among the Democrats in Morris County, most of whom were new to the Eleventh District, and to try to mend fences with Essex Democrats and labor officials who still harbored ill feelings because of my 1982 primary challenge to Joe Minish. As a result of a totally unexpected victory by LaRouche-backed candidates in an Illinois Democratic primary, there was a fair amount of coverage in the national media of the threat posed to the Democratic Party by this irresponsible but seemingly well-financed fringe group that espoused a strange mixture of far-right and far-left rhetoric, along with a program that focused on the development of nuclear fusion technology. For me, the LaRouche opposition provided a convenient opportunity to test the efficiency of my nascent campaign organization and to unite mainstream Democrats behind my candidacy. In both regards, the primary was relatively successful.

* * *

Any possibility of realizing my congressional fantasy died one week after the primary. Having defeated the slate backed by Ray Durkin for county offices, Peter Shapiro decided to try to replace Durkin as the county Democratic chairman. The chairman is selected once a year by the thousand-plus county committee men and women elected at each primary. I had been a member of the committee from West Orange for about four years.

Aware that Shapiro was gearing for a battle over the party leadership, I had been urging him to find an African- American candidate to run against Durkin. Since black voters constituted a substantial part of the Democratic constituency in Essex County, I had long felt that as long as the Democratic county executive was white, the party chairman should preferably be black. In addition, it seemed to me that such a candidate could facilitate a winning alliance between Shapiro's white suburban base of supporters and the black party leadership from Newark and East Orange. However, at a meeting with Shapiro's political chief of staff a few days before the crucial county committee meeting, I was told that Shapiro had the votes to elect anyone he wanted, and he was going to support Steve Edelstein, a white suburban lawyer in Shapiro's own mold and with whom Shapiro felt comfortable. Not surprisingly, Durkin made his own alliance with a number of black Democratic leaders and was reelected by a comfortable margin.

The major consequence of this turn of events was that Nicholas Amato, the incumbent county surrogate who had been part of the losing Durkin slate at the June primary, made himself available as the Republican candidate for county executive against Shapiro. The Republicans jumped at the opportunity and convinced their original candidate to withdraw in favor of Amato. At the same time, Shapiro was facing a tax revolt among Essex County voters because of a sudden sharp increase in the county tax rate. The reasons for the tax rise were not totally clear, but the county's old-line Democrats joined with the newly energized Republicans to place the entire blame on Shapiro's county administration. Since both Democrats and Republicans seemed to agree that it was Shapiro's fault, the taxpayers did not need a lot more convincing. Suddenly, Shapiro's coattails had become an albatross. Our agreement to share office space for the campaign—which had so encouraged my staff a few weeks earlier—no longer seemed like such a great idea.

*   *   *

Aside from the incessant need to raise money, the campaign was even more exhilarating than my 1982 primary run. First of all, I was now the official candidate of the Democratic Party and not a "spoiler." My Democratic and labor friends no longer had to avoid me, nor did I have to feel constantly angry with them for doing so. I was able to get major Democratic figures such as Senators Bill Bradley and Frank Lautenberg to make occasional campaign appearances. On one occasion, Bradley joined me for an hour greeting voters outside a supermarket.

I was surrounded by my children, who were the mainstay of my campaign staff. Andrea had returned from California to serve as my scheduler and events coordinator. Steve returned temporarily from Africa, where he had been working as a journalist for about four years, to be the deputy campaign manager. Jonny, who had been graduated from Harvard on the day of the primary, was the press secretary. And Danny, who was an undergraduate at Rutgers College in

New Brunswick, worked as the coordinator of volunteers until he returned to school in the fall. Aside from my campaign manager, Carla Horton, and Carol Schafler, a friend from West Orange who served as the fund-raiser, they represented my entire paid staff—although what my kids received was more like an allowance than a salary. No candidate ever had a more devoted or hardworking staff. The campaign was a family gathering.

The local press took substantial interest in the race because of the clear-cut choice that Gallo and I represented on most issues. About the only issue we agreed on was abortion. Since his days in the state legislature, Gallo had distanced himself from most of his fellow Republicans by adopting a pro-choice stance—although he sometimes voted against government funding of abortions for poor women. When the primary was past, Gallo lost no time trying to label me as a wild-eyed radical. In his first public statement, he was quoted as saying, "If Frank Askin were any further to the Left, he'd fall off the face of the earth."

I responded as follows: "I always thought Gallo was living in the nineteenth century, now I realize he lives in the fifteenth. Since then, people have realized that the world is round and there's no danger of falling off. . . . I don't know what Gallo thinks I'm Left on. I'm for the environment, for education, in favor of cutting waste in the Defense Department, and want to bring about arms control. I don't know whether those issues are Right or Left."

* * *

My campaign's single biggest expenditure was for a poll by a leading national political consulting firm. I decided to make this investment because I had been told that no potential funding source would take me seriously unless we did. Anytime a candidate seeks support from a political action committee or other large contributor, the first thing demanded is a poll that demonstrates how the candidate can win with the right kind of campaign. So we commissioned a telephone poll that tested the attitudes of four hundred likely voters. In addition to being a fund-raising tool, the major purpose of the poll was to discern what kinds of information provided to voters during the campaign might convince them to vote for me.

The results indicated that 42 percent of the voters were likely to vote for the Republican candidate in the Eleventh District that November, and 28 percent were likely to vote for the Democratic candidate. The poll also found that voters in the Eleventh District strongly approved of Ronald Reagan's record as he entered the final two years of his presidency. The encouraging news was that after a series of hypothetical questions based on information supplied to the respondents about the two candidates, 27 percent of those

who initially preferred the Republican nominee for Congress said that they
would consider voting for the Democrat.

It came as no surprise to me that in 1986, environmental protection was
the leading issue on the minds of voters—the one issue that our consultant
thought offered the best opportunity to take votes away from Gallo. There
were two other extremely positive findings. First, most respondents agreed
with my point of view on the need to reduce federal military spending even
more than domestic spending. Second, the poll found that my role as a leader
of the nuclear freeze movement played very well among prospective voters.
The bottom line was that I really did have a chance to beat Gallo—if I could
convince voters that I was the environmental candidate while widely publiciz-
ing my role as an advocate of a sound military policy that would reduce federal spending and ease the threat of nuclear holocaust. All I needed were the
resources to saturate the Eleventh District and its half a million inhabitants
with that message.

*   *   *

Modern political campaigning has largely come down to media battles, with
the bulk of expenditures being budgeted for television and radio advertising.
However, a campaign first has to cover the basics—staff salaries, rent, telephones, postage, and printing of basic materials. Unfortunately, my campaign
never got beyond the basics. All told, over the course of the primary and
general election, we raised about $165,000, a substantial amount in my eyes,
but a drop in the bucket for a modern congressional campaign in the New
York area. And since most of our money was raised by direct-mail appeals
from small contributions, the cost of fund-raising was quite high. Although
we prepared a few radio scripts, there was never enough money to purchase
any airtime.

We did reasonably well with what political consultants refer to as "free
media"—space in the news columns of the local press and occasional mention
on radio news and interview shows. A number of editors and reporters were
intrigued by the campaign of an outspoken law professor and social activist
who had never held public office and whose children were the backbone of his
campaign staff. It resulted in number of highly favorable feature stories. However,
such exposure couldn't begin to compete with the media campaign of my
opponent, who spent in the neighborhood of $700,000 on his reelection, in
addition to all the assistance he derived from his status as an incumbent, including the mailing of frequent newsletters at taxpayer expense. The district
covered forty-nine separate municipalities that were serviced by about seven
daily newspapers and dozens of weeklies. Most people probably received their
main political messages from the three television networks, whose local affiliates

broadcast from New York and paid relatively little attention to New Jersey politics. Under such circumstances, occasional favorable stories in various local newspapers looked good in a montage and elated our supporters but had only minimal impact on public awareness of our campaign.

We were constantly looking for gimmicks to attract media interest, always trying to come up with an idea that might entice a television assignment editor to dispatch a camera crew in the hope of making the six o'clock news. One of our most successful efforts involved stationing my children along busy highways at rush hour with the equivalent of old Burma Shave signs. One such message was:

> Do $600 toilet seats make you mad?
> Then come out and vote for our dear old Dad.
> Frank Askin for Congress—11th District.

Speaking of $600 toilet seats, we arranged for an appearance by Christopher Cerf and Henry Beard, the authors of a satirical book about bloated defense contracting costs called *The Pentagon Catalog*. We held a press conference with them in front of a local subsidiary of the Lockheed Corporation, the vendor of the infamous $640.09 commode cover, to confer the Golden Toilet Seat Award. When I held another press conference to support federal campaign financing reform and attack Gallo for accepting huge contributions from the defense industry's political action committees (PACs), we conducted it in front of the headquarters of one of his prime industrial benefactors.

I was constantly seeking ways to visually portray environmental issues, which our polls showed were the primary concern of voters in the district. That was especially important, because Gallo and I were in sharp competition for the blessing of the environmental community, which he claimed to support. I was constantly trying to point out that although Gallo pretended to be a supporter of the federal Superfund to clean up the many hazardous waste sites in New Jersey, his refusal to support legislation to place the main cost of cleanup on the polluters themselves belied his pretensions as an environmentalist. My major ally in this effort was New Jersey Citizen Action, which had been waging a door-to-door campaign in support of the Superfund in communities throughout the district. It was also clear that Gallo, the realtor, had long been an opponent of wetlands protection, a major concern of environmentalists.

We also tried to publicize my role as a member of the official West Orange Radon Task Force, a municipal advisory group working to rid radon contamination along the West Orange–Montclair border. Homes had been built on the site of a former radium dumping ground, and the cleanup posed difficult and costly problems related to the removal and disposal of contaminated soil. Several homes had actually been evacuated and left untreated for several years, and the relocated families remained in motels as a result of the abandonment of the original cleanup plan. I did research and discovered that the abandoned plant where the waste originated had gotten its start after World War I making luminous dials for gun sights under contract with the U.S. Navy. I proposed that the navy be made responsible for financing the cleanup.

We were unsuccessful in our efforts to get the major environmental organizations to endorse me and allocate their substantial resources to help my election. They were afraid of offending the Congressman, whom they expected to be reelected, so they pretty much sat out the election.

I was able to get the anti-handgun lobby to target my campaign for support, however. Because of Gallo's receipt of substantial contributions from the National Rifle Association and his terrible voting record on the issue, the gun-control community was glad to do what it could to mobilize support for me among those parts of the law-enforcement community that were especially upset by the proliferation of handguns. If I had had money for radio advertising, gun control would have been one of the main topics of my commercials.

One thing I had to credit Gallo for was his willingness to debate. We had six or seven of them during the course of the campaign. Despite the fact that he did not fare well in the first few, he kept coming back. I think he started making some headway in the latter sessions, when his staff began to plant questioners in the audience who would confront me with statements from the policy guide of the American Civil Liberties Union, with which I was closely identified. They would search out those positions of the ACLU that were particularly unpopular and ask me whether I supported the ACLU view and whether I had voted as a member of the national board to adopt them. The hostile questioners focused on issues such as pornography, legalization of drugs, free speech for Nazis, and capital punishment. Although my responses generally made for interesting philosophical discussion, they were not issues on which I was likely to win wide support. On occasion, I accurately pointed out that I had voted against adoption of a specific ACLU policy, just as Gallo might oppose some specific planks in the Republican platform.

*　　*　　*

I divided my time between raising money and greeting voters. Since we could not afford media advertising, I had to reach voters the old-fashioned way—door-to-door, on street corners, at commuter stops and plant gates, in front of supermarkets, and at house parties. We also had lots of volunteers out on the streets handing out printed literature, since it was a lot cheaper than buying postage stamps.

Unlike 1982, I did have a few substantial PAC contributions, mainly from labor unions. The United Automobile Workers union was my best financial supporter, with the International Union of Electrical Workers (IUE)—my onetime nemesis when I was a UE leader in Baltimore in my youth—and the Communication Workers of America (CWA) a close second.

As in 1982, I spent lots of time trying to enlist popular entertainers and celebrities to appear at fund-raising events. Ed Asner finally fulfilled his 1982 commitment, and we had a great party at the home of my West Orange friends Herb and Annamay Sheppard. Marilyn organized a chorus to serenade Ed "Lou Grant" Asner with the old Newspaper Guild song "Newspapermen Meet Such Interesting People." Mandy Patinkin—who at the time was starring on Broadway in *Sunday in the Park with George*—came across the river for a party we called "Sunday at Tim's with Mandy" at the home of Tim Hull, a local leader in the liberal community. Mandy had been a member of the delegation I traveled with to El Salvador and Nicaragua in 1985. Chanteuse Martha Schlamme performed for the campaign at a cabaret night at the spacious South Orange home of NOW leader Connie Gilbert-Neiss. We had two fund-raisers in Greenwich Village—one with Father Robert Drinan, the liberal Jesuit who retired from Congress at the order of the Pope, and one with former U.S. Attorney General Ramsey Clark, with whom I had worked on several civil liberties cases. My brother Stan suggested that I try to contact his old friend Harry Belafonte, who had been best man at Stan's first wedding in 1949, when they were both students at the Dramatic Workshop in New York City, but Belafonte never responded.

Also, as in 1982, I found the legal community to be my most consistent base of economic support, and we held a number of successful cocktail parties directed at that constituency. One, held in the exclusive Llewellyn Park section of West Orange, the former Thomas Edison estate, featured an appearance by my old friend the former Governor and former chief justice Richard J. Hughes. Governor Hughes was in his declining years and his memory was obviously fading. When I first contacted him about making an appearance, he said yes and then dropped me a note asking me to detail our past associations. "Frank, I know I have very positive feelings about you," he wrote, "but remind me why."

The parties were all very successful and created lots of goodwill and enthusiasm, but because of modest ticket prices, they did not generate a lot of revenue after expenses. I greatly envied those officeholders who could throw $500 cocktail parties and attract a large turnout of lobbyists and others who felt they had to attend. One such event selling 350 tickets would raise more money in one night than I did in a year.

*   *   *

As November approached and it became more and more obvious that Peter Shapiro was going to be anything but an asset in Essex County, it also became obvious that I couldn't win. Actually, the Morris County part of my original game plan was on target—a Gallo majority of eighteen thousand votes. However, my projected Shapiro majority of twenty thousand in the Essex part of the district turned into a twenty-thousand-vote deficit as Peter lost to Democrat-turned-Republican Amato. Overall, the Gallo victory margin was about two to one.

I think the whole family was glad that it was over and people could return to their normal lives. Steve went back to Africa; Andrea to California. Jonny took off for Las Vegas and played poker professionally for six months until enrolling in Rutgers Law School the following September. Danny had already returned to school in New Brunswick. I returned to full-time teaching and lawyering, and as the Iran-contra scandal unraveled in Washington, I felt frustrated that I could not be where the main action was.

17

Back to Capitol Hill:
The Iran-Contra Affair

If I couldn't get back to Capitol Hill as a member of Congress, I was willing to be some one else's water carrier. As the Iran-contra scandal unfolded in the winter of 1986–87, I longed to take part in the investigation of what promised to be an important episode in U.S. constitutional and political history. From early reports, it seemed to involve one of the most egregious abuses of power in our country's annals.

The backdrop for what history now refers to merely as "Iran-contra" was the political movement that emerged in the country in the first half of the 1980s to put a stop to U.S. efforts to overthrow the government of Nicaragua. I felt that my own trip to Central America in 1985 and my activities upon my return had made a modest contribution to that effort. After vigorous open public debate, Congress was convinced that funding the Nicaraguan civil war was not in the best interest of the United States and passed the Boland amendment, which forbade the expenditure of public moneys for military assistance to the contras. Despite that mandate by the nation's lawmaking body, people in Ronald Reagan's White House had managed to continue contra aid by surreptitious means. As Iran-contra events began to be publicly exposed, it became increasingly clear that one of the fund-raising methods utilized by the contra backers was the illicit sale of surplus U.S. military equipment to our Iranian enemies, allegedly to bribe Iranian government officials to release the American hostages who had been held since the end of 1979.

As a lawyer and legal educator who had spent most of my professional life in activities designed to make public officials obey the law and the Constitution, I viewed Iran-contra as a classic challenge to the oft-repeated cliché that "ours is a government of laws." Was it in fact possible for our political system to deal with a lawless White House?

I wrote to Peter Rodino, who had been appointed a member of the joint congressional investigating committee, to inquire about a staff position. I also let it be known through friends with Capitol Hill contacts that I was willing to spend the summer in Washington working on issues related to Iran-contra. I finally got word through my colleague Arthur Kinoy that Congressman John Conyers Jr. was interested in talking to me. Conyers, who represented most of the city of Detroit, was not a member of the Iran-contra panel, but he was the chairman of the Criminal Justice Subcommittee of the House Judiciary Committee. I had never met Conyers, but I was well aware of him by reputation as the senior African American member of Congress, a founder of the Congressional Black Caucus, and one of the most outspokenly liberal members of the House. I also remembered him as a charismatic and articulate member of the Judiciary Committee when it had considered the articles of impeachment against Richard Nixon more than a decade before. After meeting with Conyers's chief of staff, Julian Epstein, I agreed to spend the summer working in Conyers's office focusing on issues related to public accountability and aspects of criminal and constitutional law implicated by Iran-contra.

For me, working in Conyers's office was like letting a kid loose in a candy store. Our political tastes ran along similar lines, and he was excited by the same issues that captured my attention. His political effectiveness tended to be diminished, however, by the same traits that made him such an eloquent spokesman for progressive social causes. Conyers was something of a loner who advocated bold and sweeping initiatives in a system that venerated collegiality and compromise. The legislative process works very slowly, and Conyers was somewhat short on patience.

*   *   *

As the formal congressional hearings into Iran-contra got under way in the summer of 1987, we set up our own independent operation to monitor the hearings and attempt to influence public response to them. In part, my job was to make Conyers, although not a member of the committee, a player in the process. More importantly, our aim was to try to put our own spin on the hearings and goad Congress into taking aggressive steps to make sure that the plotters were properly punished and, if necessary, to enact new legislation to prevent the recurrence of such behavior in the future.

Our efforts were necessitated in part by the fact that the formal investigation and hearing process being employed by the joint House-Senate Iran-contra committee had a built-in flaw that practically guaranteed failure. In an effort to make the process bipartisan, a single staff had been created by each house, with the minority Republicans allowed to choose some of the staff members. The consequence was that the investigation was constantly being undermined internally. It was as if a criminal defendant were allowed to place his own lawyers on the prosecution team. It was impossible for the investigators to shield their plans and strategy from their targets, and the majority faced constant obstruction from within. One result of this unwieldy process was that the committee capitulated to the Republicans' demand for a deadline for the completion of the hearings. Aided by this deadline, the White House was able to delay the delivery of key documents to the committee's investigators until the hearings were over and it was too late to recall witnesses and confront them with new information that cast doubt on their public testimony.

To facilitate our own agenda, I organized an ad hoc Advisory Committee on Government Accountability, composed of leaders of the public-interest community. Among a revolving group of participants were Ralph Nader; Morton Halperin of the ACLU; Marcus Raskin and Bob Borosage of the Institute for Policy Studies; Tom Blanton from the National Security Archives, a nonprofit group dedicated to openness in government; Nan Aron of the Alliance for Justice; Eleanor Smeal and Mollie Yard from NOW; Ann Zill, representing liberal philanthropist Stewart Mott; and occasional representatives from People for the American Way, the Center for Constitutional Rights, the Christic Institute, and the National Lawyers Guild. Occasionally, staff members from other congressional offices would also sit in.

Early on, we focused on two ideas: impeachment of key government figures involved, and new criminal legislation to promote accountability by executive branch personnel. Our first big debate was whether we should work for the impeachment of Ronald Reagan. It seemed certain that Reagan had been aware of and sanctioned at least the major elements of the plot and should be held principally accountable. Rep. Henry Gonzalez of Texas had already introduced a Reagan-impeachment resolution in the House, but opposition ran along two lines. First, Reagan was still highly popular in the country, and very few members of Congress would be willing to attack him personally. Second, the impeachment process was so unwieldy that a serious effort would tie up Congress until past the next presidential election.

There was general agreement, however, that we should make an effort to impeach some lesser officials in the Reagan administration, as well as try to reform the impeachment process through legislation that would make it a more viable tool for use against wrongdoing federal officers. The two officials most appropriate for impeachment, it was agreed, were Eliot Abrams, my onetime colleague in Senator Moynihan's office who served as assistant secretary of state for inter-American affairs, and Attorney General Edwin Meese.

The constitutional provision for impeachment is cryptic. Article II, Section 4 states: "The President, Vice President and all civil Officers of the United States shall be removed from office on Impeachment for, and Conviction of Treason, Bribery, or other high Crimes and Misdemeanors." Other provisions provide that it is up to the House to vote a bill of impeachment, after which a trial before the Senate requires a two-thirds vote for conviction and removal from office. It is generally assumed that the "civil officers" mentioned in Article 4 who are subject to impeachment are those who have been nominated by the president subject to confirmation by the Senate. On only a handful of occasions has it ever been invoked against anyone but a federal judge.

Abrams, who seemed to be universally despised by congressional Democrats and the entire public-interest community, was everyone's first choice for impeachment. He was a State Department official who had required Senate confirmation for his position. Meese was viewed as something of a buffoon, and Oliver North, the fanatical marine colonel who had been the key organizer of the Iran-contra plot, was not a federal "officer" subject to impeachment. It was clear that Abrams had deceived and misled Congress when he was questioned about the administration's efforts to provide aid to the Nicaraguan rebels. The animosity toward Abrams was fed by the obnoxious manner in which he attempted to publicly justify crassly illegal conduct in the name of a higher good—opposition to the communist menace. North had used the same justification in his televized appearance before the Iran-contra committee. In fact, it was clear that Abrams and North viewed their real enemy as the U.S. Congress.

Part of our objective was to prevent the White House and its congressional supporters from obfuscating the real issue in Iran-contra: the rule of law. The Republicans followed a two-pronged defense: (1) they had violated no laws, and (2) if they had, it was justified in the war against communism. The Conyers office would issued almost daily press releases pointing out the laws that had been violated in the process of illicitly selling U.S. weapons to the Iranians and then converting the proceeds for the use of the contras.

Oliver North and his co-conspirators seemed to take the position that what belonged to the U.S. government belonged to them to do with as they would. They saw nothing wrong with selling surplus U.S. missiles to Iran and putting the proceeds in Swiss bank accounts for transfer to the contras, with possibly some commissions for their middlemen taken out along the way. Of course, they had ignored the provisions of the Arms Export Control Act, which had clear provisions regulating the sale of weapons to foreign nations, as well as laws that unambiguously forbade the conversion and misappropriation of funds and property belonging to the United States.

The most extraordinary claim made by North and the White House was that the Boland amendment, which forbade direct or indirect assistance to the Nicaraguan contras by any intelligence agency, did not apply to the minions of Oliver North, who operated through the National Security Council, because the NSC was not an official *intelligence* agency. That contention defied not only rationality but also Reagan's Executive Order 12333, which provided that the NSC "shall act as the highest Executive Branch entity that provides review of, guidance for and direction to the conduct of all national foreign intelligence, counterintelligence, and special activities, and attendant policies and programs."

I do not intend to set forth a detailed history of Iran-contra or provide an exhaustive exegesis of the wrongdoings of the Reagan administration. For readers who care to pursue such inquiries, I highly recommend Theodore Draper's *A Very Thin Line: The Iran-Contra Affair*. Another comprehensive and damning indictment of the Iran-contra plotters and the ensuing White House cover-up is contained in the final report of special prosecutor Lawrence Walsh, a former federal judge whose tenacity and grit in the face of obstruction and ridicule by his former Republican colleagues represented an extraordinary profile in courage.

Walsh was also highly successful in the courts, securing convictions of or guilty pleas from many high-level Reagan administration officials, including North and Abrams. North's conviction was later overturned by an appellate court on the ground that it had been tainted by his immunized testimony before the congressional committee. One of the ironies of the entire affair is that, as a general counsel of the ACLU, I supported its efforts in behalf of North's appeal due to the violation of his right against self-incrimination. President Bush, of course, pardoned all the Iran-contra plotters before leaving office, thereby precluding a trial of Secretary of Defense Caspar Weinberger, which might have revealed the scope of Bush's own involvement in illegal activities.

* * *

As the public hearings continued, John Conyers, despite the skepticism of most of our advisory committee, became convinced that he wanted to move to impeach President Reagan. On July 27, we issued a press release entitled "Finger of Blame for Iran Arms Deal Now Points to Reagan." He asked me to draft an impeachment resolution and a "dear colleague" letter seeking cosponsors. A "dear colleague" is a time-honored method of communication between members of Congress who are soliciting support for a piece of legislation or other policy initiative. My files do not indicate whether the "dear colleague" was ever actually circulated, but I think not. I know that we never formally introduced the Reagan impeachment resolution.

Two things intervened. During the August congressional recess, members found their constituents largely divided over Iran-contra, and there was little support for an all-out assault on Ronald Reagan. Then a new threat to civil liberties and the Constitution appeared: the nomination of Robert Bork to the U.S. Supreme Court. After Labor Day, with little enthusiasm being displayed for a new impeachment battle, Conyers and the public-interest community turned their full attention to the Herculean task of keeping Bork off the Court.

18

Un-Borking the Supreme Court

I am absolutely convinced that if not for John Conyers, Robert Bork would be a justice of the U.S. Supreme Court. Bork was rejected because all but one southern Democrat voted against him, and the southern Democrats did that because of the extreme pressure they received from their African American constituents. That pressure, in turn, resulted from the intensive efforts of the Congressional Black Caucus, which were successful because of the leadership of John Conyers and his personal commitment to that campaign in the late summer and fall of 1987. John Conyers therefore deserves the eternal gratitude of every liberty-loving American. Make no mistake: the confirmation of Robert Bork would have transformed U.S. constitutional history—and not for the better.

In so stating, I do not mean to belittle the efforts of the Leadership Conference on Civil Rights and its constituent groups—particularly the Alliance for Justice and the ACLU—in mobilizing the Bork opposition. Their contributions were also crucial. But having been involved on a daily basis in that battle for nearly three months, I say without hesitation that without John Conyers, it would not have succeeded.

My notes indicate that it was August 11 when we held a meeting in Conyers's office with members of our public-interest advisory committee, which originally had been established to deal with Iran-contra matters. By this time, our participants were concerned about the long-term threat to democratic rights posed by Robert Bork. Bork, who had been appointed by Ronald Reagan several years earlier to the U.S. Court of Appeals for the District of Columbia, was the guru of the conservative legal movement. He had been carefully grooming himself for a quarter of a century to be the Radical Right's favorite for a Supreme Court appointment. He had paid his dues most spectacularly in 1973, when he was the only senior Justice Department official willing to do Richard Nixon's bidding and fire Watergate Special Prosecutor Archibald Cox rather than resign in what came to be identified in history as the "Saturday Night Massacre." In his first official comment on the Bork nomination, Conyers reviewed the events of the Saturday Night Massacre in a speech on the House

158

floor on August 3. After noting that those events had given rise to one of the articles of impeachment against Nixon, Conyers's statement concluded:

> At a time when the Nation celebrates its 200-year-old commitment to the Rule of Law, President Reagan wishes to place upon our highest court the man who executed one of the most arrogantly lawless acts in the Nation's history. To place this man among the ranks of the defenders of our Constitution is the equivalent of installing one of the foxes among the guardians of the chicken coop.

Bork was also an inveterate foe of all civil rights legislation. He seemed to consider the right to discriminate against others Americans' most important civil right. He actively opposed just about every major civil rights law enacted in the wake of the 1960s civil rights revolution, including the Voting Rights Act.

When our advisory committee came together, it was about a week and a half after the Leadership Conference, a coalition of labor and civil rights groups based in Washington, had begun to organize a stop-Bork campaign. In a wide-ranging discussion, there was strong feeling that the only way to stop Bork would be through a filibuster. Many thought that enough conservative southern Democrats would be willing to join the majority of Republican senators to provide the necessary fifty votes for confirmation. Some wanted to begin organizing the filibuster immediately. Ralph Nader was clearly of that view. However, a majority felt that it was premature, that we should first try to sway the southerners who held the balance of power—focusing initially on the senators from Florida, Arkansas, Alabama, and Louisiana.

My minutes of the meeting indicate that it was Ellie Smeal of the National Organization for Women (NOW) who first articulated the need for the Congressional Black Caucus (CBC), an organization of twenty-three African American House members, to assume a role as the "conscience of the Congress." The southern Democratic senators had to be reminded that every one of them owed their election to solid black support—not one had received more than 40 percent of the white vote in the last election. It was time to call in those chips. Since there were no black senators, we talked about designating John Conyers the "101st senator" for purposes of the Bork issue. John, who may have been thinking of someday running for the Senate and becoming the first African American member of that body since Ed Brooke of Massachusetts a decade before, liked the idea. Before our meeting broke up, Conyers had already made a call to the Democratic Senate whip, Alan Cranston of California, to set up a strategy meeting.

The following day, Conyers and I met with Ralph Neas, chair of the Leadership Conference, and Dick Conlon, executive director of the Democratic Study Group, an alliance of liberal House Democrats, to coordinate strategy. Among the items we discussed was arranging meetings between key senators and members of the CBC, along with leaders of the public-interest community. Meanwhile, Conyers was preparing to take the anti-Bork campaign to the home turf of the swing southerners. Conyers was on his way to New Orleans to address the Southern Christian Leadership Conference (SCLC), the organization founded by Martin Luther King Jr., to enlist its help in the anti-Bork movement. Neas provided Conyers with information packets prepared by the Leadership Conference for distribution to grassroots organizers.

Although the emphasis in the African American community was on Bork's opposition to civil rights, other campaign materials emphasized his consistent support for corporatist interests in disputes with unions, workers, and consumers. One theme was his opposition to the rights of "the lame, the blind, and the widowed." Everyone was basically agreed that although it was political pressure from black voters that would be needed to carry the day with most of the southerners, the senators would need to publicly justify their anti-Bork votes in terms that would be acceptable to broader constituencies.

Conyers returned from the SCLC meeting with his spirits buoyed by the reception he had received. He felt confident that the SCLC would help ignite an anti-Bork campaign in black communities throughout the South. He told me to alert his office staff to expect to work through the weekend on our anti-Bork activities. We had a number of projects in the fire aimed at spreading our message through the black media all over the country, and especially in the South. The staff had been gathering lists of African American newspapers and radio stations. We prepared a series of opinion pieces on Bork for distribution to the press. I began spending some of my own time calling newspaper editors directly to make sure that they had received the Conyers statement and trying to convince them to run it.

In addition, we had Conyers tape a series of sound bites for black radio. We made fifteen-, thirty-, and sixty-second tapes. We had voice couplers installed on the phones in Conyers's office so that we could feed his statements directly to equipment at the radio stations. Staff members would then call the newsrooms and ask if the stations were interested in an audio feed from Congressman Conyers, on behalf of the Congressional Black Caucus, on the Bork nomination. Most of them were interested. The voice of John Conyers began to be heard on black radio throughout the South explaining why Robert Bork was a threat to continued progress in the area of civil rights.

Meanwhile, Conyers began to make the rounds of key senators, starting with Hal Heflin of Alabama and Bennett Johnston of Louisiana, both of whom exercised strong influence over the other southern Democrats. We felt that if we could get Heflin and Johnston on our side, we'd be halfway home.

* * *

At the same time, I was laboring mightily on my own to get the ACLU to join the anti-Bork movement. Immediately upon his nomination by Reagan, I had sent a memo to all members of the ACLU's national board explaining why Bork's appointment would be a disaster for civil liberties and calling for a special board meeting in August to decide what to do. The next regularly scheduled meeting wasn't until October, when it would be too late to have any impact on the nomination.

Opposition to nominees for public office is a ticklish issue for the ACLU, which throughout its existence has prided itself on its nonpartisanship. The ACLU's only prior involvement had been its unsuccessful opposition to the nomination of William Rehnquist, which had been pushed through by my colleagues and I in the board's "activist" wing. And many leading board members, including president Norman Dorsen, thought that opposing Rehnquist had been a terrible mistake that should never be repeated. I knew that I would run into strong opposition to my proposal to take a stand on Bork. My memo to the national board calling for a special meeting to change our policy to permit us to lobby against the Bork nomination focused on the threat Bork posed to abortion rights and argued as follows:

> The constitutional right of reproductive freedom, for which ACLU is probably more responsible than any other agency in our land, is now in dire peril; yet we are disabled by our own rules from doing anything about it. . . . If this were a legislative battle to amend the Constitution to overrule *Roe v. Wade*, we would be in the thick of it. But [ACLU] Policy 519 says that if the President nominates one person who can accomplish that same result, ACLU must stand on the sidelines and let it happen—even though ACLU's willingness to participate in a confirmation fight might well be crucial to its outcome. . . .

> Can we really afford to sit back and watch Ronald Reagan scuttle the right of reproductive freedom (and affirmative action) and do nothing—in the name of nonpartisanship? We are extremely partisan toward the Constitution; it is our fundamental reason for existence. But for a long time to come, we will be playing the game of constitutional protection blindfolded and with both hands tied if the Reaganites get to stack the umpire crew. . . .

> I do not undertake this campaign lightly. I realize there are many in the organization who sincerely believe that Policy 519 is crucial to the credibility of our organization. I respect their viewpoint; but I believe they are wrong and unwittingly undermine everything else we stand for.

The ACLU executive committee accepted my proposal and scheduled a special meeting of the national board on the weekend of August 29 and 30.

After a heated debate, the board voted to revise Policy 519, recognize the unique role performed by the U.S. Supreme Court in interpreting the Constitution, and authorize opposition to any Supreme Court nominee "whose record demonstrates a judicial philosophy that would fundamentally jeopardize the Supreme Court's critical and unique role in protecting civil liberties." Although the vote on adoption of the new policy was relatively close, once the policy was accepted, the board voted almost unanimously that Bork fit the newly established criteria and that the ACLU would oppose his confirmation. Since the ACLU has one of the most effective nonprofit lobbying operations in Washington, its contribution to the anti-Bork effort over the next several months was significant.

* * *

The anti-Bork campaign picked up momentum after Labor Day. Conyers devoted the bulk of his efforts to it throughout September. He divided his time between trips south to meet with local black leaders and address anti-Bork rallies and trips across the Capitol to meet with undecided senators and try to sway their votes. The formal hearings before the Senate Judiciary Committee began in mid-September. Bork turned out to be one of his own worst enemies. In his efforts to defend his narrow and restrictive views about personal privacy and other individual rights under the Constitution, he convinced more and more Americans that he was not a man they wanted on their court of last resort. In addition, his demeanor in the nationally televised hearing came across as arrogant and elitist. Opinion polls began to reflect declining public support. He was making it easier for undecided senators to join the opposition.

On September 29, Conyers testified on behalf of the Black Caucus to formally explain the reasons for its opposition to Bork. His testimony emphasized Bork's opposition to every expansion of black Americans' right to participate in the political process through the courts and Congress. And he explained that it was those laws and judicial decisions that had made it possible for there to be a Congressional Black Caucus. "If Robert Bork had had his way, none of these decisions would have occurred and there would be no Black Caucus," he asserted. "And it is likely I would not be here today as a senior member of the House of Representatives." Conyers's statement, which I had drafted, concluded:

Judge Bork's public career has spanned the period in which our society has made its greatest strides in extending the premise of equal justice to all its citizens and eliminating many of the vestiges of a polarized past. Many Americans played heroic roles in this historic forward movement toward an integrated society. Millions of others who were once skeptical of the civil rights movement have now come to terms with it and endorsed its objectives. During this entire period, Robert Bork has been in effect an active heckler along every step of the forward march toward civil rights. And, from all that appears on the public record, he remains so to this day....

In a way, this debate is as much about ourselves as it is about Judge Bork. Not only is he being tested, but we are as well. Hopefully, we, not he, will point the way to our country's future. At a time when we pride ourselves on the advances brought about by the civil rights movement, his confirmation would represent a major step backward and would polarize and divide Americans as his nomination has already started to do.

We reproduced Conyers's testimony and distributed it widely. There were special mailings to key black community leaders, including ministers and college presidents. Eloquent testimony had also been delivered by three other prominent African Americans: Andy Young, former ambassador to the United Nations; Barbara Jordan, the highly respected former member of Congress; and William Coleman, a Republican who had been secretary of transportation in Gerald Ford's administration.

One by one, key senators, including more and more southern Democrats, began making public announcements that they intended to vote against Bork. Johnston of Louisiana was one of the first, and he began to round up support from his colleagues. The papers reported that Bork could not gain a favorable vote from the Judiciary Committee. My notes for October 2 reflect, "Bork stampede starting." On October 5, I noted, "Nomination appears dead." Strangely, Senator Heflin was still being noncommittal. But it turned out that we really didn't need him. By the time he finally came on board, there were more than fifty senators on record in opposition. By October 9, the press had declared that the Bork nomination was dead. Many were publicly urging Bork to withdraw his name rather than be embarrassed by a negative Senate vote. Bork issued a statement refusing to withdraw and demanding a full Senate vote in the face of almost certain defeat. That vote on October 23 was an anticlimax. It was fifty-eight to forty-two against confirmation. The only two Democrats to vote for confirmation were Fritz Hollings of South Carolina and David Boren of Oklahoma. Six Republicans voted against.

It had been a remarkable two and a half months. It was one of the most extraordinary accomplishments of the public-interest community in the entire decade of the 1980s.

19

Tales of the National Security State

Iran-contra is history. The final report of the congressional investigation had something for everyone. As stated in John Conyers's first public reaction to that report: "Despite its restrained tone, the Select Committee report on the Iran-Contra Affair sets forth a chronicle of official lawlessness that is probably unprecedented in our nation's history." The truth is that the good guys won the rhetoric, but the Republicans won the bottom line. For those who actually sat down and read the narrative, it was clear that the report set forth a pattern of conduct emanating from Ronald Reagan's White House that was even more lawless and reprehensible than the Watergate episode, which had led to Richard Nixon's resignation. But in its operative detail, the Iran-contra report recommended only mild prophylactic actions to prevent future abuses. As a result, it left the public totally confused.

Iran-contra was an example of the excesses of a national security state that had grown out of control during the Cold War era. The threat of Soviet communism was used as an excuse for all manner of antidemocratic foreign policy initiatives, which were immediately stamped "classified" to prevent disclosure to the American public. On the home front, the guardians of the Free World, operating through the FBI, CIA, military intelligence, and the rest of a far-flung surveillance network, kept close watch on suspected critics—labeled "subversives"—and did their best to exclude them from federal employment through obnoxious loyalty oaths and obsessive personnel screening programs.

From the fall of 1987 through the spring of 1992, I continued to explore such issues as a part-time consultant to John Conyers and the House Government Operations Committee, which he chaired beginning in 1989. During the academic year, I would put in an average of one day a week in Washington, and during summer breaks, I spent most of my time on Capitol Hill. I purchased a small condo in a building at DuPont Circle, which was cheaper and more convenient than staying in hotels. As interest in Iran-contra waned, we kept agitating for enforcement of the rule of law against freewheeling executive

164

branch officers. For the next several congresses, Conyers introduced the Official Accountability Act, which would have provided specific criminal penalties for government officials who committed "national security offenses." We modeled it on a bill that had originally been introduced in the mid-1970s following Watergate and related revelations of government wrongdoing. Mark Raskin of the Institute for Policy Studies, who had helped draft the original bill a decade earlier, and Mort Halperin of the ACLU were particularly helpful in the redrafting.

The operative section of the proposed legislation provided that "no person subject to this chapter shall order or engage in the planning of, preparation for, initiation or conduct of any intelligence activity which violates any statute or executive order in force." It further provided that it was no defense that the accused was acting "pursuant to an order of his government or superior . . . unless he did not know and could not reasonably have been expected to know that the act ordered was unlawful." In other words, the bill would have abolished the "Eichmann defense" of "I was only carrying out orders." To me, the bill embodied a rational and reasonable principle for a system that proclaimed itself a government of laws. But most people in Washington considered it revolutionary and naively idealistic.

The proposal continues to languish in the congressional archives. Conyers held one extremely enlightening hearing on H.R. 3665 before the House Subcommittee on Criminal Justice on June 15, 1988, the proceedings of which were transcribed in a Government Printing Office document listed as Serial No. 147 of the Second Session of the 100th Congress. In addition to supporting testimony from a number of constitutional and international law scholars, the hearing record includes a letter from a former director of the CIA, Stansfield Turner, who wrote:

> I certainly agree with you that officials of our government cannot be above the law and should be held criminally accountable if they fail to conform with law. It is only a shame that we appear to need a bill like this one because of the flagrant disregard of law in recent years. I think your bill is particularly necessary today because of the recent willingness of high executive branch officials to condone acts of their subordinates which transgress the spirit, if not the letter of the law.

Strangely enough, Turner's views were not widely shared in Washington.

*   *   *

Through the end of the Bush administration, I worked on a variety of other issues that were remnants of the Cold War era. In their Iran-contra wheeling and dealing, the president's operatives had lied and cheated and concealed the public's business from both the public and Congress, all in the name of "national security." But Iran-contra was only the tip of an iceberg that I spent most of my time in Washington chipping away at. As consultant to the Government Operations Subcommittee on Legislation and National Security, I dealt with issues involving excessive government secrecy and the withholding of information from Congress and the public, including press censorship during military actions, protection of federal whistle-blowers who were being punished for exposing waste and corruption, surveillance of political activists by the FBI and other intelligence agencies, and intrusive investigations into the private lives of employees who held so-called sensitive positions in the federal government or private industry.

One of the few matters on which we actually achieved some tangible success was the government personnel security system. Even before I began working for Conyers, I had been consulted by federal employees who found the government's security questionnaire unnecessarily intrusive. Standard Form 86, which had to be completed by all employees in so-called sensitive positions, required job applicants and employees up for periodic review to provide—in addition to traditional information about employment and residential history—detailed information about organizations to which they belonged; foreign travel; medical histories, including treatment for any "mental condition"; past use of drugs and alcohol; and the financial affairs of themselves and their spouses. Such intrusiveness might have been justifiable if it were limited to employees with access to highly classified information. In fact, an overwhelming number of federal employees with absolutely no access to classified information were designated "sensitive." The original federal workers who had consulted me were lawyers employed by the National Labor Relations Board who were concerned about the consequences of revealing their past use of marijuana, as required by SF 86. They also objected to the fact that they were required to sign a blanket waiver of any right to redress if the information they were required to supply to their employer was misused in any way.

SF 86 was administered by the Office of Personnel Management (OPM; formerly the Civil Service Commission), which was under the direction of a career civil servant, an African American woman named Constance Berry Newman. Just how Ms. Newman had achieved a position of some power and influence in the Bush administration was something of a mystery to me, but it was clear from the first moment that she walked into John Conyers's office at our invitation that she was something of an anomaly. First of all, she came alone. I had never before seen the head of an executive department come to a meeting on Capitol Hill without an entourage. We had set out in advance some of our objections to SF 86, and no sooner had she sat down than she told the chairman that she shared most of his concerns. She also made it clear that she had limited influence within the Bush administration and would require pressure from Congress to bring about any significant changes.

My subcommittee colleague Amit Pandya and I pursued a two-pronged strategy. We organized a hearing to allow advocates of change—consisting primarily of government employee associations—to make their case for reform by setting out the personal hardship and embarrassment their members had suffered as a result of intrusive background investigations. In addition, we conducted an extensive survey of federal agencies to determine the scope of the use of "sensitive" classifications and the need for such detailed personal information by the various departments. Armed with the survey results, we drafted a committee report called "Federal Employee Privacy Rights and Standard Form 86." To my pleasant surprise, the report was adopted by the full Government Operations Committee on September 26, 1990, with only minor and insubstantial amendments.

The report's major recommendation was that the OPM should revise its personnel manual to state that the only federal jobs that should be designated as "sensitive" were those "directly concerned with the protection of the Nation from foreign aggression and not those which contribute to the strength of the Nation only through their impact on the general welfare." The committee even went along, without dissent, with the staff's recommendation that the OPM cease asking employees about the use of illegal substances until it sought and received congressional authorization to provide immunity from prosecution for any employee who made incriminatory admissions.

Shortly after the committee's action, the OPM announced a substantial revision of its personnel security system that implemented many of the recommendations contained in our report. However, I was unsuccessful in clarifying the scope of the background investigation carried out by OPM's investigators beyond the information sought on the employment questionnaire. For example, although the questionnaire did not inquire about sexual orientation, and even questions about association memberships had been dropped from the revised form, we occasionally received complaints that investigators were inquiring about employees' sexual habits. The chairman had wanted such gratuitous snooping stopped.

* * *

It is said that doctors bury their mistakes. The intelligence agencies classify theirs. Secrecy has been an obsession within the executive branch since the start of the Cold War. And even with the collapse of the Soviet Union, the national security bureaucracy resisted weaning. In response to increasing public criticism of its continued passion for secrecy after the end of the Cold War, the Bush administration announced that it was rethinking the security classification system and was prepared to declassify millions of documents. Even the CIA proudly announced that it had convened an "openness task force."

Conyers conducted a hearing in the spring of 1992 and invited a number of administration spokespeople to testify about plans for revising the security system. When he asked the CIA representative for a copy of the report of the openness task force, he was told that it was "classified."

The star witness at that hearing was Theodore Postol, a physics professor from the Massachusetts Institute of Technology who had formerly been a weapons adviser to the Pentagon. Postol had published in a Harvard University journal a study of the effectiveness of the Patriot missiles during the Persian Gulf War. Contrary to the army's extravagant claims about the accuracy of the Patriots in destroying Iraqi Scuds, the professor concluded that very few of the missiles had hit their targets. Several months later, he was informed by the Department of Defense that his published findings had been classified and that he could no longer talk about them publicly. Following the hearing, the government acted to revoke Professor Postol's security clearance but relented under pressure from Conyers.

*   *   *

The Postol incident was symptomatic of the executive branch's method of dealing with both failure and criticism. The censors always claimed that they were protecting sensitive information from our nation's enemies. Usually, they were protecting only their own asses. Invariably, the concealed information was well known to our foreign adversaries. Only the American people were kept in the dark.

One of the greatest shocks to me was the discovery that the White House administered an entire body of secret law kept concealed even from Congress. These secret laws were embodied in a series of national security directives whose designations changed slightly from administration to administration but whose importance had been growing ever since the Kennedy administration. The NSDDs (National Security Decision Directives), as they were known during the Reagan and Bush administrations, were supposed to involve only foreign intelligence operations, but they sometimes influenced significant domestic policies. Although they appeared to be serially numbered, there was no official record of these directives.

Iran-contra began, it was belatedly revealed, with an NSDD issued by President Reagan in an apparent attempt to evade the Boland amendment's prohibitions on aid to the contras. I was unable to discover exactly how many NSDDs Reagan had signed, but it is known that the first Reagan directive was numbered 1 and that number 298 was issued before the end of his administration. Only a handful of the directives had been declassified. The National Security Council (NSC), which oversaw their issuance and implementation, would permit chairs of congressional committees (who happened to learn of a directive's existence), upon request, to read directives dealing with matters within their committees' jurisdiction. However, the member was not permitted to make notes for aides, who were generally more knowledgeable than the member about the particular subject.

We tried unsuccessfully for two years after the Iraqi invasion of Kuwait to determine whether there had been an NSDD issued by President Bush encouraging Saddam Hussein's Persian Gulf objectives. It subsequently turned out that there was. But we could not get the NSC to even confirm or deny the existence of an NSDD dealing with Persian Gulf policy, let alone discover its contents.

Conyers had me prepare a bill that we entitled the "Presidential Directives and Record Accountability Act." The bill would have permitted the executive branch to continue to classify its directives but would have provided for their sequential numbering and the submission of copies to the office of the *Federal Register*, the Speaker of the House, and the president pro tem of the Senate. At least this would have provided a paper trail and a historical record, in addition to a guarantee that someone in Congress was made aware of a directive's existence. The NSC was adamantly opposed to our bill and claimed that it would interfere with the president's constitutional prerogatives. I was still attempting to arrange hearings on the bill when my consulting contract expired in April 1992. My contract could not be renewed because of a combination of factors exacerbated by congressional gridlock in a presidential election year and an obsession with budget cutting in every area, including congressional administration.

*   *   *

The passion for concealment reached such lengths that the Reagan administration required government personnel to sign a variety of secrecy agreements. Some officials were required to execute "lifetime" agreements to submit for censorship and approval any writings or speeches dealing with anything they had worked on during their government service. Shockingly, the U.S. Supreme Court upheld the constitutionality and enforceability of such coerced contracts to conceal the public's business from the public. In addition, some two million lower-level federal employees were required to sign agreements that they would never disclose any confidential information without the prior approval of their superiors. That meant that if they wanted to expose fraud and waste in a government program to a congressional committee, they had to get permission from the superior they were attempting to expose. Indeed, the agreements went so far as to prohibit the disclosure of "classifiable"—in addition to classified—information, putting federal employees at risk for revealing information they had no way of knowing was confidential.

These secrecy agreements were originally imposed in one of Reagan's secret NSDDs, but when Congress found out about it, it attempted to regulate them by legislation. That launched a tug-of-war between Congress and the White House that continued throughout the Reagan and Bush administrations. The White House and Justice Department challenged Congress's authority to control presidential initiatives in the area of information security, but congressional leaders were reluctant to let the issue be decided by the federal courts, which Reagan and Bush had filled with neomonarchists who consistently sided with the President in such interbranch disputes.

In the fall of 1989, President Bush signed an appropriations bill enacted by Congress that included a provision restricting the use of secrecy agreements. However, the president issued a statement questioning the constitutionality of the restriction and indicated that he would not abide by it. This set up a stunning confrontation with Congress. Conyers issued a press statement challenging the authority of the president to enforce only those laws with which he agreed and called Steven Garfinkel, the director of the president's Information Security Oversight Office (the administrator of the secrecy agreements), to testify before the Government Operations Committee.

The hearing was scheduled for December 20, 1989. Since most of Congress was shut down for the Christmas holiday, we figured that we would have the entire Washington press corps to ourselves. The media exhibited great interest in the issue, and all the television networks had called in advance to arrange to cover this classic confrontation between Congress and the president. It looked like this would be the public confrontation we had been hoping for and would give us a chance to challenge the administration's secrecy policy in the court of public opinion.

I awoke that morning to discover that President Bush had ordered the invasion of Panama the night before. It was a great hearing, but like the tree that fell in the forest, there was practically no one around to hear about it. In the middle of the hearing, Conyers got so disgusted with Garfinkel's refusal to provide information that he just got up and walked out of the hearing room, not to return. Sitting at the congressional rostrum, I was suddenly reminded of the occasion some thirty-five years before when a congressional committee had walked out on me en masse because I refused to answer whether I was a "Communist." Of course, on that occasion, I was a defenseless twenty-three-year-old who had come to express my views, not a representative of the White House summoned to report to Congress on the country's business.

*　*　*

One of the most pleasurable aspects of my work for the subcommittee was that I got to harass the FBI a bit. As it used to watch over me, I made it part of my job to watch over the FBI. John Conyers had long shared my antipathy for the FBI's surveillance of political activists. As a member of the Judiciary Committee, he had been a consistent thorn in its side. He was glad to bring some of that oversight into the Government Operations Committee, where we worked in tandem with Rep. Don Edwards's Judiciary Subcommittee on Civil and Constitutional Rights. Edwards was a former FBI agent who also happened to have great regard for the First Amendment and freedom of speech and association.

As a result, I worked closely with the Edwards subcommittee's chief counsel, Jim Dempsey, in an ongoing quest to keep the FBI out of the political process. The two major issues that arose during my tenure were the CISPES investigation and the Library Awareness Program. The latter had to do with the FBI's efforts to enlist librarians across the country in a program to keep tabs on persons with foreign-sounding names and accents who showed special interest in scientific and technical information publicly displayed on their shelves. The librarians were outraged but also frightened that refusal to cooperate would somehow get them placed on the FBI's "shit list." Under pressure from Edwards and Conyers, the FBI backed off and said that it didn't really mean it.

The CISPES investigation was a bigger story. The Committee in Solidarity with the People of El Salvador was one of many groups that opposed U.S. assistance to the autocratic El Salvadoran government in its battle with left-wing guerrillas. Based on unreliable reports of one witness who had infiltrated a CISPES chapter in the Southwest, the FBI decided that CISPES was involved in subversive activities throughout the country, and it launched a campaign to surveil and undermine the activities of its far-flung chapters. It compiled dossiers on thousands of individuals who were merely exercising their constitutional right to protest U.S. policy in Central America. While Conyers and Edwards were hounding the FBI over the CISPES investigation, the Center for Constitutional Rights had brought a lawsuit on behalf of CISPES and its members. Under this two-pronged assault, the FBI finally conceded that it had erred and that most of the CISPES activists were doing nothing more than exercising their rights of political protest.

Trying to stop the FBI from engaging in political surveillance can only be compared to cleaning out the Augean stables. It seems to be a never-ending task. Each time the FBI is caught doing something it should't be, it says that it will stop, but there's always a next time. In the mid-1970s, Congress included a provision in the Privacy Act prohibiting the collection or maintenance of information describing how individuals exercised rights protected by the First Amendment. But at last look, the FBI still maintained millions of such files. For several sessions of Congress, Edwards and Conyers introduced the First Amendment Protection Act, which would have done what the Privacy Act failed to accomplish and make it illegal for the FBI or other agencies to gather information on political activists without cause to believe that they had committed or were planning illegal acts. However, I must admit that increasing concern about terrorist conspiracies by fanatics with an ideological cause makes it difficult to engender significant public support for such legislation. Ironically, such proposals now seem to have the support of militant right-wingers who used to applaud government surveillance policies when they were aimed only at left-wing activists.

*   *   *

Although John Conyers never got to impeach any Reagan administration officials for their Iran-contra wrongdoing, he played a substantial role in another impeachment proceeding—that of U.S. District Court Judge Alcee Hastings. In a bizarre twist, Conyers came out in that matter as the hero of his usual adversaries, the FBI and Department of Justice. Since there was a special impeachment staff appointed by the Judiciary Committee, I had only peripheral involvement in those proceedings, providing advice and counsel when Conyers requested it. But I at least had a front-row seat for one of the most unusual and interesting events of the 100th Congress.

The Hastings impeachment, which had been recommended by the Judicial Conference of the United States pursuant to statute, was a politically and racially sensitive matter. Hastings, a civil rights lawyer appointed to the federal bench by Jimmy Carter, was the first African American judge ever to sit on the federal bench in Florida. Outspoken and flamboyant, he clearly did not fit the picture of southern WASP gentility normally associated with the federal judiciary in the Deep South. He had been accused and acquitted by a jury of conspiracy to solicit a bribe from a criminal defendant who was up for sentencing in his court. The bribe scenario was an FBI fabrication. The only difference from Abscam was that another career criminal had allegedly informed the local U.S. attorney's office that Hastings was on the take. The FBI proceeded to test that allegation by setting up an elaborate bribe scheme that involved Hastings's alleged "bag man," a close personal friend named William Borders.

As the scheme unfolded, Borders did agree to accept $50,000, in exchange for which Hastings was supposed to deliver a light sentence for the defendant. Hastings claimed that Borders had been trading on their friendship without his knowledge. Borders was convicted of the conspiracy charge, but Hastings, whose trial had been severed, was acquitted. At that point, several of Hastings's colleagues brought a charge before the federal judicial council, which led to the impeachment recommendation following a lengthy investigation. Among other things, Hastings was accused of perjuring himself at his own trial. His accusers said that it would be indecent to allow him to remain a federal judge.

Never before had a judge been impeached after being acquitted of the misconduct forming the basis of the impeachment, and African Americans felt that Judge Hastings was being treated discriminatorily because of his race. Among the Congressional Black Caucus, feeling was strong that had Hastings been white, he would never have been targeted for a bribe offer in the first place, and that after acquittal, he would certainly have been left alone. I am inclined to think that both of those claims were true. But if Hastings really had been in the business of soliciting bribes, it was unthinkable to allow him to remain on the federal bench.

Because of the sensitivity of the issue, Chairman Rodino asked Conyers, the senior black member of Congress, to chair a special committee to consider the impeachment resolution. I think that Conyers's initial view was that Hastings was a victim of racial bias and that he had to accept the task in order to protect Hastings. However, as the hearing unfolded, it became increasingly clear that Conyers's faith in Hastings was eroding. The circumstantial evidence against him was quite compelling. It was clear that Hastings and Borders were deeply involved in some kind of personal maneuvering, and the prosecution's claims provided the most likely explanation. Why else, for example, would a federal judge leave his office and use a pay telephone in the corridor to call his good buddy? That was only one piece in a complex mosaic constructed by the Department of Justice to demonstrate Hastings's culpability.

There was, however, one gigantic flaw in the case against Hastings. None of the money received by Borders was ever passed to him. The FBI had arrested Borders as he was allegedly on his way to meet Hastings. At best, the FBI's behavior was grossly incompetent. At worst, it was part of a deliberate scheme to frame Hastings. If the FBI was concerned that Borders might have been acting on his own but wanted to ensnare Hastings anyway, it would have acted in precisely the manner it did. If competent law enforcers truly wanted to make sure that Hastings was in on the deal, they would have waited until Borders arrived at his destination and shared the payoff with the judge.

Conyers was clearly undecided up to the end of the hearing before his special panel. But as the hearing neared a conclusion, he found that the circumstantial evidence was overwhelming, despite the FBI's mishandling. He began to make it clear in conversations that if Hastings wanted to rebut the government's case, he would have to testify in his own defense and explain away his incriminating behavior. Hastings declined to testify.

After further wrestling with his conscience, Conyers came down on the side of guilt, and the panel voted unanimously to impeach. As a result, he became an instant hero to the Democratic leadership, which no longer had to fear a black backlash. Indeed, since John Conyers had provided his stamp of approval, the Congressional Black Caucus voted unanimously for impeachment. I ran into Peter Rodino at Newark airport a day or so after the impeachment vote, and he commented to me, "John sure did himself a lot of good with that Hastings decision." A sentence that I had suggested for Conyers's public statement was even designated "quote of the week" by the *New York Times*. After reciting the way that southern courts had once been stacked against black people before the civil rights revolution, the statement continued: "We did not fight the civil rights revolution in order to replace one form of judicial corruption with another."

It was the next year before the House's impeachment resolution was acted on by the Senate, where a twelve-member committee was appointed to hear the evidence. Hastings testified at the Senate trial, and he came close to winning acquittal again. On most of the eighteen counts of impeachment, the Senate panel split seven to five for conviction. In the full Senate, most of the counts barely received the two-thirds vote necessary for conviction. Indeed, Hastings's lawyers spent the next several years trying unsuccessfully to overturn the impeachment in the courts on the grounds that the Constitution requires the full Senate, not a panel of twelve, to hear all the evidence and that at least it requires the senators who sat as the "jury" to convict by a two-thirds vote.

In one of the most bizarre twists in U.S. history, Alcee Hastings, after being removed from the federal bench, got himself elected as a member of the Congress that had impeached him. That was possible only because, for inexplicable reasons, the resolution of impeachment failed to include a provision that Hastings should henceforth be disqualified "to hold and enjoy any office of honor, Trust or Profit under the United States." Article I, Section 3 of the Constitution permits a judgment of conviction to include such a disqualification but does not require it. So impeached judge Alcee Hastings is now the distinguished gentleman from Florida.

20

How I Got Blamed for the "October Surprise" Investigation

On July 26, 1991, the right-wing *Washington Times*, the daily newspaper dominated by the Rev. Sun Myung Moon's Unification Church, had a front-page exposé of me under the headline "Hill Democrats Hid 'October Surprise' Probe." The lead paragraph stated:

> Key Democrats have been secretly investigating the so-called "October Surprise" scheme for at least 18 months, more than a year before their own party leaders made known their interest in such a probe.

The Moonie ravings went on to explain in revelatory prose that some nefarious Democrats had secretly commissioned the General Accounting Office, Congress's investigative arm, to examine allegations that the 1980 Reagan-Bush campaign had made a secret deal with Iranian leaders to delay the release of the fifty-two American hostages until after the 1980 presidential election. The story went on to explain:

> The probe was run by Julian Epstein and Spencer Oliver, staff directors of the House Government Operations and Foreign Affairs Committees, respectively, and Frank Askin, a $252-a-day consultant from Rutgers University who specializes in constitutional law.

I found the most embarrassing part of that story the revelation that I was working for Congress for $252 a day, less than most first-rate lawyers make in an hour. (Of course, the story did not explain that my congressional duties were a labor of love.)

Several months later, the story escalated. As the independent biweekly Capitol Hill newspaper *Roll Call* reported, the Republican minority on the House Rules Committee failed in an effort to subpoena me to testify on a resolution authorizing a formal investigation of the so-called October Surprise allegations. The Republicans on the Rules Committee explained that they wanted to get to the bottom of efforts to falsely accuse the Reagan and Bush administrations of having attained office by immoral—and indeed criminal—means.

They wanted to prove that the purpose of an October Surprise investigation was to hurt President Bush's reelection chances. In one sense, I suppose they were right. I wasn't trying to smear anyone with false charges, but I had little doubt that back in 1980 the Republicans had been playing footsie with the Iranians to convince them that they'd be better off if they held the hostages until after the election and dealt with a new Reagan administration. And I would have been quite happy if we could have proved that to the satisfaction of the American voters prior to the 1988 election.

As I watched on C-SPAN, I was totally frustrated when Rules Committee minority leader Rep. Gerald Solomon looked out over the committee's hearing room and demanded, "Is Frank Askin in the room?" I would have liked nothing better than to testify but had been forbidden to do so by the Democratic congressional leadership on the grounds that it would set a bad precedent to allow the Republicans to subpoena a committee staffer to testify at a formal hearing. The Republicans had ignored John Conyers's offer to have me meet with them privately.

Let me now try to set the record straight about how I came to be in the middle of what remains one of the most explosive and, to my mind, still unresolved episodes of recent political history.

*　　*　　*

The "October" in the October Surprise refers to the month before the 1980 presidential election in which Ronald Reagan was attempting to unseat Jimmy Carter. The "Surprise" refers to the fear rampant among Reagan-Bush campaign honchos that Carter would work a last-minute deal with Iran to free the American hostages and create a feeling of euphoria among the electorate that would sweep Carter back into office. Put together, the October Surprise refers to a theory that the Reagan-Bush campaign had managed to sabotage the Carter administration's efforts to free the hostages by making its own bargain with Iranian leaders to hold the hostages until after the election in exchange for a promise of military assistance from the new Reagan administration.

I first heard of the October Surprise scenario in a column by Flora Lewis in the New York Times on August 3, 1987, when I was working in John Conyers's office. Lewis related an interview with Abol Hassan Bani Sadr, the first prime minister of Iran after the overthrow of the shah. Bani Sadr claimed that his political foes had undermined his efforts to release the hostages to the Carter administration and had secretly met with representatives of the Reagan-Bush campaign to arrange a deal to delay their release until after the election. Of course, it is official history that the Ayatollah Khomeini's government actually sent the hostages flying home at the very moment that Ronald Reagan took the oath as president on January 20, 1981.

I pointed the column out to Conyers and commented that if it were true, it meant that top officials in the Reagan campaign—if not the president and vice president themselves—were guilty of something akin to treason. How could American politicians justify contriving with a foreign enemy to extend the internment of Americans to further their own political ambitions? It would, at least, constitute a violation of the Logan Act, which made it a crime for private citizens to negotiate privately with foreign governments, and it might provide an interesting focus for hearings by Conyers's Criminal Justice Sub-committee. Conyers expressed interest, mentioned that he knew Flora Lewis personally, and suggested that I call her for additional information.

When I reached Lewis in Paris, she expressed her belief in the substance of Bani Sadr's allegations and said that she thought the story was "dynamite." She had tried to convince her editors at the *Times* to assign some investigative reporters to the matter, but the *Times* appeared to be uninterested. She mentioned that two high officials in the Reagan-Bush campaign who later held high posts in the administration, Robert McFarlane and Richard Allen, had admitted meeting with a self-styled Iranian emissary in a Washington hotel lobby in September 1980 but denied that anything of substance had come of that meeting. They also said that they could not recall their visitor's name. She warned me that I would need subpoena power to get anywhere. I knew that there was no chance of getting a House committee to authorize subpoenas in connection with such a politically sensitive subject, but I decided to do a bit of investigating on my own.

I was aware that there had been a congressional report issued in the early 1980s about something referred to as "Debategate," which had made reference to a so-called October Surprise. Debategate involved the theft of President Carter's briefing book from the White House prior to one of his televised debates with Ronald Reagan. The Carter book had then been used to prep Reagan for the debate. The investigation had been carried out by a subcommittee of the House Committee on Post Office and Civil Service chaired by former Rep. Don Albosta.

The Albosta committee concluded that the theft of the briefing book had probably been accomplished by a Reagan campaign committee known as the "October Surprise Group." The group had been established to monitor the efforts of the White House to negotiate the release of the American hostages, who had been in captivity since the previous December. The report pictured the Reagan-Bush campaign officials as being obsessed with the hostage issue since their pollster Richard Wirthlin had advised them that the hostages' release just before the election would greatly enhance Carter's popularity and probably result in his reelection.

The October Surprise Group, which included most of the Republican campaign's top brass, met almost daily during the last several months of the 1980 campaign to receive reports from moles within the White House and the military commands. They wanted to be sure that they would have as much advance warning as possible about any impending hostage deal. The Republicans debated various ways of negating a Carter coup should his negotiations succeed. The issue not considered by the Albosta committee was whether the October Surprise Group might have advanced beyond a mere spy system into a proactive effort to sabotage the Carter negotiations and even engage in independent negotiations with Iran to prevent the release of the hostages. The theft of Carter's briefing book had been a by-product of the work of the White House moles. At least a few people I spoke to considered Donald Gregg, a National Security Council staffer assigned to the Carter White House (who became Vice President Bush's national security adviser), the most likely suspect.

I decided to question the individuals who had worked on the hostage negotiations on behalf of the Carter White House to determine what they thought about Bani Sadr's allegations. I spoke directly to three of the major players: Warren Christopher, Carter's chief hostage negotiator, who subsequently became secretary of state in the Clinton administration; Harold Saunders, Jimmy Carter's undersecretary of state for Middle Eastern affairs; and Gary Sick, who had been a political analyst on the staff of the National Security Council. All of them expressed great skepticism about Bani Sadr's claims, but none absolutely ruled out the possibility.

The general feeling was that the Iranian government was in such a chaotic state that there would have been no one for the Republicans to negotiate with. Christopher told me that the White House could barely determine who had authority to negotiate a deal. "The problem was, nobody could really speak for the Ayatollah Khomeini, although there were lots of entrepreneurs running around claiming they could free the hostages," he said. According to Christopher, the Iranians seemed to lose interest in the negotiations toward the end of September 1980—which was consistent with Bani Sadr's claims that his political opponents in Iran were negotiating with the Republicans— but Christopher attributed the breakdown to the confusion caused by the onset of hostilities between Iran and Iraq on September 22.

My conversation with Saunders provided an interesting piece of information. A self-styled Iranian emissary had, in the fall of 1980, approached the campaign of independent presidential candidate John Anderson about a hostage deal. I searched out John Anderson's 1980 campaign manager, Michael MacLeod, who confirmed such a meeting among himself, the Iranian, and several other Anderson campaign officials, including the campaign's general counsel, Washington lawyer Mitchell Rogovin. In the course of that meeting, MacLeod had decided that the discussion was totally inappropriate and insisted on taking the Iranian to the State Department for debriefing. I found two things of special interest about that disclosure. First, it seemed to parallel the meeting that Allen and McFarlane had admitted having, but unlike the Anderson people, the Republicans had never considered disclosing it to anyone until several years later when confronted by a newspaper reporter. Second, it occurred to me that the Iranian "negotiator" might have been the same person in both instances.

I requested from the State Department copies of all documents relating to its debriefing of the Iranian who had approached the Anderson campaign. It took several months, but the documents were finally produced. The emissary was identified in the documents as Houshang Lavi, an Iranian businessman living in the United States. The papers also revealed that Rogovin, who had been a special counsel to the CIA during Senate investigations of the agency in 1974–75, had been Lavi's personal attorney, and he had set up the meeting with the Anderson campaign. I wondered whether Lavi might also have met with the Republicans at L'enfant Plaza.

My efforts to track down Lavi were unsuccessful, so I decided to talk to Rogovin. That meeting was unrevealing. Rogovin had little to add to the State Department documents, and he was absolutely certain that Lavi was not the one who met with the Republicans. Based on Rogovin's assurances and the extremely limited time and resources I had to devote to this inquiry, I abandoned any further efforts to locate Lavi. It was sometime later when journalists who had begun investigating the issue reported that Lavi—who has since died—claimed that he was indeed the man who met with Allen and McFarlane at L'enfant Plaza. Since all my preliminary inquiries had run into dead ends, and since my other responsibilities more than filled up the limited hours I spent on Capitol Hill as a part-time consultant, I had pretty much abandoned the elusive October Surprise quest by the beginning of 1988. Indeed, if it had not been for one extremely revealing interview, I would have been fairly satisfied that there was no merit to the allegation of a Reagan-Bush deal with the Iranians.

The one person who made me believe that there was substance to the tale was Mansour Farhang, an Iranian expatriate who had been Iran's ambassador to the United Nations during the first part of 1980 and had returned to Iran later that year to serve as Bani Sadr's foreign policy adviser. Before ever meeting Farhang, who was a member of the Bennington College faculty in Vermont, I made inquiries about him and learned that he was extremely well respected by his American colleagues.

Farhang was equally impressive in person. And although he could not be certain what kind of deal might have been worked out, he was absolutely convinced that Bani Sadr's clerical opponents within the Iranian government— led by Mohammed Beheshti, leader of the right-wing Hezbollah faction, and Interior Minister Ali Akbar Hashemi Rafsanjani—had engaged in extensive discussions in 1980 with representatives of the Reagan-Bush campaign. He said that he had been in regular contact with the Beheshti-Rafsanjani forces throughout the summer of 1980 and that they as much as admitted their contacts with Reagan representatives.

There was one other piece of circumstantial evidence that gave credence to an October Surprise scenario. There was much evidence that the United States' ban on arms shipments to Iran was quietly lifted as soon as the election returns made Ronald Reagan president-elect. Most of those renewed shipments were routed through Israel, and many people considered it unlikely that Israel would have permitted that without authorization from the incoming Reagan administration. Indeed, a former director of the American Israel Political Action Committee (AIPAC), Morris Amitay, confirmed that Richard Allen, one of those involved in the L'enfant Plaza meeting and the national security adviser–designate, had so indicated to him in December 1980. Amitay told me in a phone conversation that he had asked Allen, at the behest of the Israeli government, whether it was all right to send arms to Iran and that Allen had indicated tacit approval.

*   *   *

Although I had given up any active interest in the October Surprise investigation, I was regularly contacted during the first half of 1988 by journalists who had picked up on the story and were searching for a scoop that might impact the presidential election. My own involvement had been grossly exaggerated in a book on the subject by Barbara Honneger, a former Reagan-Bush campaign worker and Reagan White House employee, who claimed to have proof of an October Surprise conspiracy.

As a result of Honneger's false report that I was conducting an *official* investigation for Conyers's congressional committee, all journalistic paths began to lead to my door. I was happy to tell the reporters what I knew, but I had to keep explaining my limited role and limited knowledge. As each reporter provided me with additional information he or she had picked up, however, I was becoming something of a clearinghouse of information about the subject. It seemed clear to me that since there was so much smoke, there had to be at least a small fire. I had little doubt that the 1980 Republican campaign, directed by future CIA chief Bill Casey, had had direct discussions with the Iranians about the hostages. Whether they had arrived at anything that could be described as a deal and whether there had been a specific quid pro quo for delaying the hostages' release were more elusive questions.

One of the journalists who contacted me was Jonathan Silver, a freelancer who was doing a story with ex-Yippie Abby Hoffman for *Playboy* magazine. The story came out in the October 1988 issue under the title "The Election Held Hostage." Meanwhile, there was an increased flurry of journalistic activity around the issue as the 1988 presidential race came down to the wire. I spent more and more of my time responding to reporters' questions. I did background interviews on camera with both NBC and ABC News, although neither network ever aired the story. All the networks and major newspapers were looking for a smoking gun, and I kept having to explain that there was no smoking gun, only a lot of circumstantial evidence plus direct allegations from individuals of questionable credibility. The 1988 election ended without the story's ever making it to the front pages or the evening news. A few papers printed brief accounts of the "rumors" buried on inside pages.

Meanwhile, I made one last investigative effort. The *Playboy* article reported that Bani Sadr claimed to have documents that would prove his allegations and that he was willing to turn them over only to a congressional investigator. I had no authority to accept his documents on behalf of Congress and no resources to obtain them, but I did have a friend, Norma Levine, who made regular trips to Paris as a fashion buyer. She volunteered to stop by Bani Sadr's house and pick them up for me if he would agree to turn them over to her. I was aware that a member of Conyers's staff was a Turkish American who spoke Farsi. What I did not know when I approached her to try to contact Bani Sadr by telephone was that Miriam's family was actually related to him. With no difficulty she was able to arrange for Norma to see him on her next trip to Paris. Unfortunately, when we got Bani Sadr's documents translated, they turned out to be useless. There was no hard evidence, only his speculations.

* * *

It was about a month after the election when I received a call from Abby Hoffman, to whom I had never spoken before. It was obvious that his coauthor Silver had done the bulk of the work on the *Playboy* article. Abby's knowledge of details was minimal. He wanted to know why the issue had not received more visibility in the major media after the appearance of the *Playboy* article. His frustration was obvious, and it was clear that Abby had expected the article to have a real impact on the presidential election. About three months later, he called me again to pursue the issue. I explained both the strengths and the weaknesses of the conspiracy allegations. Several months later, Abby died in what was ruled a suicide. The media reported that he had been seriously depressed.

I assumed that the October Surprise was dead and buried. Then an amazing thing happened. One of the shadowy figures at the center of the alleged 1980 hostage dealings, a self-proclaimed ex-CIA operative named Richard Brenneke, was indicted by a federal grand jury in Denver for perjury as a result of his allegations that representatives of the Reagan-Bush campaign had met with Iranians in Paris in October 1980 to conclude a deal to delay the hostages' release. Not only did a jury in Portland, Oregon (the trial had been moved close to Brenneke's hometown because of his ill health), acquit Brenneke, but the jury foreman told the press that the jurors believed his allegations. The October Surprise theory was alive and well.

Brenneke's perjury indictment grew out of his testimony in connection with the criminal prosecution of another self-identified CIA contract agent, Heinrich Rupp, for alleged bank fraud. Rupp contended that the allegedly fraudulent scheme was actually a CIA money-laundering operation, and Brenneke came to testify that Rupp had indeed worked for the CIA. Brenneke then told the federal court in Denver an extraordinary tale about how he and Rupp had been contract pilots for CIA proprietary airlines and had flown American participants to an alleged secret meeting with Iranian representatives in Paris in the third week of October 1980. Brenneke claimed that William Casey and Donald Gregg had flown on his plane and that a man he thought was George Bush had flown on Rupp's plane. Through ineptness or otherwise, the prosecution in Brenneke's perjury trial was unable to demonstrate to the jury's satisfaction that the people Brenneke identified could not have been in Paris at the time indicated and that Brenneke's testimony had been fabricated.

I took the reports of the Brenneke acquittal as an opportunity to finally institute a semiofficial inquiry into the whole episode. Spencer Oliver, chief counsel to the Foreign Affairs Committee, was also urging me to get the General Accounting Office (GAO), Congress's investigative agency, on the case. Oliver told me that his own boss, Dante Fascell, was interested but couldn't be associated with such an effort because it would anger his huge right-wing Cuban exile constituency in Miami. In a memo to Julian Epstein, who was now staff director of the Government Operations Committee, I suggested that we ask the GAO to initiate some preliminary inquiries focusing on the Brenneke trial and the government's inability to discredit him.

Julian agreed but was concerned that when the Republicans found out what we were doing, they would accuse Conyers of engaging in a partisan effort to discredit the president. I carefully worded the GAO's mission so that we would be able to deny allegations that we were out to "get" George Bush. We did not ask the GAO to determine whether there had been an October Surprise deal; we asked it to investigate the conduct of the Brenneke trial and figure out why the U.S. attorney's office in Portland had been unable to prove the whereabouts of Casey, Gregg, and Bush during the third weekend in October 1980 and convince the jury that Brenneke had lied. By the terms of our request, the GAO was asked to investigate only the competency of the U.S. attorney's office in the Brenneke prosecution. Of course, any evidence that Brenneke was telling the truth would reflect on the credibility of the October Surprise allegations.

Although the limited nature of the request gave Conyers some wiggle room in case the investigation backfired, it also ensured that the investigation would come up short. Since we were not prepared to go public with our suspicions, we could not seek authorization from the committee for the GAO to use its subpoena power. The GAO investigators warned us that denying them the ability to compel testimony and seize documents would be like sending them out handcuffed and blindfolded. We decided to go ahead anyway on the slim chance that something useful could be turned up, one way or the other.

*   *   *

Brenneke's acquittal began a new flurry of October Surprise journalism. But the real bombshell exploded on April 15, 1991, when the *New York Times* printed an opinion piece by Gary Sick under the headline "The Election Story of the Decade," in which Sick set forth his belief in the October Surprise allegations. This was the same Gary Sick who had told me four years earlier that he was extremely skeptical about Bani Sadr's claims. Sick explained that his research for a book on the Iranian hostage negotiations had uncovered evidence that caused him to change his opinion. The next night, PBS aired a story called "The Election Held Hostage," based mainly on the work of Bob Parry, an experienced journalist whom I had spoken to on a number of occasions about the case. For the first time, members of Congress began to take the issue seriously. Formal resolutions were introduced in both chambers to authorize an official investigation of an October Surprise.

Over the next several months, the Republicans on Capitol Hill fought a losing battle to prevent an investigation. I never quite understood why. If they were confident that the allegations were spurious, they should have welcomed an investigation, which was the only way to put them to rest. Instead, they insisted that Congress and the country close their eyes to the possibility. Their main argument was that since I had been "investigating" the issue for four years without being able to prove anything, further investigation would be a waste of public money. Of course, the irony was that I had never been able to do any real investigating because nobody would provide me any resources for fear that the Republicans would holler.

The GAO had come up with nothing particularly useful one way or another. Casey was dead, and his 1980 journals were less than conclusive about his travels during October. Gregg claimed to have been with his family at a friend's beach house in Delaware on the weekend of the alleged Paris meeting, a claim that the Brenneke jury had apparently disbelieved. The GAO was no more successful in pinning down the truth.

I had never put much stock in the claim that George Bush could have flown off to Paris incognito two weeks before the election, but the documentary

evidence only compounded the mystery. There was a twenty-two-hour period
from Saturday night to Sunday evening when the vice presidential candidate
had no formal campaign appearances. Secret Service travel records indicated
that he had gone to the Chevy Chase Country Club on Sunday morning, but
the club was unable to verify that. Belatedly, one of Bush's Secret Service
bodyguards, who had subsequently become chief of White House security,
recalled that the Bushes had met Supreme Court Justice Potter Stewart and
his wife for brunch at the country club. At first I thought that this might
close one gap in the mystery. However, Stewart was dead, and his 1980 dia-
ries were missing from his memorabilia, which had been donated to the Yale
University library.

On the other hand, the GAO could not verify any of Brenneke's claims,
and there seemed to be fairly conclusive evidence that Brenneke himself could
not have been in Paris at the time he claimed. However, the fact that Brenneke
was not at the Paris meeting did not preclude the possibility that there had
been one. Brenneke seemed to be extremely well versed on the cloak-and-
dagger activities of the netherworld of international intelligence agents. It was
not inconceivable that he had learned about a clandestine Paris meeting and
invented a role in it for himself. There is little doubt that there were numerous disaffected CIA agents at the end of the Carter administration who would
have been glad to use their special talents at international intrigue to help
elect the Reagan-Bush ticket and remove Carter-appointee Stansfield Turner
as the agency's boss.

*   *   *

The report of the October Surprise Task Force established by the House
over Republican objections was issued on January 3, 1993. The 250-page report, with 700 pages of appended documents, concludes that the Reagan-Bush
campaign was not guilty. Although conceding the near impossibility of proving a negative, after an exhaustive investigation, the task force found no credible evidence to support allegations that the Republicans had attempted to
negotiate a delay of the hostages' release.

I have no reason to believe that the task force was either incompetent or
deceptive. But I am not completely convinced of the Republicans' innocence,
and, according to public comments, neither are Gary Sick or Bob Parry, who
published the results of his own research in a book entitled *Trick or Treason*.
Although I agree that it is significant that the investigators could find no evidence to corroborate the allegations of specific meetings between Reagan-Bush
emissaries and the Iranians, a firm determination that those meetings did not
take place is a stretch. In too many instances, the task force seemed to make
factual findings on the basis of incomplete evidence. The inability to prove

the occurrence of events a dozen years earlier was too often made the basis for definitive conclusions that they never occurred.

Based on my own limited investigation, I found a few significant flaws in the report. The biggest gap was the task force's apparent failure to interview Mansour Farhang. As I reported earlier, he was the one person who had made a believer of me. I had told Lawrence Barcella, chief counsel to the task force, that it was essential he speak to Farhang to get a real feel for the political intrigue that was going on in Iran during the summer and fall of 1980. I found nothing in the report to indicate that Farhang had ever been interviewed.

I am not a big believer in conspiracy theory. I think that it is quite possible that Lee Harvey Oswald was a lone assassin. But I wouldn't be shocked if that turned out to be wrong. Historical events can be elusive, even when the investigation of them is contemporaneous. When it takes twelve years to begin tracing a cold trail, the chances of mistake are multiplied. For me, the October Surprise conspiracy remains unproved but not wholly improbable.

PART IV:

REFLECTIONS

21

ACLU Days

As a lawyer, my professional life has revolved around two hubs—Rutgers Law School and the American Civil Liberties Union. Both institutions have been dear to my heart for many years, even though each has often viewed me as a prodigal son rather than a devoted member of the family.

The ACLU is a big tent. The basic ideological tension is between those who consider themselves pure and nonpolitical "civil libertarians" and those of us whose commitment to civil liberties is rooted in a larger commitment to a just and egalitarian society and who tend to identify with politically progressive or "leftist" political movements. The latter faction has been a minority within the organization but has exerted significant pressure on its policies and programs over time. I believe that the symbiotic mixture of these two tendencies has made the ACLU one of the country's most important and effective private, nonprofit organizations. The purists (often referred to as traditionalists) have ensured the organization's fidelity to principle; the activists have prevented it from degenerating into an irrelevant debating society.

I have served as a general counsel of the organization for almost as long as the legendary Arthur Garfield Hayes, whose name is synonymous with the ACLU. (For four years, one of my fellow General Counsel was Ruth Bader Ginsburg, who resigned when she was appointed to the federal bench by President Carter in 1980.) My first election as one of four general counsel came in 1976, when I was an insurgent candidate against the officer slate proposed by the official nominating committee; I had to fight my way back into office, again in opposition to the official slate, in 1987. After that latter electoral contest, I commented to Norman Dorsen, then president of the ACLU, "After twenty years of loyal service to this organization, why do I still feel like an insurgent?"

*   *   *

My initial election to the ACLU national board in 1969 came as part of a revolution by a number of state affiliates against the national organization. I had been invited to join the New Jersey affiliate board about six months earlier, after handling several cases as a volunteer attorney and then addressing the local board on the not-yet-established constitutional right of abortion.

The affiliate revolt was occasioned by the national board's decision not to provide representation to Dr. Benjamin Spock and his codefendants in a federal prosecution in Boston for counseling opposition to the draft in the midst of the Vietnam War. At the time, the national board was dominated by a small group of New York–based academics and big-firm lawyers who apparently felt that involvement in the Spock trial would associate the ACLU with opposition to the war itself. Although each state affiliate was entitled to a representative on the national board, few affiliate delegates attended because of travel costs. After the Spock decision, a number of the affiliates demanded a special national board meeting and arranged to send their representatives to the meeting, at which the earlier decision was overturned.

New Jersey's national representative antagonized the state board by supporting the original national board decision, and I was elected to replace him. The argument over the Spock case also initiated a change in the ACLU's national constitution that was to have a far-reaching impact on the nature of the organization. The amendment provided that transportation to national board meetings would thenceforth be paid by the national office. As a result, the ACLU became a truly national organization as representatives from Maine to Hawaii became regular participants in national board decisions; many of the thirty at-large seats on the national board came, over time, to be filled by former affiliate representatives such as myself.

One of the first big policy fights that took place within the newly enlarged national board was over the causes and cures of racism in the United States. This battle lasted several years and was waged between those who felt that the ACLU had to remain committed to a neutral principle of complete color blindness under the law and those who believed that members of racial minority groups that had been the victims of discriminatory treatment over hundreds of years had to be given special consideration to enable them to join the social mainstream. The fight focused on the concept of compensatory or preferential treatment, which evolved over time into the principle of affirmative action.

At the time I joined the ACLU national board, I was also deeply involved in the establishment of the Minority Student Program at Rutgers Law School, which had set aside a specific number of seats in each class for qualified members of minority groups. I was quite proud of what we were doing at Rutgers to respond to the report of the presidential Kerner Commission.

I was dismayed to discover that there was strong opposition to such programs among ACLU leaders, on constitutional grounds. Even more shocking to me was the fact that Kenneth Clark and Bayard Rustin, two black heroes of the civil rights movement, associated themselves with that point of view, expressing fear that compensatory programs would stigmatize its beneficiaries and encourage white backlash. In the context of college admissions, they and their colleagues were willing to endorse individualized preferences based on specific facts of past deprivation, but they refused to support group-based remedies that would compensate individuals on the basis of racial identification. Those on my side of the debate were convinced that one-by-one remedies could not effectively deal with the mammoth racial crisis the country faced. We also believed that all African Americans, no matter their current economic or social status, had been terribly victimized by three hundred years of slavery and racial segregation. As I was to write in a debate with one of my national board colleagues in the pages of the *Civil Liberties Review*:

> Is it a necessary libertarian principle that, despite all the years of slavery and discrimination as a group, black people must now work their way into the American mainstream one by one? The historic exclusion of blacks from positions of prestige and power within society has not been done on a one-by-one basis; it has been group exclusion. It is the very essence of racial discrimination that the individual is excluded because of membership in the group. And it is not the excluded individuals alone who suffer by such social policies; the entire group suffers by a lowering of the prestige and power of the group as such.

The debate within the ACLU raged for three years. When my side lost the initial rounds, we took the issue to the floor of the ACLU biennial conference held at New York University in June 1970. The biennial conference is the only other ACLU national body that has any policy-making authority, although its decisions are subject to ratification by the national board or national referendum.

With the cooperation of leaders of the organization from New York, southern California, and the state of Washington, I successfully moved to amend the conference's agenda to take up the issue of "university admissions policy" in regard to racial diversity. After vigorous debate, the conference approved a policy that supported affirmative action, including the establishment of admission goals for minority students. Within another year and a half, the national board had adopted a policy in line with that approved by the biennial conference.

Thus, by the end of 1971, the ACLU was firmly committed to the struggle for vigorous and effective affirmative action programs throughout the country. Ever since then, the ACLU has remained dedicated to the principle of affirmative action to offset the ravages of the United States' racial history. The ACLU was probably the most significant predominantly white organization in the country in the vanguard of that movement.

*   *   *

The influx of new blood from the hinterlands plus the organizational commitment to affirmative action resulted in other changes in the composition and functioning of the national organization. As the women's movement flowered in the early 1970s, the ACLU recognized that it could not continue to advocate civil rights while remaining an almost exclusively male club.

When I joined the national board of directors, it included only three women. A fourth, Suzy Post of Louisville, Kentucky, joined the board shortly after I did. Suzy became an insistent advocate of gender diversity and goaded her male colleagues into aggressively recruiting women board members. Suzy was soon joined by other women—including Ellen Feingold of Massachusetts, Faith Seidenberg of New York, Margie Pitts Hames of Georgia, Gwen Thomas of Colorado, and Tasia Young of New Mexico—in a women's caucus that, over the next decade, became the spearhead for diversifying the organization and instituting aggressive policies in defense of racial and sexual equality in the country. Practicing what it preached, the national board instituted procedures—including gender and minority goals—to guarantee the election of women and members of minority groups to its ranks. In a relatively short period, the once overwhelmingly white male board began to resemble a more accurate cross section of the population.

*   *   *

The 1970s was a watershed decade for the ACLU in many ways. The newly influential female, nonwhite, and generally younger affiliate representatives on the national board found themselves in regular contests with the older white male traditionalists who had previously dominated it. The southern California affiliate, under the leadership of a fiery former mayor of Beverly Hills, George Slaff, and the New York affiliate, under the guidance of its executive director Ira Glasser (who was soon to become national director), provided much of the direction for a series of assaults on many of the ACLU's more cautious tendencies. In rapid succession, the activists pushed the organization to take positions against the war in Vietnam and in favor of the impeachment of Richard Nixon. Both were justified on the basis of fundamental civil liberties principles. The resolution opposing the war cited military conscription for an undeclared war in addition to the "many adverse domestic consequences" that had resulted from the hostilities in Southeast Asia. The impeachment resolution was based on Nixon's wholesale assault on constitutional principles, including his efforts to stifle political dissent.

Both of those decisions were accompanied by dire warnings from the old guard that the organization was signing its death warrant by expanding its

policy agenda beyond its traditional moorings of protecting freedom of speech
and religion and related constitutional values. To many of the predictors of
doom, the organization was indeed dead, and they abandoned the perceived
carcass to the young turks who had overwhelmed them. However, in the country
at large, the ACLU had found thousands of new supporters, and its membership ranks swelled. Among the new converts were thousands who had been
attracted to the organization by its leadership in the legal battle to make abortion a constitutional right and its fight for gender equality waged in the 1970s
by its Women's Rights Project under the direction of future Supreme Court
Justice Ginsburg.

The occasional internecine disputes should not overshadow the fact that in
90 percent of the issues in which the ACLU is involved, there is no serious
disagreement among the leadership of the organization. There is virtual una-
nimity when it comes to protecting separation of church and state, defending
the right of women to control their own reproductive processes, supporting
the right of consenting adults to act out their own sexual preferences in the
privacy of their bedrooms, opposing all forms of literary and artistic censorship, guaranteeing fair hearings for individuals who are facing detrimental
action, combating capital punishment, challenging all forms of discrimination,
protecting personal privacy from governmental intrusion, and providing for
open government. Even the question of defending the rights of Nazis to march
in Skokie, which precipitated the resignations of several hundred dues-paying
members, was uncontroversial within official bodies.

*   *   *

If there is a clear ideological division over constitutional rights within the
organization, it is over the appropriate scope of protection for economic and
property interests. Those of us who are considered on the "left" of the national board have consistently dissented from policies that would protect economic interests at the expense of other democratic and constitutional values.
One of the clearest illustrations involves political campaign financing. On at
least half a dozen occasions during my tenure on the national board, I have
been on the losing side of policy decisions opposing government restrictions
on campaign spending and contributions. A majority of the board has always
taken the position that money is speech and that restrictions on campaign
spending amounted to restrictions on speech itself. In one recent debate on
this issue, I commented, "I am aware there is a street saying that 'money
talks and bullshit walks,' but that doesn't mean we have to elevate that view
to a constitutional principle."

Once again, my arguments proved unconvincing to the majority. I acknowledge
that excessive regulation of political spending—especially by grassroots groups

and minority political organizations—unnecessarily intrudes on political activism, but I still believe that a properly administered campaign financing scheme based on public funding would enhance our political system.

*   *   *

It has been my perception that the traditionalists in the ACLU tend to elevate abstract principle over real-world consequences. They express great concern that any slight deviation from principle will threaten the principle itself—the oft-repeated "slippery slope" and "camel's nose under the tent" arguments. The realists tend to live by narrower, more nuanced principles that allow differential treatment for situations that may look alike but have dissimilar consequences.

This dichotomy was illustrated by the issue of affirmative action. The traditionalists were committed, for good and proper reasons, to the principle that the Constitution should be color-blind and should not treat people differently on the basis of race or skin color. That was a commendable principle when the ACLU was struggling to end overt discrimination against members of minority groups. However, it made no sense to enforce such a general principle to frustrate efforts to help the formerly oppressed achieve true equality. On our side, the basic antidiscrimination principle was that people with the power should not be permitted to oppress those without the power.

Recent debate over so-called hate speech reflects a similar division between purists and realists. The extreme purist position is reflected by Nat Hentoff, the columnist and onetime ACLU national board member. Nat argues passionately against the slightest tendency to punish or discipline racial and sexual harassers on the basis of words uttered, no matter how offensive or intimidating. On the other extreme are those who are willing to abandon protection for free speech at the point where it creates an uncomfortable environment for women or members of minority groups. Most ACLU national board members fall at intermediate positions along that continuum, and the board has struggled mightily to articulate principled positions that protect freedom of speech while recognizing that, at some point, words become weapons that inflict real and serious harm—such as causing reasonable people to be unable to function in a job or an academic setting. I am satisfied that the organization has dealt with these issues in a reasonably sound manner.

The ideological divide over so-called economic rights has formed the basis for another split within the organization—over the constitutional right to a guaranteed minimum level of subsistence for every individual. Led by the southern California affiliate—and, for a period, the welfare advocate and scholar Frances Fox Piven—the activist wing of the board has unsuccessfully advocated the ACLU's endorsement of a constitutional right to jobs, housing, food, and medical care. Although I have normally voted with the activists on such issues—on the theory that the government has so pervasively regulated economic activity that it is largely responsible for the homelessness, unemployment, and poverty that those policies help bring about—I share the opposition's concern that the organization cannot divert current resources to such vast and overwhelming challenges without diluting its more central agenda.

*   *   *

In large part, the differences between the traditional and activist wings of the organization have as much to do with style as substance. Historically, the organization was an intellectual debating society that would, on occasion, inform an appellate court—through friend-of-the-court briefs —of the reasons for the outcome of its debate on a given issue. It was this mind-set that provoked the historic conflict over the Spock trial in the national board. The old line would have been quite willing to file such an amicus brief on the abstract First Amendment issues following the conviction of Dr. Spock and his associates. They did not want the ACLU tarnished by active association with the defendants as their trial counsel. Those on the other side of the argument felt that the more important battle for free speech would be fought out in the trial court before a jury and believed that the ACLU should be in the thick of the fight.

Similarly, in the old days, legislative advocacy was not an organizational priority. It smacked too much of politics. With the end of the Warren Court era and the capture of the federal courts by the far right, my ideological associates and I helped turn the organization into one of the most effective legislative advocates in the nonprofit field. For the past fifteen years, the ACLU's Washington office has been recognized as an extremely effective voice for legislative action in support of civil rights and civil liberties. Many of the state affiliates have moved in a similar direction in their own state capitals.

The recognition that the organization had to immerse itself in the legislative process did not fully resolve the manner of that involvement. Those, like myself, who think "politically" are more apt to believe that lasting legislative achievements are realized by influencing public opinion and forging movements in support of a given cause or proposal. The nonpolitical purists tend to put all their faith in the power of their own words to sway decision makers.

The first time I proposed that the ACLU publicly criticize the Burger Court for being hostile to constitutional rights, old-line national board members—especially the lawyers—were horrified. It was considered unseemly to publicly chide the judiciary. You made your argument to the court, and when the judges ruled against you, you quietly licked your wounds. But heaven forbid that an organization committed to the rule of law would openly criticize the courts for failing to live up to their constitutional role—or even hint that a court might be swayed by public attitudes and reactions. I was considered the worst kind of heretic when I suggested that courts were "political" institutions and, as such, subject to public challenge and censure.

I made the first inroads into this mind-set in 1976 when, after lengthy debate, I convinced the organization to convene a conference on Capitol Hill, together with the Society of American Law Teachers and the Committee for Public Justice, challenging many of the policies of the Burger Court concerning access to justice in the federal courts. That was the beginning of the ACLU's active involvement in legislative efforts to make the federal courts more hospitable to claims of constitutional violation and to overrule numerous Supreme Court decisions that required the dismissal of cases on the basis of technical issues such as standing, justiciability, abstention, and immunity. One concrete success of that campaign was Congress's adoption of the Civil Rights Attorneys Fees Award Act, which provided for the award of attorneys' fees to successful federal civil rights litigants. That act gave fresh impetus to the public-interest law movement; it made it possible to bring many cases that were otherwise financially unappealing and provided a stronger financial base for public-interest law firms.

It similarly took me several years to institute a proposal that the ACLU sponsor an annual Supreme Court press briefing the week before the opening of the Court's term. Some of the more traditional types worried that such an event would deteriorate into inappropriate court-bashing. Since its initiation in 1988, however, the annual briefing has proved to be a huge success and is now a popular event both within and outside the organization.

Of course, some of the national board's most fierce contests were over proposals to oppose specific Supreme Court nominations—namely, those of William Rehnquist, Robert Bork and Clarence Thomas. The failure to get the ACLU to join the opposition to Clarence Thomas—an effort that fell one vote short of the needed 60 percent national board supermajority—is probably the most significant defeat ever sustained by my side in a board contest, especially since there is an outside chance that ACLU opposition might have changed the outcome of the narrow fifty-two to forty-eight Senate vote by which Thomas was confirmed. Thomas's service on the Supreme Court is not only a constitutional tragedy but also a daily affront to African Americans, whose lone representative on the Supreme Court has turned out to be a ventriloquist's dummy who voices the aspirations not of his people but of their worst enemies, the radical right of U.S. politics.

Overall, however, on these matters of style and technique, I have been reasonably successful in changing the way the ACLU thinks and operates. When I first proposed that a national board meeting that coincided with a national abortion rights parade be moved from New York to Washington so that board members could participate en masse, my motion was greeted with skepticism. But after some fairly serious debate, the board voted to move its meeting. Even the most conservative members of the board turned out for the march waving ACLU banners—and expressed gratification that they had done so. Several years later, there was no opposition at all to a proposal to change the time of a board meeting so that board members could participate as a group in a gay rights parade in New York City.

*   *   *

In my later life, I seem to have wound up at an awkward point on the political spectrum. My heart still sides with the passionate left, but cerebrally, I have come to respect the wisdom of moderation and incrementalism. That probably explains why I made a choice some years ago to devote my energies to the American Civil Liberties Union and not the National Lawyers Guild, the organization of the left wing of the bar. As it has turned out, most of my guild friends consider me a bit conservative, and many of my ACLU colleagues view me as being on the left.

As consolation, I take pride in the fact that I am the only person listed as a member of both the national board of the ACLU and the national advisory council of the National Emergency Civil Liberties Committee, a left-wing civil liberties legal organization that was organized during the McCarthy era because of the ACLU's reluctance to defend the rights of Communists. I consider myself the ecumenical bridge in the civil liberties community.

22

Reflections on a Life as a Constitutional Lawyer

When I was graduated from law school in 1966 and began to teach and practice constitutional law, it was exhilarating to believe that my conception of constitutional rights and the duty of the judiciary to enforce them was relatively consistent with the conception held by a majority of those who had the final say in such matters—the members of the Supreme Court of the United States.

It was a time when the Supreme Court was making it increasingly clear that racial discrimination was not to be tolerated; that freedom of speech and association occupied a preferred position in our legal value system and trumped almost any governmental claim of a need to suppress it; that notions of fundamental fairness required that individuals be given fair and impartial hearings before they could be punished or otherwise harmed by the actions of public officials; that police and other governmental agents were required to respect personal privacy; and that criminal defendants could insist upon their rights under the Constitution, even at the price of freedom for the guilty. Even the right of women to assert autonomy over their own reproductive processes, though not yet formally acknowledged, was clearly on its way to constitutional recognition.

It was the time when Justice William O. Douglas had proclaimed—without contradiction from his colleagues on the high court—that the basic purpose of the U.S. Constitution was to keep government off the backs of the people. And, most importantly, it was a time when the Court was making it clearer with each new decision that it was the essential role of the federal courts to shape judicial remedies that would best bring about such constitutional values.

*   *   *

Our federal judicial system has not always been a bulwark for individual rights. For much of our country's history, the U.S. Supreme Court, like most of the country's judicial system, was an instrument of the status quo, populated by conservative lawyers who were concerned mainly with protecting vested property interests and maintaining social order. It was the U.S. Supreme Court that, in the middle of the nineteenth century in the *Dred Scott* case, reaffirmed the property rights of slave owners and ruled that persons of African dissent in this country had no rights that a white person was bound to respect. After the Civil War, it was the Supreme Court that vitiated the new Thirteenth, Fourteenth, and Fifteenth Amendments and declared that black people could not be the social equals of whites.

Some early justices (such as Oliver Wendell Holmes and Louis Brandeis) began to articulate broader visions of the Constitution, but it was not until the Roosevelt revolution and FDR's opportunity to appoint a new breed of social thinkers to the Supreme Court that the federal courts began to take on a broader role. By the early 1940s, a new progressive majority was taking shape and beginnning to take interest in the federal Bill of Rights, which had lain largely dormant for most of the years since the founding of the Republic. However, this new constitutional spirit was cut short before the end of the decade as a result of the deaths of Justices Wiley Rutledge, Frank Murphy, and Harlan Fiske Stone and their replacement by President Truman with justices of little social vision or concern. Thus, it wasn't until Dwight Eisenhower appointed Earl Warren and William Brennan Jr. to the Court in the mid-1950s that the high tribunal again picked up the baton of individual rights jurisprudence.

After I established the Constitutional Litigation Clinic at Rutgers Law School in 1970, I used to tell my clinic students that in their other classes they would look at the law as it was and ask why. But in the clinic, we looked at the law as it never was and asked why not. Inspired by the willingness of the Warren Court to measure constitutional claims not only against conservative precedents but also against democratic aspirations, we were part of the burgeoning public-interest law movement that was developing novel theories to expand the frontiers of freedom and equality. And although we often met resistance from dull and reactionary district court judges, we more often than not found receptive ears on the appeals court in Philadelphia, which was much more attuned to the changing constitutional winds blowing north from Washington.

Of even greater importance, the Warren Court was not only changing the nature of constitutional law, it was also changing the face of the bar. Inspired by the new social-change jurisprudence, idealistic young men and women who once shunned legal careers for the humanities and social work started flocking to law school. By the late 1960s, law schools like Rutgers were crowded with students who had spent the middle part of the decade as foot soldiers of the southern civil rights movement. They were now looking forward to entering a new burgeoning professional field—public-interest law. Those were heady days for those of us who believed deeply in the promise of a Constitution that guaranteed maximum individual autonomy, protection for minorities threatened by majoritarian institutions, and minimum government interference with personal freedom.

*   *   *

Not everyone shared this vision of constitutional rights. By 1968, Richard Nixon was campaigning for president against the Warren Court. He promised to appoint to the Supreme Court "strict constructionists." Nobody knew exactly what a strict constructionist was, but it was obviously a code word for judges who would reverse the Court's decisions protecting the rights of criminal defendants as well as those of racial minorities. At times, the phrase was intended to convey something about respect for "states' rights," but that meant little more than the right of state officials and state courts to deny constitutional protection to criminal defendants or to victims of discrimination.

The Republican onslaught of the 1970s and 1980s was successful in two main particulars: (1) it wrecked the federal tax system in the interest of the rich and well-off and so enlarged the national debt as to make it virtually impossible for future administrations to fund meaningful social programs; and (2) it set back federal jurisprudence more than half a century, taking it back almost to a time when the major function of the federal courts was to umpire financial disputes between competing corporate interests.

The Burger and Rehnquist Courts have not only eroded essential constitutional rights and aborted the development of doctrine that would have extended constitutional protection to fundamental economic-based interests, such as the right to education, food, shelter, and a job. Even more significantly, they have reversed the central assumption of the Warren Court: that federal courts have an obligation to entertain claims of constitutional violation and to provide remedies for their enforcement. In the first landmark decision of the Supreme Court two hundred years ago, *Marbury v. Madison*, Chief Justice John Marshall explained that constitutional principles were meaningless unless courts were prepared to declare them and provide remedies for their breach— that without adequate remedies, there were no legal rights. The Warren Court took that principle seriously, and in its most important rulings it instructed federal courts to provide effective remedies to redress constitutional violations. The Burger and Rehnquist Courts have effectively dismantled the federal system of constitutional redress. The earliest and clearest example was the case of *Rizzo v. Goode*, in which Justice Rehnquist held for a majority of the Court that federal courts could no longer order systemic reform of local police departments to protect the constitutional rights of the citizenry.

Richard Nixon's first judicial nominee, Chief Justice Warren Burger, told us what was in store shortly after his appointment. In an interview with the

New York Times, Burger warned those idealistic young men and women who were entering law school in order to make a difference in people's lives that they were embarked on the wrong course. He emphasized the law as an instrument of the status quo and suggested that the young idealists go back to social work and the humanities.

The conservative movement did not leave effectuation of Burger's vision to chance. Over two decades, right-wing corporate foundations have poured megamillions of dollars into campaigns aimed at influencing both the personnel and the decisions of the federal judiciary. One of its major undertakings was the establishment of the Federalist Society, an organization of right-wing lawyers, teachers, and law students that was used as an employment office for a succession of Republican administrations and the think tank for the development of a right-wing legal ideology. With large sums of money available and a pipeline to jobs in the federal government and clerkship positions with federal judges, the Federalist Society was able to establish chapters in most major law schools. On a campus such as Rutgers, the favorite activity of the Federalist Society chapter was agitation against the Minority Student Program and crude attacks on the minority students themselves. The Federalists claim as their favorite sons Chief Justice Rehnquist and Associate Justices Scalia and Thomas, as well as would-be justice Robert Bork.

The aim of the right-wing crusade was not limited to a rollback of constitutional entitlements. Its corporatist sponsors were equally concerned about protecting business interests from populist juries, which tend to be overly willing to compensate maimed and injured parties for damages caused by consumer products and professional malpractice. Thus, the right-wing legal agenda includes support for caps on monetary awards in products liability cases, opposition to punitive damages, and restrictions on the types of testimony admissible in court to support damage claims. The hypocrisy of conservative politicians is no better demonstrated than in the efforts of right-wing members of Congress, who normally champion the cause of "states' rights," to federalize tort law and strip state courts of authority in an area traditionally left to local regulation.

However, what the conservative legal movement failed to accomplish is almost as significant as its successes, given the fact that it controlled just about every Supreme Court appointment for a quarter of a century. The lone exception was the appointment of John Paul Stevens by Gerald Ford during his brief interregnum presidency following Watergate and Nixon's resignation. Justice Stevens was a moderate Republican who did not have the active support of the radical right. Jimmy Carter, president from 1977 through 1980, never got to appoint a member of the Supreme Court.

Of course, some selections—most notably Justice Blackmun—turned out to be disappointments to their right-wing sponsors. But I believe that this was as much a consequence of public revulsion against the conservative agenda as a miscalculation by the political gurus of the right. The fate of Robert Bork perfectly illustrates that principle. Bork was the only right-wing nominee who clearly and publicly expounded the conservative agenda. As a result, he became politically unacceptable.

I suggest that the same thing happened to large parts of the conservatives' substantive agenda. Even lifetime-appointed Supreme Court justices have a constituency to answer to: the bar from which they come; the social and cultural elite with whom they mix; and the general public, whose acclaim they desire. Nobody likes to be a pariah. Faced with disapproval from close associates and disdain from others, only the hardiest ideologue remains true to the faith. It turned out that only Rehnquist, Scalia, and Thomas adhered strictly to radical right-wing orthodoxy. The nation was fortunate that Bork was not permitted to join them. Thus, for example, a woman's right to choose abortion has withstood the right wing's assault. Abrogation of that right was just too unpopular in too many circles—especially among the bar and the media opinion molders.

*　　*　　*

I explain to my students that the ethical rules counsel them against trying their cases in the media. I further explain that I have probably won as many cases in my press statements as in my briefs. My favorite example is a case involving the right of a long-haired, twelve-year-old Little Leaguer to play in the all-star game without getting a haircut, as ordered by the league commissioner. I needed a temporary restraining order to require that my client be allowed to play in the game, scheduled for the day of the court hearing. I had my students stay up all night writing a brief on the constitutional right of personal appearance. But I also tipped off the local reporters about the interesting dispute that would be heard the next morning in the New Jersey Chancery Division. When the judge called the hearing to order, representatives of all the local papers were in court, pencils at the ready. When the judge issued his ruling from the bench, it was obvious that he was not addressing me or my adversary but the assembled reporters. "This boy's hair is no longer than Sparky Lyle's" (New York Yankee relief ace), His Honor intoned. "It is my ruling that the plaintiff be allowed to play in the all-star game."

It had always been a great puzzlement to me that one of the most far-reaching civil rights decisions of the Supreme Court was a unanimous opinion written by Chief Justice Burger in a case called *Griggs v. Duke Power Co.* For years, *Griggs* was the basis for most successful employment discrimination lawsuits. Yet before and after *Griggs*, Chief Justice Burger never gave anyone reason to believe that he was a friend of civil rights. Then I read *The*

Brethren, the book by Woodward and Armstrong about the inner workings of the Supreme Court. It was a revelation. The authors explained that Burger had been stung by public criticism of his antipathy to civil rights and the unfavorable comparisons of him to Earl Warren, the author of the unanimous opinion in *Brown v. Board of Education*. They reported that he was determined to demonstrate that he was just as much in favor of civil rights as Earl Warren was; as a result, he orchestrated events so that he could write a strong pro–civil rights opinion. He spent most of his remaining years on the Court working to undermine his own *Griggs* opinion.

When the conservative agenda truly reflects popular opinion, however, such as in the case of capital punishment for heinous crimes, there is little that civil liberatarians can do to prevent it.

*   *   *

This is being written in the second half of the (first?) Clinton administration, a time when it is hard to predict what the future holds for the federal courts. I find the New Jersey state courts much more hospitable to the advancement and protection of human and political rights, so I avoid litigating in the federal courts as much as possible. However, I remain optimistic that I will live to see a time when the federal courts will, in the words of Justice Brennan, again become places where "human rights under the federal constitution are always proper subjects for consideration." Even though the New Jersey courts and the Constitution provide substantial protection for rights in one state, that is of no use to people in need of judicial protection for their rights in other parts of the Union. That is why it is important to reestablish the unitary federal judicial system as the first line of defense for human rights.

The question is, what is the proper role of the federal courts in the third century of our nation's history? Did the justices of the Warren Court have it right, or were they usurpers and judicial activists, as their critics maintain? Have Burger, Rehnquist, and the Federalists been responsible for a proper correction in the exercise of federal judicial power by restricting it to what was actually intended by the founders of our nation? Such queries obviously merge two separate questions: (1) In the best of worlds, what should be the role of our federal court system? (2) What was the original intent of the drafters of our basic charter of government, the U.S. Constitution?

Original intent is obviously an elusive quest. Try as we might, it is probably impossible to divine what the founders really thought about specific issues that were remote from their consciousness. Does anyone really believe that Thomas Jefferson and James Madison ever considered the phenomena of television communication and cyberspace when they talked about freedom of speech and of the press? Moreover, the original document and the structure of relations it established between governments—state and federal—and individual citizens were substantially altered in the aftermath of a bloody civil war.

Despite the ambiguities, I have little doubt that Jefferson and Madison and their founding colleagues would feel quite at home among modern-day public-interest lawyers and civil libertarians. What the founders established was a constitutional structure that provided maximum protection for personal autonomy in the context of a government that could provide for the common welfare. The essential difference between the system established under our Constitution and all those that went before was the notion that sovereignty resided in the people, not in the government. No longer was the government in full charge, doling out such justice as it saw fit or was wrested from it over time. For the first time in human history, the people deliberately established a governing structure with limited powers to promote the common good without unnecessarily infringing on individual liberty. And in Article III, the founders established a judicial system to enforce that compact. What the Warren Court did—and what the Burger and Rehnquist Courts undid—was acknowledge that most constitutional decisions should flow from that simple proposition. There remains some room for disagreement as to the resolution of specific issues, but those disagreements are minimized once we accept the paramaters of debate.

It is for all these reasons that I remain something of an optimist. I believe that time and history are on my side. The conservative movement may have temporarily captured the courts, but the spirit of constitutionalism has captured the fancy of the public, and especially the legal profession. The bar is no longer the bastion of the status quo. These days, the American Bar Association most often sides with the ACLU and the public-interest community, and seldom with their adversaries. This is no doubt due in large part to the changing face of the bar as a result of the number of women and nonwhites who have joined the profession in the last two decades. Although the Federalist Society is well financed and vocal, its adherents in the nation's law schools are a small minority—in large part because conservative lawyers with the intellectual credentials to gain faculty appointments tend to be too materialistic to accept academic wages. And the few who did were immediately appointed to the federal bench by Reagan and Bush.

The major concern that tempers my optimism is the race problem. There can be little doubt that right-wing politicians have made huge gains in recent years by playing the race card, and especially by exploiting the fears and anxieties of so-called angry white males. If the conservative movement is successful in convincing both the legislatures and the courts to end affirmative action and return race relations to the 1950s status quo, it does not bode well for the future of this nation.

In the nineteenth century, Lincoln said that the nation could not exist half slave and half free. In the twentieth, the Kerner Commission warned us that we could not endure as two nations, one black and one white, separate and unequal. If we abandon efforts to end the racial divide and to create a truly multiracial society based on equal opportunity for all, I worry that we may wind up with a permanent civil war—à la Northern Ireland.

One of the most perceptive observations about U.S. society was made by my son Danny when he was about seven years old. He and his older brother had taken a bus from our home in West Orange to meet me in Newark for a trip into New York City. As he stepped off the bus, Danny wanted to know why, in our suburban neighborhood, almost everybody was white and prosperous, and as the bus got closer to Newark, almost all the new passengers, as well as the people on the streets, were black and appeared poor. He had made the same discovery as the members of the Kerner Commission—that the American melting pot was a myth and a dream.

This is surely the major challenge for all who aspire to use law to create a better society in the twenty-first century. I hope to be a part of that effort.

Index